What Your Colleag[illegible]

Richard D. Sorenson and Lloyd M. Goldsmit[illegible] outstanding book to include the latest information in a h[illegible] engaging format. Their illustrative stories and case studies help new leaders learn how to apply knowledge and skills to bring about improvements in schools so that all learners can succeed. I highly recommend this guide which all educational leaders will want to keep as a ready reference.

—Michael Fanning, Instructor
Educational Leadership Program
California State University, East Bay
Hayward, California

Perhaps the most powerful element of this edition is the humanistic approach to budgeting which addresses issues such as equity, cultural responsiveness, and diversity. As school demographics and needs change, school administrators must understand their stakeholder's evolving fiscal requisites. It also addresses the current political climate and technologies that are now a permanent part of leading schools.

—Angus S. Mungal, Assistant Professor
Department of Leadership and
Counselor Education, School of Education
The University of Mississippi
University, Mississippi

I strongly recommend this excellent and comprehensive guide to everyone from the novice principal to the most experienced school leader. This text is vision and values driven. The authors use case studies to illustrate the importance of both the leader's values as well as those of all the stakeholders, to create a school community marked by ethics, integrity, fairness, and equity. Sorenson and Goldsmith are especially sensitive to issues in contemporary diverse communities.

—Arturo Pacheco, Professor Emeritus
Educational Leadership and Foundations
Former Dean, College of Education, University of Texas at El Paso
El Paso, Texas

The Principal's Guide to School Budgeting, 4th edition is an invaluable resource for campus principals and school leaders. Building on established budgeting procedures, the authors move from theoretical principles into practical applications. The case studies are especially beneficial in assisting novice administrators in solving the everyday challenges of developing a school budget.

—Virginia L. Mosier, Retired Public School Administrator
Abilene, Texas

The Principal's Guide to School Budgeting, 4th edition offers busy principals discussions of the realities of budget constraints and cuts, thought-provoking discussion questions, rich case studies, checklists, the connection of school budgets to vision and planning, a message of accountability, and a discussion on school budget audits.

—Louis Lim, Principal
Bur Oak Secondary School
Markham, Ontario, Canada

The school budget is where school leaders will likely struggle and spend the most time. This bible will be the school leader's best friend. When the fiscal environment is shaky, this book will provide the necessary assurance regarding best practices. It includes great case studies, wisdom, and resources.

—Ken Darvall, Principal
Tema International School
Ghana

This book serves as a desktop reference regarding the ins and outs of school budgets. It is a must read for school administrators and those working toward their administration degree. Each chapter offers a plethora of ideas, structures, and information about budgets for a school administrator.

—Tanna Nicely, Executive Principal
Knox County Schools
Knoxville, Tennessee

The Principal's Guide to School Budgeting

Dedicated to Xavier Barrera and Louise Moser.
Both were mentors who helped shape us into effective school leaders.
They are genuinely missed.

—The Boys

The Principal's Guide to School Budgeting

Fourth Edition

Richard D. Sorenson

Lloyd M. Goldsmith

CORWIN

CORWIN
A Sage Company

FOR INFORMATION:

Corwin
A SAGE Company
2455 Teller Road
Thousand Oaks, California 91320
(800) 233-9936
www.corwin.com

SAGE Publications Ltd.
1 Oliver's Yard
55 City Road
London EC1Y 1SP
United Kingdom

SAGE Publications India Pvt. Ltd.
Unit No 323-333, Third Floor, F-Block
International Trade Tower Nehru Place
New Delhi 110 019
India

SAGE Publications Asia-Pacific Pte. Ltd.
18 Cross Street #10-10/11/12
China Square Central
Singapore 048423

Vice President and Editorial Director: Monica Eckman
Senior Acquisitions Editor: Tanya Ghans
Content Development Manager: Desirée A. Bartlett
Senior Editorial Assistant: Nyle De Leon
Project Editor: Amy Schroller
Copy Editor: Shannon Kelly
Typesetter: C&M Digitals (P) Ltd.
Proofreader: Dennis Webb
Cover Designer: Scott Van Atta
Marketing Manager: Melissa Duclos

Printed in the United States of America

ISBN 978-1-0719-1585-1

This book is printed on acid-free paper.

SUSTAINABLE FORESTRY INITIATIVE Certified Sourcing
www.forests.org
SFI-00756

24 25 26 27 28 10 9 8 7 6 5 4 3 2 1

Contents

Preface to the Fourth Edition

In the film classic *Fiddler on the Roof*, the character Tevye speaks honestly to God about his monetary situation. He laments, "You made many, many poor people. I realize, of course, that it's no shame to be poor. But it's no great honor either! So, what would have been so terrible if I had a small fortune . . . would it have spoiled some vast, eternal plan if I were a wealthy man?" (Jewison, 1971) The authors of this new edition suspect every reader has, at some point in life, had the same thought.

Likewise, principals speculate as to why some schools seemingly have more riches than others and reflect on how they too would like to gain more bang for the buck. These are common concerns, and their solution typically relates not necessarily to more funding but to a greater utilization of effective, efficient, and essential budgetary practices. Unlike Tevye in *Fiddler on the Roof*, who woefully expresses his financial predicament, prudent principals focus on appropriate budgetary visioning, planning, analysis, needs assessment and prioritization, and strategic expenditure procedures.

The result? A realization that better budgetary preparation and practices can readily equate to a more balanced and equitable acquisition and distribution of funds to better enhance instructional programs and activities. Greater riches? That all depends on a school leader's perspective. Better management of funds? Definitely! An increase in student achievement and organizational improvement? The authors believe so, but you must be the judge. Therefore, permit this revised edition to lead the way with good advice, compelling information, and solid budgetary guidance and practice.

Prudent principals focus on appropriate budgetary visioning, planning, analysis, needs assessment and prioritization, and strategic expenditure procedures.

Welcome to the newly revised fourth edition of *The Principal's Guide to School Budgeting,* which succeeds the first three editions, all of which have been national best-sellers. Today, possibly more than ever before, principals and teams must be cognizant of where funding is derived from, how these dollars can best be incorporated, and by what means fiscal resources can not only enhance a school's curricular and instructional program but also ensure a more open culture and positive climate.

Consequently, the fourth edition is purposefully written for practicing and aspiring public and private school administrators who want to improve their instructional, technical, and managerial skills not only as the school's leader but also as the school's visionary, planning coordinator, and budgeting manager. The authors provide the reader with a critical understanding of the interwoven relationship between two independent yet distinctly connected accountability systems: academic and fiscal.

School leaders—from a financial and budgetary perspective—are responsible for understanding the equity and equality issues and fiscal consequences associated with school budgeting as well as the relationship between educational goal development and resource allocation management. The authors provide school leaders with an overview of school budgeting practices within a collaborative decision-making context.

Using school-oriented situations and the national standards for administrators as they relate to school leadership and budgeting, readers will acquire the necessary practical skills to plan and develop a budget; allocate, expend, and monitor funds; manage and evaluate budget reports; and prepare school action or improvement plans aligned with a fiscal accountability system. They will also develop a "real" school budget (see Resource A).

To improve the book's usefulness as a desk resource, it has been purposely organized into chapters focused on single topics. Each chapter begins with an appropriate quote and general overview and includes numerous visuals, tables, and relevant activities. These activities include utilizing accounting codes, projecting student populations, conducting a needs assessment, implementing a budget calendar, and building, amending, and defending a school budget.

Enhancements to the fourth edition include an overview of how national and state reform and political practices are affecting school allocations, as well as new and updated fiscal information and relevant budgetary materials and vignettes.

Enhancements to the fourth edition include an overview of how national and state reform and political practices are affecting school allocations, as well as new and updated fiscal information and relevant budgetary materials and vignettes. Moreover, a technology overview and how technology affects budgetary practices in this digital age is included, along with a section on school fraud and credit card abuse, phishing scams, fundraising, and how school funds can be misappropriated if the school leader is not readily focused and engaged in the budgetary process. Finally, real-life school and budgeting applications and/or situations can be found throughout the newly revised text.

- Chapter 1, "The Budget–Vision Relationship and the National Standards," presents and reviews the Professional Standards for Educational Leaders (PSEL) in relation to the correlation between budget and vision and the planning, knowledge, and skills necessary to be an effective school leader. It also examines three keys to ethics in school leadership.
- Chapter 2, "Culture, Data, Conflict Resolution, and Celebrating Success," reflects upon the importance of school culture, data-driven decision making, and types of data and assessment as related to academic planning and school budgeting. It also looks at the importance of conflict resolution and celebrating successes.
- Chapter 3, "A Model for Integrating Vision, Planning, and Budgeting," showcases an eight-component model related to budget and vision implementation and concludes with a real-life planning metaphor that connects with the elements of an educational action plan.
- Chapter 4, "Understanding the Budgeting Process," examines the delineation between school finance and school budgeting, budgeting in troublesome times, and other school funding concerns and considerations, including school vouchers and privatization. It also examines the future of school funding, the politicization of education and the related funding impact, and the effects of inadequate, inequitable, and unequal funding. Furthermore, it looks at how school leaders can still find hope by developing an optimistic work environment that places students first when it comes to instructional and budgetary planning efforts.
- Chapter 5, "School Funding and Steps to Budgeting Success," scrutinizes school funding sources (federal, state, and local) and the debate over voucher systems. It also offers ten steps to budgeting success: (1) Determine the allotment, (2) identify fixed expenditures, (3) involve all stakeholders, (4) identify potential expenditures, (5) cut back, (6) avoid continued debts, (7) develop a plan, (8) set goals and manage time efficiently, (9) evaluate the budget, and (10) abide by the budget.
- Chapter 6, "Effective, Efficient, and Essential Budgeting Practices," details certain aspects of the practical side of budgeting, such as the budget plan itself and how to analyze both school action or improvement and budget plans. It also covers how to conduct a needs assessment and perform an information analysis. Additionally, the effects of inadequate, inequitable, and unequal funding are examined. Budgeted dollars for school safety is a new inclusion within the text.

  The chapter also examines technology in schools today in relation to budgetary practices and reveals how to generate income sources by means of grants, fundraising, and crowdfunding. Expenditure accountability and control, along with accounting procedures such as collection and deposit structures, and the school activity account are examined, and a review of the advantages and disadvantages of cashless schools is offered. The budget amendment process is demonstrated.

- Chapter 7, "Accounting, Auditing, Risk Factors, and Leadership Behaviors," delves into auditing procedures, fraudulent practices, and frequent types of fraud. It includes a new section on phishing scams. Chapter 7 also looks at embezzlement and other risk factors and offers tips to help prevent common schemes. The chapter concludes with an analysis of the leadership role, specifically an examination of ethical and moral behaviors.
- Chapter 8, "Site-Based Decision Making, the Budget Coding Structure and Applications, and Other Budgetary Considerations," surveys the significance of site-based decision making and budget coding and applications. It offers a description of different specialized digitized school budget forms. Finally, ten important budget considerations are revealed.
- Chapter 9, "Building the School Budget: Budgetary Applications and Specialized Forms and Procedures," showcases thirteen budgetary components and five associated tables. The procedures of budget allocation are evidenced. Additionally, restricted funds are identified, and the process of projecting student enrollment is examined. The chapter concludes with a budget calendar example and an explanation of how to prepare for and successfully proceed through the budget hearing and defense process.

Special features of the book include the following:

- in-chapter vignettes with "Pause and Consider" questions
- discussion questions at the end of each chapter
- case study applications and problems
- experiential exercises including but not limited to a budget development project (see Resource A)
- a budgeting checklist for administrators
- selected templates and forms
- references and resources

School budgeting is a daunting process for many school leaders because most are not trained as bookkeepers, accountants, or financial planners. Many have received minimal training in the budgeting process, which involves not only digital accounting procedures and programs but also vision and goal development, instructional planning, and decision making. This can intimidate even the best educational leaders due to a lack of understanding of the school-based budgeting process and its integrative approaches. This often explains the willingness of some leaders to ignore, avoid, or pass on to others certain budgetary and planning responsibilities.

For these reasons the newly revised fourth edition of *The Principal's Guide to School Budgeting* has been written by two former school administrators with a combined ninety years of experience in the public school arena. These educators have extensive practical experience working with site-based decision-making committees to develop instructional goals and objectives and campus improvement plans for school and district budgets and in defending instructional and budget outcomes to superintendents and school boards.

The Principal's Guide to School Budgeting is not designed to be an exhaustive study of the budget and planning subject, nor is it designed to merely provide a basic understanding of the topic. Instead, the contents provide the necessary information and tools needed to incorporate the ideas set forth into real-life applications. As a result, readers will be able to take the integrated budget, vision, and planning concepts presented and incorporate them in a practical and relevant manner in their own school settings.

A caveat: The authors have made every effort to provide accurate and up-to-date online, technological, and digital information throughout the text. However, technology and digitally posted information are continuously changing. Therefore, it is inevitable that certain websites and other technology-oriented sources, resources, and materials listed within this text will change or become obsolete.

Acknowledgments

We would like to express our appreciation to several individuals who contributed to the development of our book, *The Principal's Guide to School Budgeting*, in its several editions—the first (2006), second (2013), third (2018), and now fourth (2024). So many people have influenced our lives and careers as school administrators and university professors. To those special individuals and friends, we publicly extend our respect and gratitude. An important acknowledgment is extended to the fine folk at Corwin, especially Tanya Ghans, our fourth edition senior acquisitions editor; Arnis E. Burvikovs, our second and third edition editor; and Lizzie Brenkus, our first edition editor, all of whom believed in helping us fulfill another goal in our professional lives. Also, we are appreciative of the guidance we received for this edition from Desirée A. Bartlett, content development manager; Nyle De Leon, senior editorial assistant; Amy Schroller, project editor, and Shannon Kelly, copy editor. The fourth edition of this text is all the better because of each of these fine individuals.

—RDS & LMG

Each edition of this book has been strengthened by the contributions of our dear friend and former colleague, Alice Frick—now retired, a school finance wizard extraordinaire—and two very special research assistants: Adriana E. Spencer and Mary F. Sholtis. These three individuals—Alice, Adriana, and Mary—provided invaluable advice and assistance. Adriana and Mary, as did my wife, Donna, conducted exceptional research for me, and they actively and accurately followed my credo: "Dig, and dig deep!" Thank you, ladies!

Finally, for allowing me to try out all of my budgeting "stuff," over the years, a special note of appreciation is extended to all of the former graduate students in the Educational Leadership and Foundations Department at the University of Texas at El Paso. Serving you was always an honor and a privilege. One concluding remark: Thank you, Lloyd. You are a very dear friend and an amazing writing partner!

—RDS

I would like to thank Mary, my wife and confidant, for having patience with me through this process. I want to thank my colleagues, Dr. Karen Maxwell and Dr. Bruce Scott, for their invaluable support and advice. A special thanks to my colleagues on the Texas Council of Professors of Educational Administration executive board for their friendship and support. I thank Bob and Montie Spaulding for being spiritual advisors to me for most of my life, helping me to keep first things first. I also want to acknowledge and thank all the congregants at the Freedom Fellowship inner-city outreach for teaching me so much about life and giving.

—LMG

Publisher's Acknowledgments

Corwin gratefully acknowledges the contributions of the following reviewers:

Louis Lim
Principal, Bur Oak Secondary School
Ontario, Canada

Ken Darvall
Principal, Tema International School
Tema, Ghana

Tanna Nicely
Executive Principal, Knox County Schools
Blaine, Tennessee

About the Authors

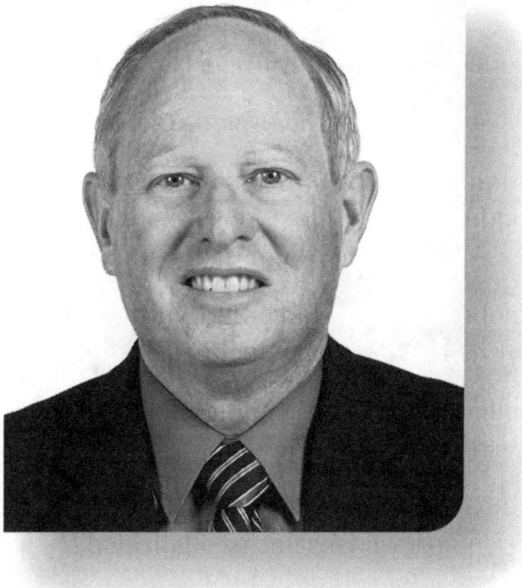

Richard D. Sorenson, professor emeritus, is the former director of the Principal Preparation Program and chairperson of the Educational Leadership and Foundations Department at the University of Texas at El Paso (UTEP). He earned his doctorate in educational leadership from Texas A&M University at Corpus Christi. Dr. Sorenson served public schools for twenty-five years as a social studies teacher, assistant principal, principal, and associate superintendent for human resources.

Dr. Sorenson worked with graduate students at UTEP in the area of school-based budgeting, personnel, educational law, and leadership development. During his twenty-year tenure, he was named the UTEP College of Education professor of the year, and he remains an active writer, with numerous professional journal publications. Dr. Sorenson continues to author other principal-oriented textbooks. He has also developed teacher resource guides and workbooks in the area of elementary and secondary social studies curricula. He has been actively involved in numerous professional organizations, including the Texas Elementary Principals and Supervisors Association (TEPSA) and the Texas Association of Secondary School Principals (TASSP), for which he conducted annual academy seminars for new principals for a decade.

Dr. Sorenson has been married to his wife, Donna, for the past forty-eight years and they have two adult children, Lisa (a school counselor with the Cypress-Fairbanks Independent School District in Houston, Texas) and Ryan (an exercise physiologist in Dallas, Texas); a wonderful son-in-law,

Sam (a petroleum engineer in Houston, Texas); and a delightful daughter-in-law, Nataly (the executive director of a Christian center in Dallas, Texas). Dr. Sorenson also has four amazing grandchildren: Savannah, Nehemiah, and Amelia, and one little guy, Oliver—all of whom are the pride and joy of his life. Dr. Sorenson and his wife, long-time residents of El Paso—the mountain and desert region of "true" West Texas—now reside near their grandchildren in Cypress (northwest Houston), Texas.

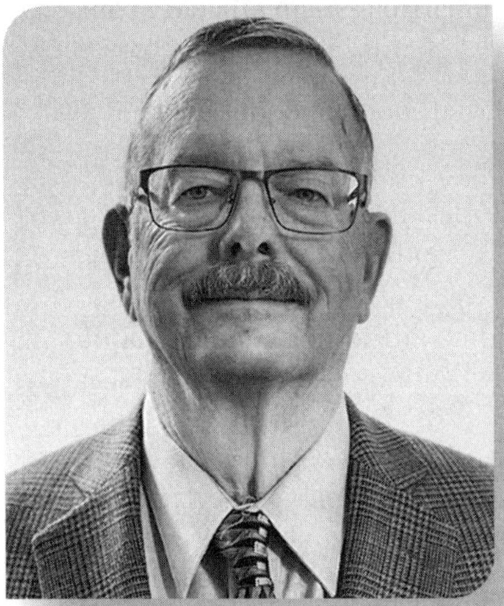

Lloyd M. Goldsmith, professor emeritus, earned his EdD in educational leadership from Baylor University. He was a professor for twenty years at Abilene Christian University (ACU), some of those years at ACU Dallas, where he taught doctoral courses in leadership theory. He also served as an admissions officer and a former director of the Principal Preparation Program and as a department chairperson at ACU. Dr. Goldsmith taught school budgeting, instructional leadership, and leadership theory. He served public schools for twenty-nine years as an elementary science teacher, middle school assistant principal, and elementary school principal.

Dr. Goldsmith and a fellow chemistry professor codirected a program facilitating high school chemistry teachers in developing effective instructional strategies. Dr. Goldsmith served on several state committees for the Texas Education Agency. He also served two terms as president of the Texas Council of Professors of Educational Administration.

Dr. Goldsmith is an active member at his church and enjoys serving others. He spends time volunteering at his grandchildren's schools and supporting their activities. He also enjoys traveling and attending ACU sporting events.

Dr. Goldsmith has been married to his wife, Mary, for the past forty years. They reside near their three children and their families in Abilene, Texas. Mary is a retired high school biology teacher, serving students for forty-one years. Lloyd and Mary have three adult children: Abigail (active in the PTO where she serves as president), who is married to Andrew (works in business development for a nuclear research lab); Eleanor (a second-grade Title I teacher), who is married to Kris (a chef, restaurant owner, and culinary arts teacher); and Nelson (a licensed professional building inspector), who is married to Kristen (a microbiologist and lab technician at Abilene Environmental Laboratory). He also has four grandchildren: Luke, Hilary, Levi, and Oliver. Plus, the Goldsmiths' have six granddogs! Life is good!

Introduction

Budgeting and accounting intimidate many individuals, whether related to work or home finances. In this book, you, the reader, will learn about numerous budgeting processes that all connect to the national Professional Standards for Educational Leaders (PSEL). However, before delving into the school budgeting process, the authors encourage you to examine the resources available at the conclusion of the text. A description of each resource is detailed below.

Resource A—The Budget Development Project: A Hands-On Experiential Exercise

Resource A offers the reader an opportunity to have a hands-on experience in developing a school budget. The project is a practice in application that brings all of the detailed book knowledge into one experiential exercise and project.

Resource B—Selected Forms

Resource B provides the reader with a couple of selected forms, the Budget Development Spreadsheet and the Strategy Page, designed to aid in completing the budget bevelopment project in Resource A.

Resource C—Experiential Exercises

- The Budgeting Codes Activity

This activity within the pages of Resource C provides the reader with four scenarios by which the budget accounting codes can be learned and incorporated.

- Accounting Codes Reference Sheet

The reference sheet permits the reader to apply a coding structure to the above-noted Budgeting Codes Activity as well as to other learning activities in Chapter 8.

Resource D—Budgeting Checklist for School Administrators

This checklist ensures that the reader has a successful budgetary year by identifying bookkeeping tasks and responsibilities, budget manager tasks and responsibilities, fundraising considerations, site-based team and budget development indicators, and important budgetary questions—all of which are worthy of perusal.

1 The Budget–Vision Relationship and the National Standards

Empowering those around you to be heard and valued makes the difference between a leader who simply instructs and one who inspires.

—Adena Friedman,
President and Chief Executive Officer, Nasdaq
(Nasdaq, 2020)

School Leadership: Inspirational, Empowering, and Visionary

School leaders face the challenge of improving student academic achievement in a time of inadequate, inequitable, and unequal funding as well as contracting resources. They also confront a host of other challenges, including

- maximizing scarce resources,
- making budget adjustments without adversely impacting student achievement,
- fiscal equity, equality, and efficiency, and—far too often—the lack thereof (an issue specifically associated with vouchers and school privatization),
- stretching human capital (recruitment, retention, and empowerment),
- retirements, resignations, and replacements,
- political polarization (LGBTQ+ issues, critical race theory, book bans, and opt-out students from instruction),
- threats against educators,
- serving an increasingly poor and diverse student population,
- providing individual instruction more quickly and prudently,
- using funding as a lever to spur innovation,

- aligning instructional goals and strategies with funding,
- providing teachers what they need, how they need it, and when they need it,
- meeting the high expectations held by top-performing nations in reading and mathematics, and
- increasing parental involvement (Douglas, 2022; Jochim et al., 2023; Sorenson, 2022; Sorenson, 2024)

Inspirational and empowering leadership, as noted in the opening quote by Adena Friedman, the president and chief executive officer of Nasdaq, combined with visionary approaches enables school leaders to not only arouse and motivate teams but also to overcome the numerous school-related challenges when developing, maintaining, and assessing a school budget.

School Budgeting, School Vision

Budgetary and visionary leadership: these are two issues school leaders must confront on a daily basis. The relationship between school budgeting and vision is as intertwined as is love with marriage. In both cases, you can't have one without the other. These two forces, budget and vision, come with their own accountability systems. The former is fiscal; the latter is academic. Technology gives rise to greater and more complicated accounting procedures. Leaders can become overwhelmed when trying to make sense of a sea of data being spewed from a variety of sources. With all of these and other demands, what is a school leader to do? A different approach to the situation is required. Lead by being inspirational, visionary, and by always empowering others.

It is the integration of vision within the school budgeting process that transforms school budgeting from merely number crunching to purpose-driven expenditures supporting academic success for all students.

School budgeting is certainly about spreadsheets, reports, tracking the expenditure of funds, and the completing of a myriad of accounting forms (see Chapters 6 and 9). It is easy to get caught up in the accounting dimension of budgeting and neglect its companion: vision. It is the integration of vision within the school budgeting process that transforms school budgeting from merely number crunching to purpose-driven expenditures supporting academic success for all students. An articulated and shared vision creates the environment necessary for planning for academic success and for all students to flourish.

Principals must rethink their approach to school budgeting. School budgeting must not be thought of as merely an accounting responsibility. Leaders must leave the primary accounting responsibility to certified public accountants (CPAs) and the business office. These individuals must be allowed to provide the technical expertise and support necessary to meet the regulatory requirements associated with state and federal fiscal accountability standards. Principal leadership skills must carry the school budgeting process to the next level. This is achieved by integrating the school vision with the budgeting and academic processes for the purpose of achieving academic success for all students.

Imagine a train heading down a track. The track is time; the train is the school. The locomotive represents the school leader. This individual leads the local motivation to create a shared vision for the school. The remaining cars are the school's vision and budget and planning process. The movement of the train down the track is the school year. Like the locomotive, the leader is key to moving the school "down the track." Bringing along the cars of vision, budget, and planning is essential—so essential, in fact, they are recognized and supported in the Professional Standards for Educational Leaders (PSEL).

The Professional Standards for Educational Leaders

The PSEL provide a logical place to commence a discussion of the relationship between leaders and school budgeting and planning. Sometimes in the school budgeting and planning process, the PSEL can appear distant to leaders and stakeholders. That should not be the case. Rather, these standards provide leaders with a firm foundation for exploring and growing leadership development and practice.

A brief examination of the PSEL provides an overview of the authors' assertion that all standards address budget issues and do indeed speak loudly to leaders and other stakeholders engaged in the budgeting process. The lofty goals of these national standards *are* connected to the reality of leading schools. These standards are crucial in making a difference in student success as well as in student well-being and learning (Sorenson, 2022).

Future-oriented standards provide guidance in the fast-changing global arena where educational leaders reside. The PSEL demand active, not passive, leadership. These standards promote leaders that are collaborative, inspiring, empowering, inspirational, and inclusive in leading their schools. However, leadership is stronger and more effective when other stakeholders are involved, such as teachers, counselors, and paraprofessionals. Such collaborative and empowering leadership demands cultivating and improving the leadership growth and development in all stakeholders. The PSEL "reflect the importance of cultivating leadership capacity in others" (National Policy Board for Educational Administration [NPBEA], 2015, p. 4).

The PSEL demand active, not passive, leadership. These standards promote leaders that are collaborative, inspiring, empowering, inspirational, and inclusive in leading their schools.

The PSEL provide a clarion call for collaboration between all stakeholders within the school and its community. The standards are "a compass that guides the direction of practice directly as well as indirectly through the work of policy makers, professional associations, and supporting institutions" (NPBEA, 2015, p. 4).

Covey (2020), in his classic book, *The Seven Habits of Highly Effective People,* encouraged leaders to begin with the end in mind. In essence, this is exactly what the PSEL call on school leaders to do, as every standard promotes *each* student's academic success and well-being. *Each* means all students, 100 percent. *Each* also implies individual attention to all students. Can school leaders walk down their school's hallways and look at students and determine which ones they do not want to meet with success? What moral choice do school leaders have but to "promote *each* student's academic success and well-being"? This "*each* student" dimension of the PSEL demands a train trip for planning big and promoting success. It requires another visit to two longtime friends—school budgeting and vision—and an examination of their often-overlooked relationship in the planning process.

The PSEL are examined through a school budgeting lens in an effort to explore how the national leadership standards address the school budgeting process. This examination provides school leaders with guiding principles for school budgeting.

Initially, a leader might be criticized for taking such a utopian train trip. Critics will accuse the leader of not living in the real world. School leaders will suffer through the criticism and cynicism of these sarcastic and skeptical voices because they understand every student meeting with success is, by its very nature, a utopian goal. Visiting utopia provides us with a perfect vision for our schools. It is imperative to begin with this perfect vision. To begin planning for academic success for each student with a vision that is less than ideal dooms a leader and team in their quest for academic success for each student.

The PSEL define the practice for educational leaders. They offer guidance for professional practice as well as inform how educational leaders are "prepared, hired, developed, supervised and evaluated" (NPBEA, 2015, p. 2). The PSEL provide greater emphasis on student learning and provide strong guidance to guarantee each student is prepared for success in the 21st century. The PSEL clarify and offer greater specificity for educational leaders.

While in utopia devising a plan for academic success for each student, give primary consideration to the interrelationship between school budgeting and vision. While neither of these concepts is new, it could be argued school leaders have not given due consideration to the significance of the symbiotic relationship they have on the academic success of students and schools. It is essential to consider budgeting and vision simultaneously in the planning process in order to increase our understanding of their influence on each other and the fulfillment of the national standard's clarion call for "academic success and well-being for *each* student." It is imperative the discussion of school budgeting and vision begin with an introductory overview of each PSEL. It is also essential the overview of the standards be accomplished through a school budgeting and vision lens.

An Introduction of the PSEL Through a Budget–Vision Lens

A macro-view of the PSEL provides an appropriate introduction to these standards and their elements. The PSEL influence how leaders perceive the manifestation of campus leadership behavior.

PSEL 1: Mission, Vision, and Core Values

> Effective educational leaders develop, advocate, and enact a shared mission, vision, and core values of high-quality education and academic success and well-being of *each* student.

PSEL 1: Mission, Vision, and Core Values, like all of the standards, includes the phrase "success and well-being of each student." This phrase requires leaders to approach budgeting and vision with the expectation *each* student will meet with success, not only those students who come to school prepared and nurtured by their families but also those who come with little nurturing and minimal preparation. Leaders might do well to stop and reread the previous statement and allow the significance of it to sink in. "Success and well-being of *each* student" does not allow leaders or other stakeholders to rationalize or explain away their responsibility to have each student meet with success. The focus is no longer on organizational effectiveness; rather, it seeks success for each student.

Kouzes and Posner (2023) identified five practices of strong leaders. One of those practices is inspiring a shared vision that guides all of the organization's stakeholders. Leaders are those who have the obligation to help stakeholders visualize goals and outcomes. Likewise, leaders must help those they lead by providing a positive example. This requires leaders to keep their word on commitments they make with others. Doing so moves the organization forward.

Budgeting, visioning, empowering, and academic success are intertwined with each other in the planning process. They are not isolated variables operating independently in a school's culture. When leaders accept this coupling of budgeting and vision and understand their combined effect on academic achievement, budgeting expands from a fiscal responsibility to a fiscal visioning opportunity that in turn drives planning for the academic success of each student.

PSEL 1: Mission, Vision, and Core Values is at the very heart of this book's purpose in that it calls for the melding of mission, vision, and core values within the budgeting process. Not only must a school leader facilitate the development, articulation, and implementation of a school vision, the leader must also be a steward of that vision. Stewardship is the administration and management of the financial affairs of another. A school leader ensures the school's resources are allocated in a manner that supports the school's vision. The school's budget does not belong to the principal or any other leader. It belongs to all the school's stakeholders. It belongs to the public who sacrifice through the payment of taxes, thus providing the budget revenues.

Principals once focused attention on the school facilities and ensured the school was managed in an orderly fashion, with students sitting quietly at desks. Principals spent little time or energy on instructional practices or encouraging a culture of continuous improvement or a student-centered education. The vision and mission were ignored or, at best, posted somewhere in the building, never to be reviewed or discussed.

Principals, today must focus on student learning and achievement. Principals delegate managerial and other routine duties to supplementary individuals. Principals tout the vision and mission statements frequently so all stakeholders know and understand the vision, mission, and core values.

PSEL 2: Ethics and Professional Norms

> Effective educational leaders act ethically and according to professional norms to promote *each* student's academic success and well-being.

PSEL 2: Ethics and Professional Norms is essential in growing the integrated budget–vision–planning process. It is noteworthy that this standard immediately follows *PSEL 1: Mission, Vision, and Core Values*, which established the importance of having a school vision. Core values and ethics must be melded in order to be an ethical and moral professional leader.

The *Ethics and Professional Norms* standard is a reminder that character does in fact matter. Principals must examine personal motives and their treatment of others as well as how they carry out their personal and professional missions and lives. Leaders must decide what they are not willing to do in order to achieve personal and school goals.

Integrity, fairness, and ethical behavior are a trio of concepts school leaders often struggle to define. Former United States Supreme Court justice Potter Stewart, commenting in the *Jacobellis v. Ohio* case concerning the issue of pornography, stated he could not attempt to define pornography yet acknowledged, "But I know it when I see it" (Linder, n.d.). Like Stewart, educators know integrity, fairness, and ethical behavior when observed but struggle to define this trio of terms.

This trio can be analyzed utilizing the works of Plato, John Locke, Immanuel Kant, Niccolo Machiavelli, and others, but that might seem detached from the day-to-day challenges school leaders face. Leaders must depend on their personal judgment and experiences in determining how to react to given situations (see the fraud and embezzlement issues discussed in Chapter 7, along with "Case Study #2: Fiscal Issues and the New Principal" in Chapter 4 and "Case Study: Sex, Money, and a Tangled Web Woven" in Chapter 7).

Readers must take time from their busy schedules to consider integrity, fairness, and ethical behavior. After all, the in-the-face demands of academic accountability, student discipline, per-pupil expenditure, and a host of others provide a variety of excuses for bypassing an examination of these terms. Cooper (2012) suggests school leaders often make administrative decisions using rationality and systematic reflection in a piecemeal fashion. Cooper asserts leaders are ad hoc problem solvers, not comprehensive moral philosophers who only resort to the next level of generality and abstraction when a repertoire of practical moral rules fails to assist in reaching a decision. Sound familiar?

Examining Three Key Terms—The Trio

It is important to examine *PSEL 2: Ethics and Professional Norms* in the light of budgeting and vision and to pay close attention to the three key terms found in this standard: *integrity, fairness,* and *ethics* (see Table 1.1).

TABLE 1.1 Key Terms in PSEL 2: Ethics and Professional Norms

Integrity	Soundness of and adherence to moral principle and character
Fairness	Free from bias, dishonesty, or injustice
Ethics	A system of *moral* principles

Source: Stein (1967).

Integrity. Integrity, the first of the trio of ethical terms, is an important dimension of leadership. Leaders who value integrity are not only interested in results but are also interested in relationships. This is easily illustrated in the world of high-stakes student assessment. Each year, educators are under increasing pressure to meet a mandated level of academic performance for their students. The consequences for not achieving these defined goals are increasing. The temptation from a variety of schemes for school leaders to manipulate these data is also increasing.

Principals must not only consider integrity within the sphere of academic goals. To be successful, they must also consider the integrity of their relationships with all of the school's stakeholders. For integrity to exist, leaders must show genuine concern for others and their personal goals. When concern and integrity exist, trust flourishes and further empowers the leader to lead the school toward fulfilling its shared vision.

Stories abound in which school leaders succumb to temptation and misrepresent themselves, inappropriately use school funds, or manipulate data (see Chapter 7). When this is discovered, these leaders lose their reputation and effectiveness along with their dignity. It takes a lifetime to build a good reputation and only a minute to lose it.

High-stakes testing is a prime area for leaders to be tempted to cheat by manipulating data. Variables such as test security, student exemptions, and test preparation become factors. In one highly publicized case, systematic cheating was uncovered in Atlanta's public school system. Forty-four schools and at least 178 educators, including the superintendent, were involved in this alleged cheating incident (Blinder, 2015; Severson, 2011). Cizek (1999) compiled a list of euphemisms that have been used by educators in attempts to soften the term *cheating*. Sadly, two of the more creative euphemisms were *falsely reporting success* and *achievement similarities not attributable to chance.*

Samuel Johnson, one of the most quoted moralist from the 18th century, said, "Integrity without knowledge is weak and useless, and knowledge without integrity is dangerous and dreadful" (Brainy Quote, 2001–2023). Integrity alone will not allow a school leader to meet with success. Principals must understand every facet of a school and its students. Principals must have a command of the school's vision and its budget. If a leader lacks integrity, the school is at risk; doubt and fear will replace integrity. People will revert to the selfish nature of man, and the common good of the learning community will be forgotten.

FairnessOnce again, school leaders risk their effectiveness when they separate vision from the budget, especially when it comes to fairness. It is essential to consider both budget and vision as integral parts of the planning process to completely understand the complex nature of fairness.

Fairness, the second of the trio of key terms, does not mean ensuring everyone gets the same amount of something or the same treatment. Fairness is when everyone receives what is needed in order to successfully accomplish his or her goals. Some students will need one cup of patience while others will require two, three, or even four cups of patience to reach their goals. Still others will need different resources dedicated to them to ensure their academic success, thus the continued clarion call for Title 1 funds for disadvantaged students in high-poverty schools. Another example is students with learning disabilities (often ignored in school privatization programs) who might need greater special education resources in order to reach their instructional goals than those without disabilities.

When principals accept the fact that vision is what drives the budget and shared vision is designed to help all students achieve their potential, then they begin to understand fairness requires resources to be allocated on the basis of need in order to achieve academic goals. Fairness is not dividing the financial pie into equal pieces. Common Ground (2022) reported the 2023 New Jersey per-pupil expenditure for students in special education was $32,674, compared to $19,519 for general education. The financial pie was not divided into equal pieces. Instead, it was apportioned based on meeting the individual needs of students.

Schools perish when a lack of vision exists. When money is thrown at problems, human nature takes over to demand "Give me my fair share." This usually translates into "I'll get all I can get." In the absence of an understanding of the budget–vision relationship in the planning process, greed takes control and the good of the learning community is abandoned.

Unfortunately, fairness does not become a part of a school's social fabric overnight. It cannot be ordered or microwaved into existence. Instead, the leader must keep the budget–vision relationship in front of the team and make inroads relative to fairness, especially as opportunities arise. Through persistence, fairness will become valued as part of the school's culture and will manifest itself in strong ethical and moral behaviors.

EthicsEthical and moral behaviors are an essential part of the school leader's persona. Fairness, integrity, and equity are employed to best conduct the school's business. School leaders must act in an ethical manner when handling discipline problems, implementing state-mandated accountability testing, managing school budgets, consulting with parents, supervising faculty and staff, and in a host of other situations.

Principals must ensure both ethical and moral behaviors are strong personal attributes, both regularly exhibited and frequently observed. Principals with strong moral character are honest, trustworthy, diligent, reliable, respect all aspects of the law (education code/school board policies, for example) and exhibit—as previously noted—integrity, candor, discretion, observance of fiduciary duty, respect for others, absence of hatred and discrimination, fiscal (budgetary) responsibility, and mental and emotional maturity.

Principle of Benefit Maximization

A continued examination of the national standards with regard to their implication on budgeting and vision reveals how appropriate it is to consider the principle of benefit maximization. This principle requires principals to make choices that provide the greatest good for the most people. When developing a school vision, the process must be one of inclusiveness. Shared vision is about meaningfully involving everyone in the vision development process, not only those with the greatest political clout or the loudest voices. The principal must help craft and share a school vision that not only provides each student with the opportunity to meet with success but also is truly shared by all stakeholders. The PSEL's mantra to "promote *each* student's academic success and well-being" reminds us *each* means all students (and not just some) will meet with success.

The principle of benefit maximization also applies to the budgeting process. Budgets must provide the greatest good for the most students. This requires tough decisions be made. Granted, tough decisions are not always popular decisions. But tough decisions made with integrity and fairness and in an ethical manner will propel schools toward the fulfillment of their vision. It is essential the school budget be considered in tandem with the school vision.

The budget is an essential tool in turning the vision into reality. When the budget process is divorced from the vision process, the likelihood of the vision being fulfilled dramatically decreases. Bracey (2002) provides a vivid illustration of what can happen when the budget process and the academic vision process are divorced. In his now-classic read, *The War Against America's Public Schools*, Bracey detailed the 21st-century attack on public school, notably privatization (see Chapters 4 and 5 of this book). He also wrote about a group of superintendents enthusiastically embracing a new efficiency model that changed them from scholars into managers. Bracey concluded his chiding of this particular efficiency model by writing, "Of course, one might wonder why, instead of studying ways to save money on toilet paper, superintendents didn't investigate why their charges dipped it in water and slung it at the walls" (p. 37).

Considering the toilet paper problem from a purely accounting perspective, the focus is only on the financial cost associated with providing the toilet paper for student use and neglects the possible academic issues at play in the misuse of the toilet paper. By only considering the financial issue associated with the use or misuse of the toilet paper, leaders wipe out the opportunity to get to the academic bottom of the toilet paper problem in terms of its cost to the school's vision to have all students meet with academic success.

By including the academic perspective in conjunction with the budget perspective, thus addressing the budget–vision connection, the toilet paper problem is then also considered as a potential indication of an academic failure to meet the needs of all students. Bottom line: Budgeting and vision must be considered simultaneously if schools are to reach their goal of 100 percent student success.

The Golden Rule Principle

A second principle to consider in the examination of ethics is the Golden Rule. Many might mistakenly limit the Golden Rule to the teachings of Jesus; however, there is some version of the Golden Rule in five of the world's major religions. The universal truth found in the Golden Rule is important to consider in our ethical treatment of others. It requires principals to treat all people with equal value. People are entitled to equal opportunity. Principals must value all people and respect their educational goals. People must not be considered as merely assets to be used to achieve the school vision.

Finally, leaders must respect individuals' rights to make their own choices. When including the Golden Rule as part of the code of ethics, principals are more apt to integrate the budget process with the vision. The end result: Leaders are less likely to see people as objects to be manipulated to achieve selfish purposes.

PSEL 3: Equity and Cultural Responsiveness

> Effective educational leaders strive for equality of educational opportunity and culturally responsive practices to promote *each* student's academic success and well-being.

Culturally responsive behavior is essential for today's campus leaders. Leadership is no longer limited to teaching; it requires the entire school environment to be responsive to the instructional needs of all students in general and minoritized students specially (Khalifa et al., 2016; Munna, 2023). A large body of literature focuses on culturally responsive academic instruction. Campus leaders and other stakeholders must assist in equity, equality, and cultural responsiveness by increasing their cultural knowledge, enhancing staff members' cultural self-awareness, validating others' cultures, increasing cultural relevance, establishing cultural validity, and emphasizing cultural equity (Banks & Obiakor, 2015; Sorenson, 2022).

Striving for equity of educational opportunity and cultural responsiveness requires strong campus leadership. This necessitates principals prioritize and budget time and resources to support academic achievement and moreover serve as advocates for societal change.

Striving for equity of educational opportunity and cultural responsiveness requires strong campus leadership. This necessitates principals prioritize and budget time and resources to support academic achievement and moreover serve as advocates for societal change.

PSEL 4: Curriculum, Instruction, and Assessment

> Effective educational leaders develop and support intellectually rigorous and coherent systems of curriculum, instruction, and assessment to promote *each* student's academic success and well-being.

The authors, as former principals, observed many instructional improvement programs come and go. School stakeholders frequently became jaded and skeptical of the next new curriculum plan. Regardless of how many instructional programs are adopted, they often fail because they are frequently uncoordinated, short lived, or limited in scope. Therefore, it is essential all stakeholders possess ownership of the school's action or improvement plan and recognize the importance of allocating instructional resources to achieve the desired academic results (the biggest bang for the buck) that are in line with the school's vision and mission. The learning community is literally investing its resources in its students and is thus expecting a return on its investment in the form of educated, enlightened, and productive individuals.

When schools fail to produce this product, the community resources must be reallocated to address this failure in the form of welfare, juvenile detention, and adult prison programs. The failure of schools to meet student needs creates a domino effect that is felt throughout the community. Failure to meet the campus goals for students creates an intensely competitive environment as other public institutions vying for the same limited public resources must meet the shortcomings of school programs.

An example of added costs to the public that occur when education is not successful can be found in the prison system. New findings have revealed 30 percent of prisoners in U.S. state and federal prisons have their high school diploma or an equivalent. This compares to 86 percent of the general population. This survey, the most comprehensive assessment of the educational backgrounds of prisoners in the last decade, also reported overall prison inmates with GED/high school equivalency certificates had higher literacy scores than those with high school diplomas (Ositelu, 2019).

Keeping a person in prison costs more than two and a half times the amount it takes to educate a child. The average per-pupil expenditure for students in U.S. public elementary and secondary schools in 2021–2022 was $13,701 (Hanson, 2022). Utah, at $7,591, spent the least per pupil in educating children. New York spent $24,881 per pupil, making it the largest spender per pupil (Hanson, 2022). The average cost to taxpayers to keep a prisoner incarcerated was $35,347. On average, the cost of keeping an individual in prison is $21,646 more per year than the average per-pupil cost for students in public schools (Prison Bureau in Federal Register, 2021).

The cost to the public due to unsuccessful schools is also reflected in the median earning of adults based on educational attainment. The more educated a person, the greater the person's income is likely to be. Conversely, the earlier a person drops out of school, the lower the person's income is likely to be (Ositelu, 2019).

The relationship between educational attainment and income is significant. The cost to society for students not meeting with academic success is staggering. Assuming a forty-year work career and not adjusting for inflation, the worker with a bachelor's degree will earn $1,396,480 more in a work career than the individual who left school with less than a high school education.

When school leaders and teams, and even state and federal legislative bodies, fail to achieve the PSEL's call for academic success for each student, then schools can expect other systems to compete with them for public resources. It is imperative for students to meet with academic success not only to become greater producers for society but also to lessen the need for prisons and thus increase the availability of funds to enrich the services provided by public education. It is essential, if not critical, principals and teams focus on curriculum, instruction, and assessment. Consider where you and the other school stakeholders are relative to implementing innovative and student-centered curriculum, instruction, and assessment at your school.

PSEL 5: Community of Care and Support for Students

> Effective educational leaders cultivate an inclusive, caring, and supportive school community that promotes the academic success and well-being of *each* student.

A school must have a strong community to support the students under its care. This does not happen unless leaders intentionally guide and promote the stakeholders within the school and its broader community. Gordon and Louis (2009), more than a decade ago, affirmed the importance of the democratic assumptions that underpin public education in the United States and the significance of involving as many stakeholders as possible to impact student achievement in a positive manner. Hence, openness and sharing increases the potential to solve problems in learning communities.

Trust between parents and school is important in growing a healthy school community. Trust requires ongoing and frequent interactions with all stakeholders within and across the school community. Strong social interactions provide the environment for developing trust (Sorenson, 2024). If the various school stakeholders fail to have frequent and meaningful interaction with each other, they cannot expect to grow the trust needed for a healthy environment.

Campus leaders must invest time and energy in developing the conditions necessary to produce a healthy community of care and support for the students and their parents. A note of caution: Schools that are doing well academically may not feel the need or urgency to recruit community members and parents, since their campus is functioning well. Such thinking is a mistake! Principals and other campus stakeholders must always focus on community care and support for all students and families. Examine where you and the other school stakeholders are regarding the establishment of a community of care and support for the students and their families.

PSEL 6: Professional Capacity of School Personnel

> Effective educational leaders develop the professional capacity and practice of school personnel to promote *each* student's academic success and well-being.

Educators are operating in a new era of teacher evaluation. It is important for school leaders to address the professional capacity of all school personnel. Growing professional capacity is a deliberate endeavor; it must not be a haphazard endeavor. Principals working as instructional leaders are at the very core of solid teacher practice. Principals who effectively use a sound teacher evaluation system promote a professional learning community that fosters effective teaching and learning (Childress, 2014; Toch & Rothman, 2023). This requires principals to provide human capital, social capital, cultural capital, and financial capital as well as informational resources, each as means of building capacity (Hattie, 2012; Lai, 2014; Lemov, 2021; Sorenson, 2022).

Development of professional capacity of educators remains an ongoing challenge. Darling-Hammond and McLaughlin (1995), almost three decades ago, addressed professional development concerns that remain relevant today. Three professional development designs were suggested: (1) opportunities for teacher inquiry and collaboration, (2) strategies to reflect teachers' questions and concerns, and (3) access to successful models of (new) practice.

Darling-Hammond and McLaughlin (1995) also offered ideas related to both learners and teachers. Three suggestions were provided: (1) engage teachers in partial tasks and provide opportunities to observe, assess, and reflect on the new practices, (2) be participant driven and grounded in inquiry, reflection, and experimentation, and (3) provide support through modeling, coaching, and the collective solving of problems.

Darling-Hammond and McLaughlin's (1995) suggestions for policies that support professional development continue to remain strong today, identifying needs many leaders still experience on their campuses three decades later. PSEL 6 remains an ongoing challenge not only for the campus instructional leader but for all campus stakeholders. Principals and team members must always focus on the professional capacity of school personnel. Think about where you and the other school stakeholders are growing the professional capacity of your school's personnel.

PSEL 7: Professional Community for Teachers and Staff

> Effective educational leaders foster a professional community of teachers and other professional staff to promote *each* student's academic success and well-being.

Growing a professional community must be a thoughtful undertaking. It is essential for principals to promote a professional learning community that fosters effective teaching and learning. This empowers PSEL 7's charge to "foster a professional community of teachers and other professional staff to promote *each* student's academic success and well-being" and thus helps leaders achieve envisioned outcomes. *Foster* is a well-selected word for this PSEL. *Foster* encourages. *Foster* supports. *Foster* stimulates. *Foster* cultivates and nurtures. *Foster* strengthens and enriches.

It is the responsibility of the school leader to nurture and develop the school's learning culture, be it the faculty, staff, or student body (Hoy & Miskel, 2012; Sorenson, 2024). This is a responsibility that cannot and must not be delegated. It is within the school's culture that the traditions, values, and beliefs of the various stakeholders are manifested (Deal & Peterson, 2016; Mungal & Sorenson, 2020). School leaders must seize the opportunity to define and shape the professional learning community. Leaders must be certain not to lead with reckless behavior. It is important to get teachers and other professional staff on board. If principals, teachers, and staff see the importance of a professional learning community, it will thrive.

What leaders, through time and labor, value will be inculcated in the school's culture. If principals value the importance of a professional learning community for teachers and staff, it will become part of the school's culture. Principals are likely to hear someone say, "At this school, we put our money where our mouth is when it comes to growing our professional learning community."

Resources (fiscal, human, and material) must be aligned with the school's vision during the planning process if the school's culture and instructional program are to be conducive to student learning and staff development. Anything less than aligning the budget with the vision bastardizes the process.

Resources (fiscal, human, and material) must be aligned with the school's vision during the planning process if the school's culture and instructional program are to be conducive to student learning and staff development.

One final point about professional community: Some long-term faculty and staff have acquired substantial institutional memory. Some of these individuals are burned out and have stayed past their time of effectiveness for various reasons. Others have lots of institutional knowledge they keep to themselves. Most of us have experienced interactions with long-term employees, be they faculty or staff. Long-term school employees—administrators, teachers, paraprofessionals, custodians, or others—often know where the bodies are buried. Interestingly, the 1941 classic Hollywood film *Citizen Kane* is credited with being the first known source of the phrase "knows where all the bodies are buried" (YARN, 2005–2023).

A long-term employee who holds a position of trust in a school acquires knowledge of many secrets, secrets that powerful employees would rather stay buried. Thus, a long-term employee knowledgeable of secrets can and will use those secrets to secure something of value. This behavior reminds us that one must always be waiting for the other shoe to drop; something will happen, and it is usually bad. Principals and faculty must always focus on the professional growth of the learning community. Always determine where you and team are when it comes to professional growth and development.

PSEL 8: Meaningful Engagement of Families and Community

> Effective educational leaders cultivate and engage families and the community in meaningful, reciprocal, and mutually beneficial ways to promote *each* student's academic success and well-being.

Almost four decades ago, *Beyond the Bake Sale: An Educators Guide to Working With Parents* (Henderson et al., 1986) was published. At that time, the authors' superintendent made the book a required study for all administrators. The superintendent recognized the importance of involving families and the community in a meaningful way. Through the superintendent's stewardship, campus leaders increased their engagement with their communities and families.

In the text, Henderson and her co-authors identified five family and community roles in schools, all of which remain relevant today:

1. **Partners:** Parents performing basic obligations for their child's education and social development.
2. **Collaborators and problem solvers:** Parents reinforcing the school's efforts with their child and helping to solve problems.
3. **Audience:** Parents attending and appreciating the school's (and their child's) performances and productions.
4. **Supporters:** Parents providing volunteer assistance to teachers, the parent organization, and other parents.
5. **Advisors and/or co-decision makers:** Parents providing input on school policy and programs through membership in ad hoc or permanent governance bodies (p. 3).

Henderson et al. even included self-assessment checklists for (1) key characteristics of your school, (2) key characteristics of families in your school, (3) assessing the family–school relationship, and (4) assessing the parent–teacher relationship.

Twenty-three years later, the method detailed in Warren et al. (2009) "Beyond the Bake Sale: A Community-Based Relational Approach to Parent Engagement in Schools" was significantly different from that of Henderson et al. Moreover, Ishimaru (2020) took further steps by identifying an absolute need to build equitable collaborations with families and communities. These later researchers went beyond the campus to include a community-based relational approach to fostering parent engagement in schools. A comparison between the "bake sales" of 1986, 2009, and 2020 illustrates the significant differences between the traditional school community–centered model, the community-based model,and the equitable collaborative model.

Principals and campus stakeholders must focus on meaningful engagement of families and community. Contemplate where you and the campus stakeholders are relative to growing and supporting such meaningful engagement as well as in transitioning from the traditional school community–centered model to the community-based model to the equitable collaborative model.

PSEL 9: Operations and Management

> Effective educational leaders manage school operations and resources to promote *each* student's academic success and well-being.

A casual glance at this PSEL standard could be deceptive. Reading the words *operations and management* might conjure a mental model of cleaning the building, sending notes to and from the classroom and the office, and assigning faculty load based on teacher preference. This mental model for operations and management is likely to have a weak connection to teaching and learning at best, and no connection at all at worst. This is no longer the case; PSEL 9 is much more than an old mental model of operations and management typically assigned to noninstructional items. In fact, this standard speaks directly to the premise of this book. Element D reads that "[effective leaders] are responsible, ethical, and accountable stewards of the school's monetary and non-monetary resources, engaging in effective budgeting and accounting practices" (NPBEA, 2015, p. 23) and embodies the Sorenson-Goldsmith Integrated Budget Model as detailed in Chapter 3. This standard readily relates to school leaders serving as accountable stewards when it comes to budgetary management. School leaders must engage in effective, efficient, and essential budgetary processes and practices (see Chapter 6 and the scenario titled "Budgeted Dollars and School Safety").

PSEL 9: Operations and Management also addresses the importance of developing and managing the relationships with feeder schools in enrollment, curricular, instructional, and budgetary matters. A wide range of strategies can be developed and implemented to strengthen the ties with feeder schools. These strategies include collaborating with each feeder school to receive permission to provide recruitment information such as an introductory letter or developing a section on the school's website targeting feeder school families (Independent School Management [ISM], 2017). Recognize it is essential for principals and team members to focus not only on instruction (which is critical) but also on operations and management as well. Reflect upon where you and the other stakeholders are in developing and implementing effective, efficient, and essential campus operations and management.

PSEL 10: School Improvement

> Effective educational leaders act as agents of continuous improvement to promote *each* student's academic success and well-being.

For the last three decades, there has been a clarion call for continuous improvement in areas such as instruction, technology, communication, and data analysis. Continuous improvement depends heavily on the interactions between teachers as well as interactions with the principal. Time is an important factor in school improvement (see Sorenson et al., 2016). The more time school leaders invest in instructional leadership, the greater the increase in instruction. The more time teachers are engaged with the principal in the instructional leadership role, the more improvements will occur in the instructional practice for those teachers.

The Carnegie Foundation for the Advancement of Teaching published a decade ago what continues to be a most relevant white paper titled "Continuous Improvement in Education" (Park et al., 2013). Seven overarching themes were identified. A direct public school connection has been added to each of these themes.

1. **Leadership and strategy.** Leaders of continuous improvement schools bring a strategic mindset to their work. The very best campus leaders do not believe in some magical concept as a strategy for school improvement. Rather, they focus on establishing disciplined processes for developing, testing, evaluating, and improving the school's core work streams and programs in order to build the capacity to engage in instructional leadership.
2. **Communication and engagement.** Effective communications and strategies are essential for engaging all stakeholders in the school. Many schools employ systems thinking that brings about greater collaboration between the school's stakeholders. This, in turn, allows the faculty and staff to identify and address root causes to the problems their school faces.
3. **Organizational infrastructure.** Principals must employ continuous improvement of instruction. This requires the development of structures across core processes and specific goals. Schools must identify a central organization that coordinates the work of the various groups.
4. **Systems thinking.** Using systems thinking, principals employing continuous improvement can establish structures

around specific goals or processes that encourage interactions across their campuses.

5. **Methodology.** Methodology is a must in continuous improvement. Factors such as purpose, focus on inquiry, and improvement must be targeted. Some school leaders and teams use the inquiry process for strategic planning purposes; others use an improvement process. Both processes must be constructed around student data to improve instruction.

6. **Data collection and analysis.** Tracking campus data informs stakeholders on the progress they are making toward campus goals. Data monitoring is essential. It is critical principals and teams collect outcome data while tracking student performance using local- and state-level assessments. A challenge for many, if not most, principals and teams is to develop a solid, efficient data-collection process.

7. **Capacity building.** Campus leaders must invest in faculty and staff training. This must become part of the school's culture. Not doing so is likely to impede continuous improvement. Focusing on school improvement is an imperative aspect of principal leadership. Contemplate where you and your team members are relative to implementing school improvement initiatives.

Final Thoughts

School budgeting and vision must be considered simultaneously in the planning process in order for principals and teams to increase their likelihood of achieving the PSEL's utopian goal of promoting *each* student's academic success and well-being.

The trick for school leaders is to incorporate the generalities of the national standards into practical steps to achieve the ideal of academic success for all students. This chapter at times might appear to be "Pollyannaish." Some of the examples and metaphors could illicit a "That's pie in the sky" reaction from you, the reader. However, it is essential to begin the integrated budget planning process with a "pie in the sky" perspective. To do otherwise would immediately lower expectations to less than 100 percent of the students obtaining academic success. Achieving 99.9 percent is not good enough. If 99.9 percent were good enough, then twelve babies would be given to the wrong parents each day, two planes departing daily from Chicago's O'Hare International Airport would be unsafe, and 291 pacemaker operations would be performed incorrectly every day (Snopes, 2017). The introduction of the PSEL sets the stage for further exploration as to how they impact academic and leadership performance as well as campus budgeting matters.

Discussion Questions

1. Which three PSEL influence the budget–vision relationship the most in your employment situation? Defend your choices.
2. Do you agree or disagree with the authors' contention we "must visit utopia" in creating a vision for our schools, or is this just fluff? Support your response.
3. What are your initial thoughts regarding the contention that budgeting and vision must be integrated into the planning process in order to promote the "academic success and well-being of *each* student" insisted upon in every PSEL?

Case Study

Belle Plain Middle School

The application of a case study or studies is presented at the conclusion of each chapter to provide applicable and relevant workplace scenarios so the reader can apply, in a practical manner, the knowledge acquired through textual readings.

Belle Plain Middle School (BPMS) is composed of approximately one thousand students in Grades 6 through 8. The school is 40 percent Anglo, 25 percent Hispanic, 25 percent African American, 5 percent Asian American, and 5 percent Other. Of these students, 60 percent qualify for free or reduced lunch. Twelve percent of the students are identified as limited English proficient, and the campus mobility rate is 30 percent.

The facility is twenty-five years old and is in an average state of repair. The neighborhood around the school is composed of modest homes of a similar age to the school. Many homes are in good repair and pride in ownership is evidenced. Most of the nearby businesses are independently owned small businesses with the typical scattering of franchised fast-food restaurants.

The majority of parents of the students at BPMS are employed in blue-collar jobs. A recently constructed subdivision of upper-middle-class homes in the attendance zone has created the potential of changing the campus demographics. The supermajority of students who reside in the new subdivision are either being homeschooled or are enrolled in a private school thirty-five minutes away because of parent concerns about the academic integrity of BPMS. The parents from this subdivision who have enrolled their children in the school want to meet with the principal about becoming more involved in the school and in their children's education.

The BPMS faculty is divided into two groups. The Old Pros are those teachers who have an average experience of more than fifteen years at the school. The Greenhorns are faculty and staff that have less than five years of experience at the school. The latter group has a high turnover rate. There is tension between the two faculty groups as well as a certain amount of distrust. The Old Pros perceive the Greenhorns as short on experience and long on idealism. The Greenhorns perceive the Old Pros as jaded and insensitive to the needs of the students. They also accuse the Old Pros of being unwilling to attempt innovative strategies to meet student needs because of professional bias.

A total of 65 percent of all students passed the state reading test. The passing rate for Hispanics and African Americans was 52 percent; limited English proficient students had a 47 percent passing rate. Seventy-one percent of all students passed the state mathematics test: 59 percent of the Hispanic students, 61 percent of the African American students, and 53 percent of the limited English proficient students. The percentage of students identified as needing special education services is 17 percent above the state average. The percentage of Hispanic students in special education is 53 percent higher than the Anglo rate.

You are the new principal to the campus. You are the third principal in five years. The selection process for hiring you was substantially different from that employed with previous principals. The superintendent secured a search committee comprised of parents, teachers, staff, and community members. A successful effort was made to involve individuals of all ethnic and socioeconomic groups. The superintendent screened the initial applicant list and submitted the names of five individuals for the committee to interview and then make a recommendation to her. The two male and three female finalists were ethnically diverse. Like you, all of the finalists were from outside the school district.

The superintendent and board have set a priority of turning BPMS around. You have been promised a 12 percent increase in your campus

(Continued)

(Continued)

budget for the next three years. The campus has also been allotted two additional faculty positions to be determined by you in a collaborative effort with the faculty and staff.

The previous two principals gave lip service to involving teachers, staff, and parents in making academic plans for the students. A campus academic improvement plan was developed each year but was never referred to during the school year. The previous principals usually made some modifications to the previous year's plan and ran it by the faculty for a quick "rubber stamp" vote before sending it to the superintendent.

Teachers have little or no knowledge about the campus budget. They are not aware of what financial resources are available to the campus. Currently, the primary way of securing financial resources is to ask the principal and wait until a response is received.

Three years ago, the parent–teacher organization was abandoned for lack of attendance. The superintendent has informed you the two Hispanic board members and one Black board member receive frequent complaints that Black and Hispanic parents do not feel welcome or valued on the campus. A recent parent survey compiled by the central administration indicates, among other things, many of the Old Pros believe their students are not performing well because the children do not try hard enough and the parents do not care.

Case Study Application

Use the BPMS Case Study Application Worksheet to log your responses to the case study. The worksheet provides a graphic organizer for your responses. The first column identifies a PSEL. The second column, "Action to Address a BPMS Need," is where you will insert the need(s) you identify in the case study. Should you not be able to identify an action to address a BPMS need, use the third column, "Additional Information Needed to Strengthen or Make a Recommendation." Share your responses in class.

BELLE PLAIN MIDDLE SCHOOL CASE STUDY APPLICATION WORKSHEET		
PSEL	**ACTION TO ADDRESS A BPMS NEED**	**IDENTIFY ADDITIONAL INFORMATION NEEDED TO STRENGTHEN OR MAKE A RECOMMENDATION**
1: Mission, Vision, and Core Values		
2: Ethics and Professional Norms		
3: Equity and Cultural Responsiveness		
4: Curriculum, Instruction, and Assessment		

(Continued)

(Continued)

BELLE PLAIN MIDDLE SCHOOL CASE STUDY APPLICATION WORKSHEET		
PSEL	**ACTION TO ADDRESS A BPMS NEED**	**IDENTIFY ADDITIONAL INFORMATION NEEDED TO STRENGTHEN OR MAKE A RECOMMENDATION**
5: Community of Care and Support for Students		
6: Professional Capacity of School Personnel		
7: Professional Community for Teachers and Staff		
8: Meaningful Encouragement of Families and Community		
9: Operations and Management		
10: School Improvement		

Culture, Data, Conflict Resolution, and Celebrating Success

2

Anyone could carve a goose were it not for the bones.

—Eliot (1935), *Murder in the Cathedral*

Carving a Budget Aligned With a School's Vision and Mission

Our utopian trip in Chapter 1 provided a clear view of the ideal learning environment school leaders seek. Unfortunately, no one lives in an ideal world. Instead, the world is filled with many challenges, such as shortages of fiscal, material, and human resources, and schools serve an ever-growing and increasingly diverse student population. In an opinion column, Will (2005) commented on the challenges of constructing the federal government budget when he penned, "'Anyone,' said T. S. Eliot, 'could carve a goose were it not for the bones.' Anyone could write a sensible federal budget, were it not for the bones—the sturdy skeleton of existing programs defended by muscular interests" (p. 4AA).

Noting Will's comment, the same can be said about the integrated school budget process. When school leaders become serious about aligning the school budget with the school vision, they can expect to encounter the sturdy skeletons of existing programs as they carve a budget aligned with the school's vision and mission.

The bones of programs near and dear to some stakeholders will not necessarily be germane to attaining the school's vision and mission. Besides the bones of existing programs, school leaders can also expect to encounter bones of impaired vision from stakeholders who either do not understand or choose not to accept the academic success for all as exemplified in the late Ron Edmonds's remark, still so applicable almost half a century later:

> We can, whenever we want, successfully teach all children whose schooling is of interest to us. We already know more than we need to do that. Whether or not we do it must depend on how we feel about the fact that we haven't so far. (Edmonds, 1979, p. 56)

The challenge for any school leader and stakeholders is growing a culture that supports a school's vision and mission of ensuring *all* students are important to us—*if,* as questioned by Edmonds, such a vision and mission is, in reality, actually important to us. And, just as important, if not more so, whether we actually believe it. An examination of the importance of school culture, data, conflict resolution, and celebrating success in the integrated budget model is in order.

Culture

The importance of a school culture that is receptive to the integrated budget model asserted within this book cannot be overemphasized. Wilkins and Patterson (1985) wrote decades ago that "culture consists of the conclusions a group of people draws from its experience. An organization's [school's] culture consists largely of what people believe about what works and what does not" (p. 5). The integration of the budget and vision into a single process cannot flourish unless it is woven into the fabric of the school's culture as identified by Wilkins and Patterson.

The integrated budget model requires a school culture receptive to collaboration. Schools that possess a collegial spirit and share values, beliefs, and traditions are more apt to spawn the required collaborative environment that in turn increases enthusiasm, energy, and motivation (R. L. Green, 2016; Lunenburg & Irby, 2022). This integration must be valued by the school's culture since it frequently influences people's opinions and behaviors while serving as the vehicle to turn dreams into reality.

School culture was touched upon in Chapter 1 with the examination of the *Professional Standards for Educational Leaders (PSEL)3: Equity and Cultural Responsiveness*. This national standard calls on education leaders to "strive for equity of educational opportunity and culturally responsive practices to promote *each* student's academic success and well-being." This national standard warrants closer examination because the integrated budget process cannot exist with any degree of usefulness unless it is inculcated into the school's culture.

Culture can be described as the shared values, beliefs, traditions, customs, norms, attitudes, and behaviors of a learning community (R. L. Green, 2016; Sorenson, 2024; Sorenson et al., 2016). The use of the adjective *shared* in describing culture is of importance when considering it with the *PSEL 3* edict encouraging education leaders to "strive for equity of educational opportunity and culturally responsive practices." *Shared* is a *we* thing. *Shared* implies all stakeholders in the school possess common core values. *Promote* requires school leaders initiate, advocate, nourish, and sustain the school culture in such a manner that meets the edict of *PSEL 3*.

A brief examination of a school culture's three elements—values, beliefs, and attitudes—makes a case for the integration of budget and vision.

This examination is conducted within the PSEL obligation to advocate, nourish, and sustain the school culture.

Values

Values are those ideals leaders hold near and dear. They are the ideals leaders deem important. Values shape the practice of principals, teachers, and staff. For the integrated budget approach to become inculcated within a school's culture, stakeholders must understand how this approach helps them fulfill their personal mission as well as the school's mission. It is essential for leaders to model their personal and professional values. Leaders advocate for the integrated approach to budgeting when they support it, plead its case, and assist the stakeholders in understanding it. Leaders nurture it by discussing it in formal and informal team meetings and by sharing it with parents and community members. Leaders sustain it by never allowing the integrated budget approach to be removed from the stakeholder's conscience.

Beliefs

Beliefs are what leaders hold to be true. The integrated relationship among budget, vision, and planning must become something stakeholders hold to be true. Gradually, through time and effort and by consistently keeping the integrated budget process at the center of school planning, events will unfold and stories will develop that will become part of the school's heritage. Stories will be rooted in cherished accomplishments that occur through the integrated budgetary process. Rituals will manifest themselves as ceremonies. Traditions, customs, norms, ceremonies, and beliefs are to culture what movies are to scripts. They afford the players an opportunity to act out their beliefs. Beliefs become ongoing events that sustain the integrated budget approach in the school culture.

Sad Sack School

Good, bad, or ugly, schools have a culture. The authors observed one school with a poisonous culture. A strong level of distrust existed among this school's stakeholders. Teachers didn't trust the principal. The principal didn't trust the teachers. Friction was high between professionals and paraprofessionals. No sense of community existed. The campus ran amuck. If there was a mission statement, it was likely "Take care

(Continued)

(Continued)

of yourself." Throughout the campus, an air of failure and defeat prevailed. Distrust had replaced trust. Rumors replaced constructive conversation. Data were abused and used to abuse. The school was in a hopeless freefall.

This school did not set out to become what it had become. Undoubtedly, the school at one time was quite different. It appeared that time, difficult problems, and tough situations combined with weak leadership and the lack of a plan to address the school's challenges led to the poisonous culture. It was obvious the stakeholders were not satisfied with the situation, but they couldn't overcome their sense of helplessness and frustration. Their negativity generated more negativity, spinning into a bottomless downward spiral.

However, despite this desperate situation, glimmers of hope existed in a couple of areas within this school. This story illustrates the impact of an unhealthy culture on schools. The story also offers hope for those who are trapped in unhealthy cultures. This story is for those who are hunkered down in bunkers of positive thought in an unhealthy culture. Culture can be changed! Culture changes when hunkered-down groups purposefully seek such change. Change agents identify the root causes of discontent and start addressing these root causes, gradually dismantling the negativity.

Three excellent sources related to the topic of culture are Chapter 6 in *Essentials for New Principals: Seven Steps to Becoming Successful—Key Expectations and Skills* (Sorenson, 2024), Chapter 4 in *The Principal's Guide to Time Management: Instructional Leadership in the Digital Age* (Sorenson et al., 2016), and Chapter 6 in *The Principal's Guide to Curriculum Leadership* (Sorenson et al., 2011). These sources are instructionally and culturally based texts designed for school leaders and written in the principal's voice!

Attitudes

Attitudes are how leaders feel about things. Did a parent or caregiver ever tell you "Watch your attitude"? This statement usually had "that" tone in it, letting you know your attitude was not appreciated for whatever reason. You learned as a child there were ways things were done around your home. In healthy homes, parents communicated with the family members to collaboratively develop a shared family culture respecting all of its members. In unhealthy homes, dysfunctional behavior had family members in contentious relationships. Eventually, some unhealthy families seek intervention to improve the family. Other unhealthy families never seek intervention and either dissolve or remain contentious.

Schools are a lot like families. Over time, a school's stakeholders realize their school cannot function at its best unless they develop a healthy culture. The integrated budget approach is at the core of a healthy school's planning process. The more the integrated budget process is used in planning, the more deep-seated it becomes as part of the school's culture, and the organization's health improves.

Certain attitudes develop: This is the way things are done in the school, this is how we celebrate, and this is how we appreciate each other. It takes time for ideas like these to become part of the school's culture. Enthusiastic leaders never tire in their effort to advocate and nurture the budget–vision integrated relationship as a part of the culture.

Finally, school leaders must never cease in their efforts to sustain an open school culture. How? By what means? Education Week (2023) recommends a principal do the following:

- First, **listen to teachers**. Teachers are more likely to report a disconnect between leader demands and their own instructional capacity when teachers are not consulted on decisions about school support and fiscal, human, and material resources.
- Second, **nurture a culture of self-care.** Leaders must encourage teachers to set professional boundaries. Then, leaders must shield and defend teacher conference and planning times and, just as important, serve as a protective buffer when teachers are unjustly criticized, challenged, condemned, threatened, or abused.
- Third, **provide teachers time and space to support each other,** always ensuring teachers are able to frequently collaborate with each other and with campus leadership, especially during times of decision making.
- Fourth, **never overlook exhausted or burned-out teachers and staff**. In a study conducted by the Yale Center on Emotional Intelligence, teachers experience the highest turnover rate of any professional occupation (Yale School of Medicine, 2023).
- Fifth, **lift morale and find times to celebrate**. Generously recognize staff and do it often—every time there is an opportunity to celebrate. Think of the 1980 song *Celebration* by Kool & The Gang. Play the music, turn up the sound, create a long conga dance line, and celebrate! (See the section titled "Celebrating Success" that appears later in this chapter.)

Data

Earl's (1995) school and data observation made more than three decades ago remains astute to this day:

> We live in a culture that has come to value and depend on statistical information to inform our decisions. At the same time, we are likely to misunderstand and misuse those statistics because we are "statistically illiterate" and consequently have no idea what the numbers mean. (p. 62)

Schools, at times, appear to be drowning in data. State testing data have a prominent role not only in state accountability policies but also in federal accountability policies. Leaders must ensure high-quality data are used in decision making. School leaders must work with school stakeholders in analyzing data, identifying solutions, and implementing those solutions. Time must be allocated for data gathering and analysis. Data analysis is essential to effective, efficient, and essential budget-building processes (see Chapters 3 and 6).

It is important school leaders regularly analyze data ranging from reading assessments to norm-referenced data, as well as district and campus diagnostic data and federal and state data. The plethora of data sources and questions requires an organized approach to data analysis. Examining data collaboratively encourages leader, faculty, and staff to become more involved in data-based decision making. This, in turn, quickly improves a team's ability to identify and employ different data types to best address instructional issues at hand. An essential-questions approach frequently proves highly effective in building data literacy. Ronka et al. (2009) pose eight important questions for consideration:

Time must be allocated for data gathering and analysis. Data analysis is essential to effective, efficient, and essential budget-building processes.

1. How do student outcomes differ by demographics, programs, and schools?
2. To what extent did specific programs, interventions, and services improve outcomes?
3. What is the longitudinal progress of a specific cohort of students?
4. What are the characteristics of students who achieve proficiency and those who do not?
5. Where are we making the most progress in closing achievement gaps?
6. How do absence and mobility affect assessment results?
7. How do student grades correlate with state assessment results and other measures?

Now, a serious question: Are each of the eight essential queries, as proposed by Ronka et al., a part of a principal's and team's instructional and budgetary decision-making processes? Additionally, how is data better ensuring equity and equality in schools and student achievement?

Data-Driven Decision Making

The Sorenson-Goldsmith Integrated Budget Model (see Figure 3.1) is introduced in Chapter 3. The third and fourth components of this model involve data gathering and data analysis. As to not place the proverbial cart before the horse, the authors are compelled to call attention to data gathering and analysis before introducing their model. It's okay to look ahead in Chapter 3 and take a peek at the budget model, however.

Effective use of data changes a school's culture. Data expose bias and ignorance and provide "Aha!" moments as well as debunk ineffective practices. In short, data gathering and analysis are a catalyst for changing a school's culture from closed to open. In other words, they work for the good of the school.

The authors have personal experience using data to expose ineffective teaching practices. Ineffective practices, left alone and unchallenged, become encoded within a school's culture. To be fair, school leaders must not think ineffective practices are deliberately adopted with the intent to harm or limit student achievement or potential. This noted, whether ineffective instructional practices are unintentional or intentional, the results are the same—low performance for students *and* teachers, low expectations, and a drag on the school's culture.

Data expose bias and ignorance and provide "Aha!" moments as well as debunk ineffective practices. In short, data gathering and analysis are a catalyst for changing a school's culture from closed to open.

Both authors had the opportunity to affect school culture by using data to end the practice of ability grouping into academically segregated classrooms. Providing our faculties with longitudinal as well as disaggregated student achievement data made it apparent to the stakeholders that this teaching practice was only widening the gap between the various subpopulations on their campuses. This data "Aha!" moment could not be refuted by anecdotal arguments offered by those clinging to this antiquated and long-failed instructional strategy. The dismantling of ability groups began, albeit with strong resistance from a group dedicated to the ability-grouping mantra. A data-based decision-making culture planted a foothold in the school's culture.

As time passed (cultural change doesn't happen overnight), both campuses matured in incorporating data within the decision-making process. Stakeholders seeking additional data sources evidenced this. As the use of data-driven decisions increased on the campus, so did the level of teacher expectations for all students. No longer were faculty and staff content with whole-school academic performance data. There was an expectation for data to be disaggregated into the appropriate subpopulations. Data analysis sparked imaginations as interventions were formulated to improve the performance of subpopulations not meeting campus expectations.

As data gathering and analysis continued their mercurial rise in the school's culture, so too did the concept of continuous incremental improvement. No longer would faculty, staff, parents, and community members be satisfied with maintaining the status quo. The school was now committed to continuous improvement.

One example of continuous improvement was seen in the area of student achievement. One teacher group that had been using data-driven decision making for several years was consistently witnessing its students' mastery on the state reading examination fall between the 90 percent to 100 percent passing rate. This teacher group took its data analysis to the next level. These teachers began examining not only *if* their students passed the reading exam but also *how well* they passed the exam. This led to a higher self-imposed level of expectation for student achievement. The academic goal was no longer limited to the state's mandated passing score on the exam but on how well the students scored above the state's required reading exam score. How sweet it is—incremental improvement.

This story is not over. The faculty and staff did not stop at this level of data analysis. They drilled their data analysis of student subpopulation performance down to the reading objective level. They even added an analysis of student wrong answers on the state exam questions. This analysis determined where and how the teachers refined their delivery of instruction to help the students master the reading curriculum. When faculty, staff, parents, and the community value data-driven decision making, watch out! The sky's the limit on where academic success will go.

Barriers to the Use of Data

The previous data story had a happy ending. But happy endings don't occur without hard work. Barriers block data use in schools. Stakeholders must be diligent in their quest to gather and analyze data required in the third and fourth components of the Sorenson-Goldsmith Integrated Budget Model. Likewise, stakeholders must not allow personal bias on a subject matter to interfere with identifying subjects needing improvement.

Holcomb (2017) identified six reasons why data are little used and why it is a challenge to motivate people to be data driven. Holcomb's barriers to data use comprise the following:

- lack of proper training involving others in decision making and in the appropriate use of decision making,
- lack of time,

- feast or famine mindset (anxious there are no data or panicking over too much: "What are we going to do with all these data?"),
- fear of evaluation (frightened the data are going to be used against individuals or schools)
- fear of exposure (the troubling thoughts that even though your colleagues believe you are a good teacher, the data might expose you as a fraud), and
- confusing a technical problem with a cultural problem.

School leaders and faculties all have witnessed Holcomb's data barriers and, like the authors, have personally experienced them. Developing an awareness of these data barriers is necessary to address data concerns. Holcomb (2017) further postulates collecting data for the sake of collecting data is an exercise in absolute futility.

How does a school break down its data barriers? R. S. Johnson (2002) more than two decades ago effectively described the tried and true five stages in the change process for creating stakeholders who value the incorporation of data gathering and analysis into the decision-making process. Briefly, those stages are as follows:

1. **Building the leadership and data teams.** Building leadership and data skills must be incorporated in the reform process. Training is provided on the skills needed to collect and analyze data.
2. **Killing the myth/building dissatisfaction.** Data are used to reveal false beliefs about educational practices, such as having low expectations for certain groups of students.
3. **Creating a culture of inquiry.** The school values provocative questioning and responses that use data to inspire the school change process.
4. **Creating a vision and plan for your school.** This stage requires a long-term collaborative planning process that will result in positive change. It involves establishing priorities, allocating resources, and assigning responsibilities.
5. **Monitoring progress.** Monitoring becomes a part of the school culture.

This concludes an early peek into the Sorenson-Goldsmith Integrated Budget Model.

Quality Data and Mountains of Information

Both Holcomb's and Johnson's books readily correlate with the technical expertise necessary in implementing the third and fourth components of the Sorenson-Goldsmith Integrated Budget Model, to be introduced in the next chapter. Data gathering and data analysis are challenging components of this model. Be patient with yourself and others as data skills are acquired and honed.

W. Edwards Deming believed that "quality comes not from inspection but from improvement of the process" (Walton, 1986, p. 60). Leaders improve the process when they improve the quality of the data used in decision making. Good decision making, as intimated by Deming, is only as good as the quality of data used in formulating the decisions. The challenge for school leaders today is to sift through mountains of information to construct informed decisions. The dilemma faced in this process is that schools are about the business of students, and students' needs cannot always be easily described, plotted, and analyzed on spreadsheets.

Federal and state legislation have long aimed at increasing education accountability by requiring school leaders to use new data sources. Laffee (2002), some twenty years ago, wrote,"The tools of education—intuition, teaching philosophy, personal experience—do not seem to be enough anymore. Virtually every state has put into place an assessment system intended to measure and validate student achievement and school performance" (p. 6). That statement still applies today and reveals school leaders need to not only possess the three skills Laffee references; they must go beyond them.

Data Types

Today's school leader must employ a variety of data types. Disaggregated data, longitudinal data, perception data, qualitative data, and quantitative data are five data types (see Table 2.1). Each data type provides its own unique assistance in developing an integrated budget.

TABLE 2.1 Types of Data

DATA TYPE	DEFINITION
Disaggregated	Data are broken down by specific student subgroups, such as current grade, race, previous achievements, gender, and socioeconomic status.
Longitudinal	Data are measured consistently from year to year to track progress, growth, and change over time. True longitudinal studies eliminate any students who were not present and were not tested in each of the years of the study.
Perception	Data are used to inform educators regarding parent, student, and staff views or opinions about the learning environment, which could also reveal areas in need of improvement.

DATA TYPE	DEFINITION
Qualitative	Data are based on information gathered from one-on-one interviews, focus groups, or general observations over time (as opposed to quantitative data).
Quantitative	Data are based on "hard numbers" such as enrollment figures, dropout rates, and test scores (as opposed to qualitative data).

Sources: Lemov (2021), Sorenson et al. (2011), and the American Association of School Administrators (2002).

Disaggregated Data

Disaggregated data are data broken down by specific student subgroups, such as current grade, race, previous achievements, gender, and socioeconomic status. Disaggregated data provide leaders with an additional level of specificity needed to identify the academic needs of students.

Instead of examining student achievement data from a whole-school-population perspective, school leaders now have the opportunity to examine student academic performance by ethnicity as well as socioeconomic status. This approach to data analysis provides principals and teams with priority and academic direction as to where needs to intervene may exist.

Moreover, the use of disaggregated data can assist a campus leader and the faculty with the identification of specific instructional delivery problems that may very well have not been identified otherwise. Now school funding to assist the most in need can be budgeted and more appropriately disseminated.

Longitudinal Data

Longitudinal data are data measured consistently from year to year to track progress, growth, and change over time. True longitudinal studies eliminate any students who were not present and tested in each of the years of the study. In an actual school situation, five or so years of data is recommended. Using sophisticated software, school leaders readily construct longitudinal comparisons of same groups from year to year, which provides guidance in areas of curriculum and instruction that require intervention and appropriately budgeted dollars.

Perception Data

Perception data are data that inform educators about parent, student, and staff insights regarding the learning environment, which could also reveal areas in need ofenhancement, if not advancement. Perception data can be gathered in a number of ways, such as through interviews, questionnaires, and even by observations—all designed to gather opinions, comments, and recommendations from stakeholders. Perception data is an essential aspect of the strategic planning process of any school community. This data type can be utilized to effect changes that bring about continuous instructional improvements within and across the teaching, leading, and learning environments.

Qualitative Data

Qualitative data are data based on information gathered from one-on-one interviews, focus groups, or general observations over time (as opposed to quantitative data). One exemplar of qualitative data is when a school district brings in focus groups to discuss a controversial topic such as the banning of certain library books, or sex education, or teachers carrying guns in schools. The district compiles the comments from the sessions and uses them in conjunction with information from other sources to consider revising or maintaining library content, or modifying the school's sex education program, or even recommending to the state legislature that teachers carry or not carry guns in schools for the purpose of safety.

Quantitative Data

Quantitative data are data based on "hard numbers." This data type can be counted or measured (as opposed to qualitative data). Examples include but are not limited to enrollment figures, dropout rates, and test scores. It is worth nothing that data can meet the definition of more than one data category.

Assessment

There are two basic types of assessment: formative and summative. An example of formative assessment is a pretest given in an academic area such as algebra, reading comprehension, or keyboarding skills. This information would then be used to drive the instructional strategy and the development of lesson plans.

The second type of assessment is summative. An example of summative assessment is a benchmark test given in mathematics, reading, science, or other subjects to determine individual student mastery of taught objectives. Formative and summative assessment, when planned properly, can yield all five types of data previously defined and examined. Formative and summative data used in conjunction with each other are invaluable in making program adjustments.

Acknowledging Opportunities for Growth and Development

Schools have grown in complexity and require sophisticated assessment and data analysis. The immediate cause of this phenomenon is quite simple. A powerful idea dominating policy discourse about schools stipulates students must be held to higher academic achievement expectations and school leaders must be held accountable for ensuring all students meet or exceed such expectations.

This perspective, and multiple others, subsequently dictate numerous, simultaneous, and systematic changes in leading and teaching. Such emerging viewpoints, demands, and expectations have dictated the absolute need for school leaders to be active participants in continuous and varied professional development opportunities. Data analysis is at the heart of this process.

For school leaders to be successful—whether it be in envisioning school reform initiatives, planning programmatic changes, developing a school budget, or advancing opportunities for increased student achievement—they must understand that the once-standard in-service workshop model is anything but acceptable. What is known and what research supports is professional development must be entrenched in practice and be research based, collaborative, standards aligned, assessment driven, and accountability focused—all of which serve to increase the capacity, knowledge, and skills of administrators to improve their leadership practices and performances.

Educators must recognize student learning can only be enhanced by the professional growth and development of school leaders. Educators must take this a step further by creating a professional learning community. Today, society can no longer educate the populace by employing a traditional education model. Those who have yet to make the transition must do so posthaste.

Staff development, like other facets of a school, must be data driven. Needs assessment surveys from the faculty analyzed in conjunction with data from other sources (such as student achievement data) increase the effectiveness of the training, resulting in increased performance of both teachers and students.

An example of data-driven staff development took place in a school with a high percentage of students who were not meeting with success in writing as measured by the state's assessment program. A review of the testing data by the site-based decision-making (SBDM) committee revealed this problem was evident throughout all the assessed grades.

The SBDM committee surveyed the teachers and discovered that the writing teachers felt inadequately trained to teach writing within the parameters of the curriculum and assessment program. The committee also discovered writing was only a priority for the language arts teachers in the grades that were tested by the state. Other teachers felt no ownership in teaching writing across the curriculum.

The SBDM committee members conducted a review of potential writing workshops and selected one they deemed most appropriate for their students based on an analysis of the disaggregated achievement data.

The committee also surveyed teachers throughout the district and developed a writing-across-the-curriculum plan that was supported by the faculty.

The SBDM committee ensured these two strategies were incorporated into the school action plan. Funding was secured to bring in writing consultants and to make out-of-town school-site visits where the writing curriculum and instructional practices were successful. Funds were also allocated to secure the required materials for the teachers, and the teacher training received priority on the professional development calendar.

Pause and Consider

Underground Resistance

The members of W. Nigel Bruce (WNB) Middle School's SBDM committee have grown in their understanding of the use and importance of a variety of data sources in campus planning. But unfortunately, not everyone at WNB shares the enthusiasm for increasing the use of data-driven decision making. LaKisha Galore and Stan Barrier are vocal in their effort to diminish data analysis at WNB. Their mantra is, "You can find data to prove anything." Ms. Galore and Mr. Barrier are creating a growing pocket of resistance to data-based decision making.

An excellent source pertaining to teacher resistance is the text *Responding to Resistors: Tactics That Work for Principals* (Sorenson, 2021).

- What, if anything, should be done to address Ms. Galore and Mr. Barrier's campaign against data-based decision making?
- What could the WNB SBDM committee do to proactively carry data analysis to the next level at WNB?

Conflict Resolution

Conflict will always exist in the school budgeting process. Stakeholders have special interests and agendas. Passion, resistance, and even tempers can flair in the heat of the school budgeting process. Words can be spoken that people later wish they had not said. What's a school leader to do? First, carefully consider the next two subsections for clarification on handling conflict. Also, an excellent source for new principals attempting to manage conflict is *Essentials for New Principals: Seven Steps to Becoming Successful—Key Expectations and Skills* (Sorenson, 2024).

The Negative Things About Conflict

At your next faculty meeting, ask the assembled academic warriors, "How many of you *like* conflict?" If your crowd is typical, you'll see only a few, if any, hands go up. Most of those who respond affirmatively will be your campus clowns who just want attention. In all likelihood, when confronted with conflict, the jokester is the first one to offer a glib remark and then disappear. The remainder who raised their hands are likely those who could best be called troublemakers. They feel they have power. When we were young, we called them bullies. Most people will refrain from raising their hands because they share negative views of conflict.

First, in a conflict a problem arises that challenges those involved. This initial event is necessary because it draws attention to the problem and sets in motion a rebuilding process. Second, a conflict should be *rested.* Note that *resting* and *avoiding* are not the same thing. In this context, resting refers to a conscious effort to separate people from the problem and to deal with the problem. In other words, we must work to attain and maintain a proper perspective. When we concentrate on people instead of the problem, we lose objectivity and our edge for problem solving. Finally, conflict requires proper nutrition—an appetite for mutual benefit and a penchant for understanding. Thus, the need for conflict resolution.

Conflict resolution requires the participant to be open to conflict, have perspective, and possess a desire to achieve mutual benefit whenever possible. Lacking any of these elements can lead to disaster. Even though the conflict experience may be distasteful, an effective school leader will embrace the conflict and do everything possible to bring perspective and mutual benefit to all parties. "Yeah, right," you're saying. "That won't work with my crowd."

> Conflict resolution requires the participant to be open to conflict, have perspective, and possess a desire to achieve mutual benefit whenever possible. The lack of any of these elements can lead to disaster.

True, it doesn't work out that easily all the time. Sometimes you just have to be the boss and make hard decisions. It comes with the territory. But if that's the only way you deal with conflict, you won't be viewed as an effective leader. Dictators can be extremely efficient, but in the long term, they are rarely effective. Nowhere is this more apparent than in the school.

Personnel disputes are costly, especially when left unchecked. Campus personnel disputes can lead to interrupted teaching and learning time and decreased productivity, and they certainly have a negative impact relative to morale. School leaders play a very important role ensuring conflict is minimal. Conflict resolution strategies work to mediate teacher-to-teacher, teacher-to-principal, and teacher-to-student disputes. Identified below are seven methods for resolving personnel conflict at school.

1. Ensure and maintain an open door policy.
2. Determine the severity of the issue at hand.
3. First, encourage faculty to handle the conflict on their own. If unable to do so, move on to Item #4.
4. Take action and step in to resolve and mediate the situation.
5. Listen carefully and thoughtfully to all parties. Provide each party with an opportunity to say their peace. Sometimes this involves due process.
6. Document, document, document. Remember, the incident never occurred if left undocumented!
7. Develop a solution by seeking common ground, brainstorming resolutions, developing a plan of action, and always following up after a few days and even weeks.

Remember, problems are opportunities to show sound and effective leadership. The best principals handle conflict by building trust and understanding, and by teaching others to do the same.

Celebrating Success

School leaders must not underestimate their impact on a school's culture. The leader sets the tone of a school. In an era of increased outside accountability systems, along with fiscal constraints and political intrusions if not interventions, campus leadership teams and personnel are experiencing tremendous stress. Leaders must be cognizant of this underlying current in schools. Effective leaders celebrate success as a means of mitigating stress. They must lead in the establishment of a culture that appreciates success. Leadership in celebrating success manifests itself in any number of ways. It is only limited by one's imagination.

Principals lead celebrations at their schools for achieving goals by performing out-of-character acts such as kissing a pig, shaving their heads, sitting on the roof, dancing in a pink tutu, doing an Elvis impersonation, and even riding a Harley-Davidson through the gym. These manifestations of success celebration often bring with them the side benefit of positive local media attention to schools. Sometimes a leader must let stakeholders have a little fun at the leader's expense. Leaders do this because they know a school culture with an atmosphere of love and support for stakeholders will accomplish miraculous transformations in student performance.

Principals lead celebrations at their schools for achieving goals by performing out-of-character acts such as kissing a pig, shaving their heads, sitting on the roof, dancing in a pink tutu, doing an Elvis impersonation, and even riding a Harley-Davidson through the gym.

Celebrating success is not limited to attention-getting public stunts. Celebrating success can also be private. A handwritten note of thanks is worth a million dollars to the recipient. Who doesn't treasure personal notes of gratitude? These notes are often tucked away and read again in moments of frustration or during times of reminiscing.

A face-to-face verbal compliment provides a positive benefit to the recipient as well as to the giver. Compliments need not be lengthy; they only need be sincere. As a sidebar, leaders must know how to model accepting a compliment. School leaders should not try to brush away a compliment by saying things like, "It was nothing." Instead, honor the compliment giver: "Thank you so much. I appreciate you recognizing my work and the work of my colleagues."

Celebrating success manifests itself in many other ways: awards assemblies, bulletin boards, newsletter references, marquees, parking privileges, covering a class so a teacher can have a longer lunch, T-shirts, and any other positive ideas you possess. Bathing schools in the celebration of success encourages the integration of budgeting, visioning, and planning. It also builds an open culture and positive climate!

Celebration should be an all-inclusive process. Do not limit it to teachers and students. Include everyone—the custodians, bus drivers, cafeteria help, parent volunteers, and community members. A positive, optimistic, and supportive school culture increases energy and motivation, and this is contagious to all stakeholders. School leaders encourage teachers to help their students celebrate success. So, be the head cheerleader for your school—you might even get to wear the uniform!

Final Thoughts

Cultures can change. School leaders must (1) act purposely in growing a healthy and open culture, (2) be results oriented and data driven, (3) resolve conflicts on their campus, (4) celebrate success, (5) ensure efforts are ongoing, and (6) see the value of all stakeholders. Schools are more likely to fulfill their vision and mission when they align vision, budgeting, and planning.

Fostering a shared vision of a school's purpose while taking deliberate and collective action to align their budgets and commit their resources to the school's vision is a principal's gift to the learning community. The best way to make a school successful is to foster a culture in which the stakeholders have a shared vision of the school's purpose and future.

Discussion Questions

1. Consider three values you share with your school. How have these shared values impacted your school's culture?
2. How do the beliefs and attitudes of the various stakeholders impact your school's culture? Provide positive and negative examples.

(Continued)

(Continued)

3. How do the school leaders affect school culture positively and negatively?
4. List your top ten data sources for building your campus budget. Why did these sources make the top ten list?
5. How can or does the effective use of data impact your school's culture?
6. How does the effective use of data impact your school's budgeting process?
7. How can the data types in Table 2.1 impact your campus in a constructive way?
8. How have you witnessed data being used in the decision-making process at your school? Was it used effectively? Defend your response.
9. How do the beliefs and attitudes of the various campus stakeholders impact your school's culture? Provide positive and negative examples.
10. How does this chapter relate to the Professional Standards for Educational Leaders (PSEL) as documented in Chapter 1? Which standard(s) are specifically relevant and why?

Case Study

Scarlet C. Doyle Middle School

Scarlet C. Doyle (SCD) Middle School, a school of 540 students in Grades 6 through 8, is located in a southern border state less than two hundred miles from the U.S.–Mexico border. It is 62 percent Hispanic and 38 percent Anglo. It is one of six middle schools in Kilnwood City. Juan Molina is the principal. Although SCD has always been predominantly Hispanic, Dr. Molina is the first Hispanic to be named as the school's principal in its forty-two years of existence. Dr. Molina has been enthusiastically accepted by all of the school's stakeholders. He is using this acceptance capital to make needed instructional changes to ensure all children meet with academic success.

Case Study Application

Table 2.2 contains two years' accumulation of achievement data for SCD. Recognize the table is abbreviated for the sake of brevity. Use these data to respond to the following questions:

1. Identify at least two instructional concerns at SCD. What types of data did you use to identify the concerns?
2. Examining the data provided, what would you recommend to Dr. Molina as the top instructional priority? Support your recommendation with data.
3. Recently a survey noted there was a detected increase in the positive perception of SCD by the parents between the last school year and the current school year. Is there anything in the given data that might explain the recent upward swing in the campus's public perception? Support your response.
4. What data are not provided that you would like to have to be better informed about the needs and strengths of SCD?
5. Make a connection between a PSEL standard and the SCD case study. Is there more than one? If so, identify all.
6. How might budgeted dollars be expended and in what areas specifically to enhance instructional programming and student achievement?

TABLE 2.2 Scarlet C. Doyle Middle School State Academic Performance

	STATE	DISTRICT	CAMPUS	AFRICAN AMERICAN	ASIAN AMERICAN	HISPANIC	WHITE	LOW SOCIO-ECONOMIC STATUS
Met State Standard: Grade 6								
Reading								
Second Year	87	83	86	*	87	84	89	82
First Year	80	76	83		86	80	88	74
Math								
Second Year	78	65	80	*	92	77	84	73
First Year	71	61	65		90	64	68	53
Met State Standard: Grade 7								
Reading								
Second Year	83	79	94	*	96	92	98	94
First Year	82	78	83		90	77	93	72
Math								
Second Year	71	60	71	*	80	69	76	69
First Year	63	52	57		71	52	69	43
Met State Standard: Grade 8								
Reading								
Second Year	90	88	94	*	97	89	99	84
First Year	84	79	86		91	83	93	75
Math								
Second Year	67	57	83	*	95	76	92	72
First Year	62	50	48		52	44	55	38

Notes: All numbers are percentages. * = Less than ten students.

A Model for Integrating Vision, Planning, and Budgeting

3

Alice:	*Would you please tell me which way I ought to go from here?*
The Cat:	*That depends a great deal on where you want to get to.*
Alice:	*I don't much care where—*
The Cat:	*Then it doesn't matter which way you go.*
Alice:	*—so long as I get somewhere.*
The Cat:	*Oh, you're sure to do that . . . if you only walk long enough.*

—Carroll (1993/1865)

Are We Somewhere in the Nowhere?

Alice and the Cheshire Cat in Lewis Carroll's *Alice's Adventures in Wonderland* had a provocative conversation on vision and planning. Alice is seeking direction on where she needs to go. The Cat replies he cannot help her unless Alice knows where she *wants* to go. Sadly, Alice doesn't know or even care where she goes. Alice's attitude allows the Cat to tell her it makes no difference since she just wants to go somewhere. The Cat concludes the conversation by telling Alice to keep walking and she'll get somewhere.

Unfortunately, many schools are like Alice. They are going somewhere—anywhere. These schools appear not to care much where they go just as long as they go *somewhere*. That somewhere, sadly, is often nowhere for some school leaders and teams. In this chapter, a case is made that it *does* matter where a school goes and how it gets there and that it is important to avoid the somewhere in the nowhere! The Sorenson-Goldsmith Integrated Budget Model provides a purposeful map—a GPS, so to speak—for a successful, meaningful school journey. Walking aimlessly somewhere in the nowhere might be acceptable to Alice, but it is not acceptable for our schools and our students.

In our earlier examination of the integration of the visioning, budgeting, and planning processes, school leaders learned how to make the important delineation between school finance and school budgeting. Next, the budget relationship to the Professional Standards for Educational Leaders (PSEL) was discussed. Then, a closer examination of the budgeting and vision relationship with an emphasis on culture, climate, and data-driven decision making took place. Now it is time to allow these underlying principles to manifest themselves into a practical and workable budget model.

Figure 3.1 provides an illustration of such a model—again, a map or a GPS of sorts. It is necessary to consider each component of the Sorenson-Goldsmith Integrated Budget Model individually to ensure a thorough understanding of this model's integrative nature. The model employs many principles associated with the site-based decision-making (SBDM) process. The SBDM process, a decentralized collaborative process, involves the various campus stakeholders. Stakeholders include parents, faculty, paraprofessionals, community members, and students. Typically, the campus faculty and staff elect the SBDM committee members. This process continues to be required in numerous states and school districts throughout the United States.

It is necessary to consider each component of the Sorenson-Goldsmith Integrated Budget Model individually to ensure a thorough understanding of this model's integrative nature.

FIGURE 3.1 The Sorenson-Goldsmith Integrated Budget Model

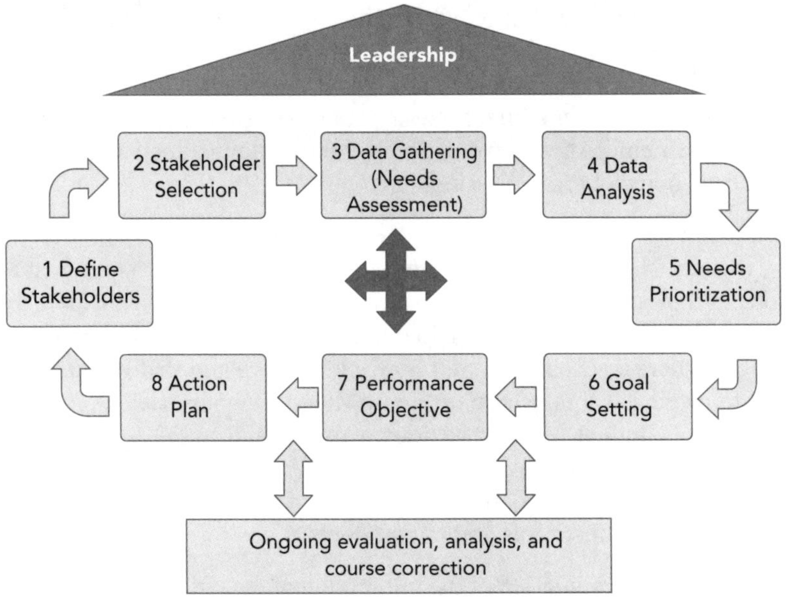

The SBDM process functions at either the campus or district level, but it functions best when applied at both levels. The term *school* in the remainder of this chapter refers to either a campus or a district. The level of planning in which the Sorenson-Goldsmith Integrated Budget Model is utilized determines which definition of *school* is employed. Campuses who employ the SBDM process expect improved student performance as a result of

- effective campus and school district planning for the purpose of improved student performance,
- improved community involvement in the school improvement process,
- clearly established accountability parameters for student performance,
- increased staff productivity and satisfaction,
- improved communication and information flow,
- consensus-based decision making,
- pervasive and long-range commitment to implantation,
- increased flexibility at the campus level in the allocation and use of human, material, and fiscal resources, and
- coordination of "regular" and special programs or service components.

The Sorenson-Goldsmith Integrated Budget Model

Leadership

Leadership is located at the top of the model not to symbolize top-down leadership but rather to represent the relational leadership exhibited between a school leader and an instructional team. School leaders must exhibit strong relationship and communicative skills as they assist and nurture their teams, always incorporating collaborative planning and decision-making processes.

Rigid top-down leadership might initially produce results, but it does so at a cost to the collaborative planning process. Decisions may be made in an orderly meeting run with firm control, but apathy and resentment may be the price to be paid (Yukl & Gardner, 2019).

Communication is an essential leadership skill in working with the school planning committee. The school leader must communicate passion for the school's mission. The leader must kindle the imagination of all the stakeholders about what can be done to help the school achieve its vision and mission. A leader cannot be a visionary without being persuasive.

The school planning committee must witness the leader's passion for the school.

Leaders must foster the crafting of a clear school vision, one resonating with all stakeholders. Leaders must inspire committee members to fulfill the school's vision. It is incumbent on leaders to provide stakeholders with opportunities to envision, understand, and experience the school's vision as they develop the school's action plan and campus budget using the Sorenson-Goldsmith Integrated Budget Model. Vision is not free. It costs time, money, and energy. The components of this model will be individually examined in an effort to make the vision a reality.

Component 1: Defining Stakeholders

If the entire learning community is to share ownership of the SBDM and budgetary processes, then all stakeholders must be involved. Expected stakeholders include

- school-site administrators (for example, principal, assistant principal, site specialist, campus facilitator, and/or instructional coach);
- school-site directors of students (band, choir, orchestra, drama, and athletic directors, for example);
- teachers and grade-level or department chairs;
- staff members including but not limited to paraprofessionals, custodians, etc.;
- other professionals;
- district or central office administrators;
- parents including but not limited to parent–teacher association (PTA) or parent–teacher organization (PTO) executive committee members;
- community members; and
- students.

Every stakeholder is valuable to the collaborative or SBDM planning, visioning, and budgeting processes as each stakeholder brings a unique perspective to these processes. SBDM is one of the most critical strategies a school leader can incorporate, and it is important to understand why it is essential to effective leadership, followership, and budget development. For additional information related to this topic, turn to Chapter 8 and the two initial sections, "Site-Based Decision Making" and "Why Site-Based Decision Making?"

Component 2: Stakeholder Selection

An examination of state and local policies is appropriate to ensure compliance with any state laws or regulations in selecting stakeholders. Local policies and administrative procedures determine the structure and authority of the school collaborative planning committee. Procedures also define the roles and responsibilities of the committee.

Committee Size and Structure

The size and structure of the collaborative planning committee must be considered. The authors believe teachers should comprise a majority to a supermajority of the committee positions. The election and selection of committee members should be as simple as possible. While it might work well to elect faculty and staff committee positions, it would be more efficient if other positions, such as parents and community members, were appointed. Once again, clear procedures must be in place.

Diversity

Careful consideration must be given to creating diversity on the committee when selecting members. Appointments should represent the community's diversity. Besides ethnic diversity, other populations should be represented. Parent representatives must also reflect the diversity of the student population. Among those populations to be considered are parents of children who

- speak English as a second language,
- have special needs,
- have special gifts and talents, or
- come from a variety of socioeconomic situations.

There are several actions administrators should take to increase the diversity of the SBDM committee. Chief among those actions are

- posting on the school's or district's websites or social media accounts,
- advertising in the local newspaper,
- securing public service announcements on local television and radio stations,
- seeking nominations from PTAs or PTOs,
- seeking nominations from local businesses, and
- seeking nominations from community organizations (such as the Chamber of Commerce) or service organizations (such as the Kiwanis or Lions clubs).

Administrators should also strive for educational diversity, which can readily correlate with equity and equality. In fact, diversity, equity, equality, and inclusion are four closely linked values held by many principals and teams that are working to be supportive of differing groups of students, including those of different races, ethnicities, religions, abilities, genders, and sexual orientations.

Members who are nominated must be willing to serve and invest time in the school's planning process. This is not the time for arm-twisting. An unwilling volunteer will likely lead to an empty seat and a missed opportunity for diverse representation.

The administrator or committee that finalizes the selection of the school planning committee members must deliberate conscientiously over the nominations. Some questions to consider include the following:

- Does this individual have the time to attend committee meetings?
- Will this individual be willing to attend site-based training on the committee?
- Does this individual demonstrate the capacity to consider all sides of an issue?
- Is the individual an ideologue or one who is considered to be open-minded?

Committee Member Training

Committee members need training to understand their role in the collaborative decision-making process. Frequently, principals and faculty members have not been trained adequately to meet with success in the collaborative planning process. The committee requires designated areas to examine budgeting, curriculum, staffing patterns, staff development, and school organization if it is to improve school performance. These areas must be clearly defined in the training process. Training prevents misunderstandings about the committee's function and authority.

Committee members must develop their listening skills, understand other cultures, and know how to use conflict resolution skills.

SBDM committee members benefit from training in team-building, consensus, and compromising skills. Committee members must develop their listening skills, understand other cultures, and know how to use conflict resolution skills. Finally, training must be provided in the collection and interpretation of data. The committee must be convinced of the merits of using data as the basis for not only creating change in the school but also for budget development.

Staggering the Terms

Consideration must be given to staggering committee members' terms. This technique ensures stability and experience over time. If members serve two-year terms, then at least 50 percent of the school planning committee would be experienced members at any given time. Three-year staggered terms allow for two-thirds of the committee to be experienced members with institutional memory. This strengthens the process as well as assists the one-third just starting to serve on the committee.

Component 3: Data Gathering (Needs Assessment)

Like businesses, schools are expected to verify their performance with solid data. Schools must gather, collect, and analyze data from a wide range of sources, requiring state education agencies to report student performance by income, English fluency, migrant status, race, gender, and disability. The increased pressure for external accountability heightens the need for schools to be data driven. A school's program success is dependent on how efficiently data measuring the change being implemented in the school are collected.

Needs assessment requires the school planning committee to ponder, "How well is our school doing in meeting our school improvement plan goals?" The answer to this question goes beyond the hunches and feelings of committee members. No longer can schools simply proclaim, "We had a great year. Our students made tremendous progress." The answer to the previous question requires the committee to gather data from an array of sources in order to complete a comprehensive needs assessment of the school (see "Conducting a Needs Assessment" in Chapter 6 for a more in-depth examination of how to effectively direct the needs assessment process). The more data collected from a broad range of sources, the greater the likelihood the committee will accurately respond to the posed question.

Data originate from a wide array of sources. A partial list for collecting school data includes the following:

- student achievement test results
- campus and district websites
- state education agencies' websites
- attendance data (student and faculty)
- dropout data
- school budget reports
- parent surveys

- student surveys
- faculty surveys
- focus groups
- volunteer logs
- transfer requests (student and faculty)
- retention data
- failure reports
- discipline data
- facilities reports
- organizational description (mission, vision, values)
- staff development needs
- staffing patterns
- accident reports
- extracurricular data
- special populations data
- mobility rate
- unusual events on the campus (for example, death of a student, fire, shooting, etc.)
- any other information useful in measuring the school's performance

As data are gathered in an ongoing process, a school profile emerges. This profile reflects the school's operating environment, key educational programs, resource allocation, and other facets of the school. Once data are gathered, the committee must sift through them to derive meaning from the sea of numbers and reports. Needs assessment never ends. Schools constantly gather data. Data gathered must go to the next step—data analysis. After all, what good does it do to gather data and not analyze it?

Component 4: Data Analysis

A discussion of measurement, analysis, and data management as keys to improving student performance began in Chapter 2 and continues in Chapter 6 (see the section titled "Performing an Information Analysis"). Data analysis takes needs assessment or data gathering one step further. Data analysis provides the crucial linkage between data examination and the development of effective strategies. In this process, the school planning committee interprets probable causal factors. These factors can be anything from a high dropout rate to a low attendance rate to low academic performance in specific curriculum areas.

In the simplest terms, the Sorenson-Goldsmith Integrated Budget Model component is the "brain center" for aligning the school's delivery of instruction and related services to meet individual student needs. This component addresses knowledge management and the basic performance-related data and comparative data, as well as how such data are analyzed and used to optimize the school's performance.

Collecting data without analysis is an exercise in futility. Data analysis can be a daunting task for the school planning committee, particularly for the members who are not school employees as they face the infamous "stack of stuff." This is where the school leader provides much-needed assistance and assurance, particularly to the committee members who are noneducators. The leader ensures educator committee members do not freely throw around acronyms and educational jargon at the expense of the noneducator members' comprehension of the data.

Educators may inadvertently speak in shorthand by using acronyms or phrases such as *ELL* (English language learner), *IDEA* (Individuals with Disabilities Education Act), *Title I*, or *two deviations below the norm*. Remember, this lingo is foreign to most noneducator committee members. The school leader must be sensitive to this issue and be certain the dialogue remains inclusive to all committee members; not doing so is a lapse in professionalism.

Data must be disaggregated to obtain the level of specificity required to ensure all students meet with success. Data disaggregation requires data differentiation by subpopulations. Examples of subpopulations include race, gender, and economic status.

One example of data disaggregation is found in student achievement data. To better illustrate disaggregation of student data, examine an abridged report on student achievement in fifth-grade mathematics at the fictitious Fort Chadbourne Elementary School (FCS) identified in Table 3.1.

In reviewing these data, several observations can be made about the mathematics achievement of students at FCS. The low SES score refers to students who are of low socioeconomic status. Low SES is typically defined as being eligible to participate in the federal free or reduced-price lunch program.

Before reading the following list of the authors' observations about FCS, stop and construct a mental or physical list of your own observations based on a data analysis of the FCS performance report in Table 3.1. Compare the findings of the data analysis with the authors' observations.

- The campus performed above state average last year and below state average this year.
- The Asian American subpopulation performed the highest in both years.

TABLE 3.1 Fort Chadbourne Elementary School State Academic Performance Report

	FIFTH-GRADE MATHEMATICS								
		PERCENTAGE PASSING							
	STATE	CAMPUS	ANGLO	AFRICAN AMERICAN	HISPANIC	ASIAN AMERICAN	LOW SOCIO ECONOMIC STATUS (SES)	MALE	FEMALE
Second Year	85	88	94	87	81	98	78	68	91
First Year	81	84	94	86	77	96	69	57	87

- The Anglo subpopulation performed second highest in both years.
- The Hispanic subpopulation increased its performance by four points in the current year.
- The African American subpopulation performed above the state and Hispanic subpopulations in both years.
- The low SES subpopulation had the greatest increase in performance (nine points) of the three ethnic groups.
- The gap in achievement between the four ethnic groups is narrowing, with the exception of one ethnic group, although a significant gain has been made in that group as well. Which ethnic group is this?
- The lowest-performing subpopulation of any is the low SES group.
- Females outperformed males each year.
- All areas listed within Table 3.1 improved their performance with the exception of the Anglo subpopulation, which remained the same.
- The profile of the most at-risk student at FCS based on these data is the male student who is potentially on free or reduced-price lunch.
- Though not noted as part of the bulleted listing, what additional area(s) based upon your analysis has/have made improvements, if any? Regressions, if any?
- What can be surmised, based on personal perception analysis, regarding the fifth-grade mathematics program at Fort Chadbourne Elementary School?

Hopefully after this brief analysis of abridged data, other questions are forming about FCS—questions requiring additional data gathering by the collaborative planning committee. Consider what additional questions would provide a better understanding of the issues at FCS based on the data. Stop and develop a list of questions about FCS based on these limited data. Consider the partial list of questions below that might come to a committee member's mind based on the data presented in Table 3.1.

- What, if any, intervention was initiated that improved the performance of the Hispanic, African American, Asian American, and low SES subpopulations?
- What was the performance of these same groups of students on the tested mathematics objectives?
- Did students perform poorly on the same math objectives each year?

- How did students at the lower grades perform on mathematics in comparison to the fifth-grade students?
- Are there problems with the same type of objectives between grade levels?
- How did this same group of students perform on the mathematics exam in past years?
- Is the FCS mathematics curriculum aligned with the concepts assessed on the state exam?
- Do the same subpopulations have the lowest scores in other areas of the exam?
- What interventions were in last year's FCS school improvement plan? How effective were they?

This initial examination of the snippet of gathered data in Table 3.1 led to some obvious observations, which in turn led to a greater depth of questioning and the need for assimilating additional data. (This required the committee to revisit the third component, data gathering.) The analysis also led to the previous year's school plan and into the arena of school plans evaluation. Hopefully, a need for additional data was raised.

Had it been feasible in the FCS example to include more data than the student performance in mathematics at one grade level over a two-year period, more questions would have been generated. These questions would likely be more specific and of greater instructional depth. With a broader array of data, a broader field of needs would be identified. Recognize data does not necessarily identify the right answers or provide quick fixes. Data does, however, offer decision makers an important glimpse through differing lenses to create opportunities to challenge longstanding assumptions and thus pose additional questions. This leads to needs prioritization, the fifth component of the Sorenson-Goldsmith Integrated Budget Model.

Component 5: Needs Prioritization

After completing the data-driven process of identifying the school's needs, the school planning committee is frequently confronted with more needs than can be realistically addressed within the confines of fiscal, human, and material resources. At this point, the committee must determine which needs receive priority. Successful school leaders and teams prioritize the needs of their schools and address a few at a time.

Data review is an integral part of prioritizing needs. Failure to use data knowledge effectively is costly to schools. Educators must learn to use data to inform academic progress. Committee members must review the data at hand and reach consensus on what needs should receive top priority in order to propel the school toward the fulfilment of its mission.

Conflict can arise while planners are attempting to reallocate resources. When needs are identified using a data-driven process, the identified needs immediately possess a stronger status than those identified from a purely partisan process.

Prioritizing limited resources for data-driven needs is no doubt a challenge for all involved. The school leader must approach the situation in a nonpartisan manner. This is a situation in which those skills and attributes embedded in *PSEL 5* are so important.

In the discussion of this standard in Chapter 1, fairness was examined. Fairness—to be free from bias, dishonesty, or injustice. Fairness necessitates principals model to the planning team how to put the interests and needs of others above their own interests and needs. It also requires leaders and their teams remember that best meeting the needs of students does not necessarily translate into equal distribution of the resources.

Leaders must allocate ample time for all to be heard and try to reach consensus. If the planning team approaches the situation with this mindset, then the chances dramatically increase for a successful resolution that can be supported by the majority. In the end, the needs prioritization process will draw the planning team closer together emotionally as well as missionally. Once the needs have been prioritized, the SBDM committee is ready to start setting goals.

Component 6: Goal Setting

Goal setting is a crucial component in the integrated budget model. Goals unify stakeholders by providing meaning and purpose. Goals are broad statements of expected outcomes consistent with the mission, vision, and philosophy of the school. Goals must be driven by student performance–based needs and must be consistent with the school's vision and mission statements.

A school leader must be sensitive when beginning in earnest to develop data-driven goals. Data will reveal differences in performance. They point their digital fingers to strengths and weaknesses in the school. This makes some stakeholders uneasy. The collaborative committee process must not ignore where data are pointing, nor can it bury the facts. Academic integrity demands the committee examine the actions dictated by the data and develop the appropriate goals.

The school planning committee must be involved in the goal-setting process because goals reflect the essence of the school's culture. When goals are assimilated into the school's culture, stakeholders are more motivated to achieve them and more likely to punish members who abandon them. In fact, goals can become so incorporated into the school's culture they continue to exist through changes of administration. Results-driven goals motivate and engage effective teams. It is imperative the collaborative planning committee (the SBDM committee) assist stakeholders in making the connection between goals and improvement if there is to be a significant chance for improving the school.

This committee has gathered data, analyzed data, and prioritized needs. Each committee member should have a greater understanding of why things are the way they are at the school. Ubben et al. (2016) provide four assumptions to guide a principal in working with the school planning committee on goal setting:

1. People at the working level tend to know the problems best.
2. The face-to-face work group is the best unit for diagnosis and change.
3. People will work hard to achieve objectives and goals they have helped develop.
4. Initiative and creativity are widely distributed across campus.

It is the leader's responsibility to keep the goals in front of the stakeholders. Goals must be distributed and displayed in a variety of forums, such as PTA/PTO meetings and community service organization meetings. Goals must be reviewed at every faculty meeting, every grade level, or every department meeting. They must appear in faculty newsletters or e-mails; they must be posted on the school's website or via the schools social media accounts. They must be embedded in parent communications. Goals must definitely drive the school budget and distribution of campus funding. Bottom line: Goals must be constantly kept in front of the stakeholders.

Component 7: Performance Objectives

Once goals congruent with the school's vision and mission are established through the collaborative planning process, performance-based objectives must be developed to provide increased definition to the course of action. Performance objectives identify specific, measurable, and expected outcomes for all student populations served. Performance objectives must be driven by student performance–based needs assessment data. Table 3.2 contains two objectives. The first objective is not a performance objective. The second objective *is* a performance objective.

The first objective is not measurable because the students are being asked to do "well" in mathematics this year. *Well* is a subjective term and can vary in definition from individual to individual. This objective is also vague in that it not only lacks specificity, it also does not prescribe a method for completing the measurement.

TABLE 3.2 A Comparison of a Nonperformance Objective to a Performance Objective

Nonperformance Objective	Students will do well in mathematics this school year.
Performance Objective	Student scores in the state assessment exam on mathematics will increase by 5 percent in each of the ethnic subpopulations with an N > 30.

The second objective is a performance objective for three reasons: (1) A data source for the assessment is identified—the state assessment exam, (2) a specific improvement of 5 percent is expected in each of the ethnic subpopulations, and (3) it adds specific accountability to subpopulations.

It is essential all objectives in the school action plan be measurable if the school is to be data driven in its planning. When objectives are not measurable, it is left up to each individual to employ personal feelings on whether the objective has been achieved. Ten different individuals could evaluate the objective ten different ways.

Component 8: Action Plan

The action plan is a *living, breathing* document that serves as a guide for all stakeholders. Emphasis was added to the adjectives *living, breathing* to call attention to the fact the action plan is not static. (If it's static, it's likely to be dead.) This point cannot be overemphasized. A quick review of the Sorenson-Goldsmith Integrated Budget Model in Figure 3.1 reminds the principal and team that much effort is required to produce this meaningful document.

The action plan is a *living, breathing* document that serves as a guide for all stakeholders. Emphasis was added to the adjectives *living, breathing* to call attention to the fact the action plan is not static. (If it's static, it's likely to be dead.)

In conclusion, at the base of the model in Figure 3.1 is a box with three terms—*ongoing evaluation, analysis*, and *course correction*. This foundational concept of the model demands the action plan be a living document. *Ongoing* means the process never ceases. Ongoing evaluation and analysis require continuous monitoring. This action manifests itself in ongoing course correction that results in editing marks appearing throughout the action plan.

A Planning Metaphor

Prior to boarding a flight in New York City to Los Angeles, the pilot has already filed a flight plan with the proper authorities. Once the plane departs New York, the pilot and copilot continually reference the flight plan to ensure the goal of the flight—to arrive in Los Angeles with all the passengers and the plane in safe condition. Despite the flight crew's effort in submitting a viable flight plan that, when implemented under static conditions, would allow the them to meet the goal, events will occur during the flight that will require the crew to make course corrections in the flight plan.

As the plane approaches Missouri, it encounters severe thunderstorms. The pilots consult and agree upon modifications to the plan so as to circumvent this unexpected weather event. Later, as the plane is approaching Nevada, a passenger becomes seriously ill. After a quick needs assessment of the situation, the crew decides to make an emergency landing in Las Vegas to secure the appropriate medical treatment for this passenger.

The plane leaves Las Vegas to finish the flight to Los Angeles. Unfortunately, air traffic is stacked up and the plane is diverted to a holding pattern until space is available. After forty-five minutes of circling Los Angeles, the plane makes a safe landing. The flight plan, along with the course corrections initiated by the flight crew, allowed everyone to celebrate the success of the plan by experiencing a safe arrival. But what about the passenger who was left in Las Vegas? This passenger received the appropriate medical treatment. The airline provided the passenger a ticket from Las Vegas to Los Angeles so he could reach his final destination. Granted, he did not reach it at the same time as the others. But through the appropriate accommodations, he achieved the goal of the original flight plan.

Several similarities exist between this flight and a school year. Like the flight crew, the school planning committee creates and files a flight plan, but it is called a *school action* or *decision-making plan*. The plane's flight is representative of the implementation of the flight plan. Likewise, the school's activities during the school year represent the implementation of the school action plan. Both the plane and the school will encounter unanticipated events that require their crews to revisit the original plan and incorporate the necessary changes to keep the plane or school on course to meet its goals. It is essential to understand that every plan developed requires constant monitoring and regular adjustments. Otherwise, the flight or the school is doomed to failure.

Planning may progress, as noted in Figure 3.1, from Component 1 through Component 8, but in the monitoring process the committee can return to whatever component is necessary to make the appropriate course correction. For example, new data might be gathered (Component 3), which will be analyzed (Component 4), which will then necessitate action in Components 7 and 8.

This is exactly what happened in the flight from New York to Los Angeles. The flight crew analyzed new data—a weather report. This analysis caused the crew to modify the flight plan to meet the goal of a safe flight. School leaders must ensure action plans (much like flight plans) are constantly monitored and appropriately adjusted.

The GOSA Relationship

Goals, objectives, strategies, and actions (GOSA) bring structure and detail to the planning process. These facets of planning are integrated on the action strategy pages in the school action plan. Understanding the relationship between these four planning facets is essential to understanding the school action plan. This relationship is detailed below.

Goals (the *G* in GOSA) were examined earlier in Component 6 of the Sorenson-Goldsmith Integrated Budget Model. Measurable objectives (the *O* in GOSA) were explained in the discussion of Component 7 of the model.

The *S* in GOSA is strategy. A strategy is a statement that assigns resources to accomplish the goal and the objective that it supports. Types of resources include but are not limited to informational, human, fiscal, material, spatial, and technological. Strategies can also be broad initiatives that cover the breadth of a school. Examples include a math-manipulative program, a new tutorial design, or a dropout prevention intervention. The strategy should be expected to significantly impact the performance of the targeted populations. An example of a strategy statement is, "Implement new reading small group/digital intervention programs targeting students who are reading one or more grade levels below their grade placement."

The *A* in GOSA is activity—a particular action is required to implement a strategy. An example of an activity to be used in the above strategy is, "The campus reading instructional coach will coordinate with teachers relative to implementing the new and innovative digital program as well as training the reading interventionist teacher at each grade level."

Examining the GOSA elements from the first (goal) to last (action) increases the specificity. The opposite occurs when they are examined from the last to the first. The elements become increasingly general. This unique relationship allows the document to be examined on four different levels of detail. Examining only the goals and objectives provides the reader with a quick general understanding of the school action plan. Examining all four levels provides the reader with the detail required for implementation of the goals and objectives.

An Example

Table 3.3 reveals the integration approach of visioning, planning, and budgeting in the Fort Chadbourne Elementary School example. Recall effective, efficient, and essential budgetary practices must be based on the premise that school budgeting will never be a successful practice if visioning and planning are not integrated within any budget development process (see also Chapter 6).

TABLE 3.3 Integration of Vision, Planning, and Budgeting in the Fort Chadbourne Elementary School

VISIONING, PLANNING, AND BUDGETING INTEGRATIVE APPROACH	
Budget	$18,500, personnel assigned, facility space assigned
Vision	Seeking mastery of the reading curriculum by all students
Planning	Use of a planning team, page from the campus action plan

Form 3.1 is a completed strategy page from the Fort Chadbourne Elementary School Campus Action (Improvement) Plan. There is one goal on the page: All students will master the objectives of the reading curriculum. The goal happens to be a broad statement supporting the school's mission of academic success for all students. It is also linked to student performance–based needs.

The objective is specific and measurable. It focuses on the reading goal and uses the results of the state assessment examination as its measure of mastery. Greater accountability is further achieved in that the objective is calling for a 5 percent increase in the performance of all identified student subpopulations.

The strategy—using the Reading It Through intervention program—assigns resources to support the goal and objective. Greater specificity of who, what, when, and where is provided with the inclusion of six specific action statements. For example, responsibilities are assigned to the principal, counselor, instructional coach, and reading intervention teacher. An accountability system is also in place for both formative and summative evaluation. The location of the evaluation data is even specified.

Finally, on this strategy page from a campus action plan, the integration of the budget with the vision and planning process is clearly in evidence (see Table 3.3). Fiscal resources have been budgeted, as evidenced by $18,500 in funds being assigned to this strategy as well as personnel (human) resources and facility resources. The allocated resources serve to support the school's vision of having all students master the reading curriculum. Planning is evidenced in the campus action or improvement plan through the strategy pages and minutes of the planning committee.

> Implementing an integrated vision, planning, and budget model does not happen overnight. It requires a significant amount of commitment and labor from all stakeholders, but students as well as all the stakeholders will reap benefits in the long run.

Remember, the school action plan is actually the integration and coordination of multiple GOSA relationships that are designed to fulfill the school planning committee's identified and prioritized school needs. The incorporation of the action plan process into the building of a school budget moves from discussion into the reality of practice in "The Budget Development Project" found in Resource A.

FORM 3.1 Strategy Page Form: The Fort Chadbourne Elementary School Campus Action (Improvement) Plan

Goal 1: All students will master the objectives of the reading curriculum.

Objective 1: Student mastery of the reading curriculum as measured by the state assessment exam will increase by 5 percent or more in each identified subpopulation.

Strategy 1: Students will use a diagnostic and instructionally managed Reading It Through intervention program to remediate specific reading objectives students are failing to master.

ACTIONS	RESPONSIBILITY	TIMELINE (START)	TIMELINE (END)	RESOURCES (HUMAN, MATERIAL, FISCAL)	AUDIT (FORMATIVE)	REPORTED/ DOCUMENTED
1. Purchase Reading It Through intervention program.	Principal	May YTD	July YTD	$7,000	Purchase order	Principal's office
2. Provide faculty training on Reading It Through intervention program.	Principal, instructional coach	August YTD	Ongoing	Consultant, $1,500	Purchase order, training agendas	Principal's office
3. Provide reading teachers with a list of identified students based on state assessment scores.	Instructional coach	August YTD	Ongoing	Instructional coach	Student listings	Instructional coach's office
4. Assign students to three forty-five-minute sessions per week for intensive intervention sessions.	Instructional coach and teachers	August YTD	Ongoing	Instructional coach and teachers	Student listings	Instructional coach's office
5. Provide teachers with progress reports (benchmarks) relative to student progress.	Instructional coach	Second and fourth Fridays	Ongoing	Instructional coach	Progress reports or benchmark reports	Teacher and instructional coach files
6. Schedule monthly planning sessions with principal, instructional coach, and reading teachers.	Instructional coach and reading teachers	Fourth Friday	Ongoing	Instructional coach and reading teachers	Agendas and minutes	Instructional coach and principal

Evaluation (Summative): State assessment reports, Reading It Through reports.

Final Thoughts

Implementing an integrated vision, planning, and budget model does not happen overnight. It requires a significant amount of commitment and labor from all stakeholders, but students as well as all other stakeholders will reap benefits in the long run. The transition to a planning process that integrates budget and vision evolves through four stages:

1. **Reactive stage.** This first stage is characterized by poorly defined goals and random strategies and activities designed to meet immediate needs. There is little to no coordination between three important factors—visioning, planning, and budgeting—since they are headed in completely different directions.
2. **Transitive stage.** This stage reveals early evidence of the alignment of goals, objectives, and strategies. Vision, planning, and budgeting are all headed in the same general direction although deficiencies in planning and coordinating between the three elements are apparent.
3. **Aligned stage.** This third stage reveals alignment has been achieved between the budget, planning, and visionary processes; however, there is no integration of all three elements.
4. **Integrated stage.** The final stage reveals an amalgam has been created using vision, planning, and budgeting. Collaboration and communication are now apparent and valued. Continuous evaluation and course correction are in place. The three elements (visioning, planning, and budgeting) are now one. Together the elements make a team, working in tandem, all aiming toward a central conclusion: success!

Schools need all stakeholders working together to ensure academic success for everyone. No family wants their child to be the student who does not meet with academic success. Integrating a school's vision with planning in coordination with the campus budget greatly increases the likelihood of achieving the school's mission. Recognize that as a school leader, it is essential patience be exercised when working with faculty during the four-stage process.

It is up to the school leaders to keep the vision and the plan in front of the stakeholders. Remember, like the flight from New York to Los Angeles, a school year will have situations requiring the school planning and decision-making team to revisit the school action or improvement plan and make regular, if not necessary, course adjustments. In the end, if everyone works collaboratively and commits to a well-constructed and managed plan, both academic and budgetary success will occur.

P.S.

Schools will never have enough resources to do everything for their students. The integrated budget model provides leaders with an opportunity to rearrange resources and use them in a more efficient, equitable, and adequate manner. Stop and think about it: This is, in reality, an *increase* in revenue without asking more from the taxpayers.

Discussion Questions

1. What are the advantages of having procedures and policies in place to define the roles and responsibilities of the school planning or decision-making committee?
2. What are the advantages of providing training to school planning committee members?
3. Describe four attributes of a data-driven school. Describe how those attributes manifest themselves on your campus. If they are not manifested, what would need to happen for them to be demonstrated on your campus?
4. Data analysis, the fourth component of the Sorenson-Goldsmith Integrated Budget Model, was referenced as the "brain center" of this model. What is the significance of this descriptor for the fourth component of this model?
5. Why is the quote at the beginning of the chapter relevant to this chapter?
6. Rewrite this nonmeasurable objective into a measurable objective: "More students will take advanced placement (AP) courses next year." Defend your revision.
7. How would the flight metaphor play out at your school?
8. Which stage is your campus at in the implementation of the Sorenson-Goldsmith Integrated Budget Model? Defend your choice.
9. Using your response to Question 8, provide three recommendations to bring your use of the budget model to the next stage. If your campus, for example, is at Stage 4, describe three actions you took to get from Stage 3 to Stage 4.
10. How does this chapter relate to the Professional Standards for Educational Leaders (PSEL) as documented in Chapter 1? Which standard(s) are specifically relevant and why?

Case Study

Shifting Paradigms With Changing Times

Note: This case study is designed to lead the reader through the Sorenson-Goldsmith Integrated Budget Model. In order to assist the reader in obtaining a global view of how this model functions, parts of the process are provided. The budget amounts are unrealistic but were kept small so the reader does not become bogged down in mathematics. Frequent references to Figure 3.1 can assist in observing the flow of the model through this case study. A continuation of this case study is found in Chapter 8.

Part I: The Deal—Components 1 and 2 of the Sorenson-Goldsmith Integrated Budget Model

The Situation

Waterview is a prosperous suburb on Pecan Bay, just south of the thriving seaport of Indianola. With a population of thirty-five thousand, Waterview has grown in the last fifty years from a sleepy coastal village to a thriving community where new industries and businesses continue to locate. Waterview is the county seat of Cade County. Cade Consolidated School District (CCSD) has two high schools, four middle schools, and ten elementary schools. While the county's population has continued to decline for the past twenty years, Waterview is an exception. As a result of the population growth, two new middle schools and four new elementary schools have been built in Waterview during the past decade.

Two years ago, Dr. Ronald Scotts was named superintendent of CCSD. Dr. Scotts, a forty-eight-year-old father of thirteen-year-old twin girls, moved with his wife, Juanita, from the upstate town of River City. While serving as the associate superintendent for finance, Dr.Scotts earned a reputation in River City as a strong and competent leader. The CCSD board hired Dr. Scotts to bring about change to the school system. Academic performance for the last ten years had been consistently mediocre. Routines had become the norm. The last major innovation in the district had been ten years ago. The board, with its three newly elected members, wants CCSD to move from an attitude of mediocrity to one of excellence.

During his first year as superintendent, Dr. Scotts started a dialogue with the administrators about a decentralization plan for the school district. At the end of that year, before the principals started taking their vacations, Dr. Scotts announced that in the fall he would provide an allocation of $25,000 to schools that wanted to receive training in a collaborative planning process. Principals would need to submit a plan outlining how the funding would be spent to train the faculty in the process. Dr. Scotts further told the principals that campuses with an operational campus planning committee would assume responsibility for the development, spending, and monitoring of the campus budget, with the exception of salaries, maintenance, transportation, and operations. With this newfound autonomy came accountability for the effective use of the budgeted funds.

Principal Hector Avila and Assistant Principal Abigail Grayson are in their second year at Pecan Bay High School (PBHS). Hector had previously been a middle school principal in an urban district before being named principal at PBHS. He is the first Hispanic principal in the district. He has been well received by the community. Hector was hired to be a change agent at PBHS and has the gift of being able to unite people behind a shared vision. Abigail has taught mathematics and served as the girls' basketball and softball coach at PBHS for the past five years. Abigail has a much-deserved reputation as an innovative classroom teacher who is willing to try new teaching strategies. Abigail attended mathematics training at a local university through a Teacher Quality Grant during the past two summers. Hector and Abigail like each other, and each one's talents complement the other's.

After Dr. Scotts annouonced his $25,000 challenge, Hector and Abigail immediately and aggressively spent two weeks on campus writing a proposal that was well documented by research and contained a detailed implementation plan based on the Sorenson-Goldsmith Integrated Budget Model. The two delivered the plan in person to Dr. Scotts, demonstrating their enthusiasm for the project. Dr. Scotts inwardly smiled and thanked the two for the proposal. Two weeks later, PBHS became the first campus in CCSD to have its collaborative planning proposal approved.

During the first day of staff development in late summer, Abigail and Hector excitedly explained to the faculty their proposal using a

(Continued)

(Continued)

PowerPoint presentation with coordinated handouts. The faculty was quiet. The principals were picking up from the body language that they were bombing. Finally, Ed Feeney, a veteran teacher of twenty-seven years at PBHS, broke the passive silence and asked, "Whose idea was this?" Ed's friend and colleague, Jonathan Hedras, blurted out, "Sounds like the superintendent wants us to do his work. I'm busy enough as it is." There was some applause. Latasha Jackson, a fourth-year drama teacher, asked, "Is this another one of those fads that goes through schools? I bet the state is up to this." Kelly Tyres, a paraprofessional, commented, "No one ever asks us what we want. They just keep shoving stuff down our throats."

The principals let the teachers go to lunch thirty minutes early (a very popular decision) and went back to their offices, surprised and feeling beaten down, if not rejected. They kept repeatedly saying things to each other like, "Where did we go wrong?" and "I can't believe they are so negative" and "Where do we go from here?"

Thinking It Through

Hector and Abigail desperately need your assistance. Where did they go wrong? Where do they go from here? Hector and Abigail have a great proposal and are very capable administrators; yet they encountered strong resistance from the faculty. As that other set of eyes, you need to stop at this point in the case study and write a step-by-step plan for these principals to win over the faculty. Some handy hints have been included to help you with this process.

HANDY HINTS

- involve all stakeholders
- talk mission and vision
- communicate
- share decision making
- identify challenges
- identify strengths
- identify outside resources

PART II: THE NEEDS—COMPONENTS 3 THROUGH 5 OF THE SORENSON-GOLDSMITH INTEGRATED BUDGET MODEL

You will discover that if you do this activity with several colleagues, your intervention plan will be stronger than if you complete it by yourself. Remember, collaboration is a critical key to success.

Thank you for your assistance in developing a step-by-step plan for assisting the PBHS faculty to reconsider and adopt the collaborative planning process! Your work is not done. Learning to use the collaborative process requires time and effort from all the school stakeholders. Read on and be prepared to provide assistance again as the process continues to unfold.

Checking It Out

By the time spring arrived, the campus planning committee had been established and the training completed. Now it was time to begin constructing PBHS's campus-based action plan with an integrated budget. The campus planning committee was provided with a data packet courtesy of Hector and Abigail. Data were gathered from a variety of sources. The two principals spent countless hours gathering these data but only did so as a way to assist and encourage the committee. The committee was free to gather any other data it deemed necessary.

Dr. Scotts was pleased to inform the campus planning committee that PBHS would receive an additional allotment of $200,000 for the next school year. Nelson Clampett, the assistant superintendent of finance, trained the appropriate individuals on the district's budgeting software. Nelson was anxious to see his old alma mater meet with success. In fact, it was seventeen years ago he led the Fighting Squirrels baseball team to the state championship by pitching a no-hitter in the championship game. Since that time, the school had not received any athletic or academic awards.

In order to assist the flow of this case study, the planning committee's work of data gathering and analysis (Components 3 and 4) has been completed for you. The committee spent several meetings analyzing the box of data provided by Hector and Abigail. They requested additional data and were provided with all the data they required.

Make a list of data you would want to have if you were on the PBHS campus planning team.

Proceed and Prioritize

It is now time to proceed to Component 5 of the Sorenson-Goldsmith Integrated Budget Model. Take a look at Table 3.4. You must take the nonprioritized list of ten identified needs by the PBHS planning committee and prioritize them. Remember, PBHS has an allocation of $200,000. The committee cannot exceed the budget allocation! Note the identified needs will cost substantially more than the campus's allocation. It is time for the committee to make some tough decisions. Assign your priority numbers to the needs using the column on the far left. Provide a written rationale to share with the faculty and administration to defend your needs prioritization.

TABLE 3.4 PBHS Nonprioritized Identified Needs (Please prioritize and then proceed to Part III.)

Next Year			
Your Priority	**Cost**	**Identified Need**	**Committee Rationale**
	$20,000	• Copier contract	• Used by all departments • Basis of many academic assignments
	$30,000	• Reading intervention plan • $12,000 for software • $3,000 for training	• Percentage of freshmen reading below grade level is twice the state rate • Percentage of Hispanics reading below grade level is three times the state rate • Teacher survey shows reading issues are the number one teacher concern
	$40,000	• General supplies	• Meet basic office/classroom needs of paper, staplers, tape, and so on
	$6,000	• Special Olympics	• Add this program since these students are unable to participate in other extracurricular events • Parent advocacy group has made an appeal to the SBDM committee

	$30,000	• New band uniforms	• Current uniforms are twenty-three years old • Uniforms were water damaged and now have a mold problem
	$12,000	• Vernier instruments, other digital equipment	• Needed in advanced science and math classes • Essential to meet state curriculum requirements • Needed in pre-AP, AP, and dual credit courses
	$17,000	• Professional travel	• New category • Teachers need to be able to expand their knowledge by attending professional development events • Number four need on the teacher survey
	$60,000	• Expanded technology (hardware and software) • $45,000 tech services • $5,000 printers • $10,000 supplies	• Students need access to innovative digital technologies • Identified by teachers of AP courses as a number one priority
	$60,000	• Ninth-grade school-within-a-school • $5,000 training • $35,000 facility upgrades • $20,000 curriculum materials	• High failure rate in freshmen classes • High disciplinary referral rate to office • High absentee rate
	$7,000	• Spring athletic banquet • $5,000 honorarium for speaker • $2,000 catered meals for 200	• Boost enthusiasm for athletics • Increase school spirit

PART III: THE ACTION PLAN—COMPONENTS 6 THROUGH 8 OF THE SORENSON-GOLDSMITH INTEGRATED BUDGET MODEL

Now that you have prioritized the needs, it is time to construct an *abridged* action plan. For the purpose of this case study, you will only use the top two prioritized needs.

Using the number one prioritized need, complete a strategy page to address that need. It may be necessary to use more than one strategy page due to space constraints. A clean copy of the strategy page is located in Resource B and is available online at qrs.ly/xgfap8g

Repeat the process for the need you designated as the second priority. Once you have completed both priorities, review your pages. Are the goals, objectives, and strategies aligned and logical? Do the actions clearly define what is being done in order to implement the strategy? Are the resources, personnel, and evaluations in place?

Now that you've experienced a brief taste of the initial budgetary process, prepare to read the next six chapters and encounter the so-called nuts and bolts of effective, efficient, and essential budgeting procedures. In these chapters, you will

- investigate the sources of school funding,
- learn the critical steps to budgeting success,
- become familiar with expenditure accountability and control as well as accounting and auditing procedures,
- examine the budgetary leadership role as related to ethical and moral behaviors,
- master a detailed examination and application of proper coding, and
- build a school budget!

One final query: What's a principal to do when it comes to faculty negativity such as that exhibited in this case study by Latasha Jackson, Kelly Tyres, and, most notably, Ed Feeney? Be explicit in your response.

Understanding the Budgeting Process

4

> *A budget will not work unless you do!*
>
> —Anonymous

The Basics of School Budgeting

School leaders have always needed to devote a vast amount of time and energy to funding and budgeting issues, but this is especially critical in today's era of continued fiscal conservatism and political partisan polarization, both of which negatively affect public education and funding. School leaders who fail to devote time and energy to the budgetary process commit a terrible disservice to their students. Why is budgeting so essential beyond the stated reason? First and foremost, the budgeting process enables school leaders to develop an understanding of the need for strong organizational skills, technical competence, and the collaborative planning process so essential to ensuring organizational trust and development.

Moreover, numerous studies have documented the importance of strong organizational skills to a leader's success and effectiveness. Hughes et al. (2021) reveal technical competence relates to a knowledge base and the particular behaviors a leader brings to successfully completing a task. School leaders generally acquire technical competence, specifically in relation to the budgetary process, through formal education or training, but, more often than not, also from on-the-job experiences (Yukl & Gardner, 2019). Thus, the reader immediately recognizes one of the primary purposes of this book is to serve as a school leader's guide to appropriate and effective school-based budgeting.

School leaders who fail to devote time and energy to the budgetary process commit a terrible disservice to their students.

Effective school leaders know how to properly develop a school budget. They also understand why budgeting and accounting procedures are integral parts of an instructional program. The best school leaders understand goal development and instructional planning are significantly impacted by the budgeting process. Appropriation of public funds for a school is ensured by adopting a fiscal year budget that includes all estimated revenues and proposed expenditures. Budget accounts, in most states, are reported electronically by means of a Fiscal Education and Information Management System (FEIMS).

The FEIMS is a codified information and management system electronically linking revenues and expenditures (for example, from school to district office to state departments of education) through an accounting process that traces and audits funding and examines programmatic considerations. The system even reviews student achievement and accountability standards as well as other important issues, all the while detecting material and human errors in the fiscal data of a school district. Therefore, recognize the significance of the adoption of a district budget by the local school board. This adoption provides the legal authorization for school leaders to expend public funds.

School leaders, early in their careers, realize that setting goals, establishing measurable objectives, developing action or improvement plans, incorporating the entire learning community in a collaborative or participatory process, developing trust, acting with integrity, and making student enrollment projections are essential components in the development and implementation of an effective school budget. Said qualities further ensure effective and strong school leadership (Mungal & Sorenson, 2020; Sorenson, 2022; Sorenson, 2024; Sorenson et al., 2011).

School leaders must recognize it is not by mere coincidence that the budget planning and development processes coincide with the instructional or school action planning process. Both processes are essential to the overall success of any school or, for that matter, any school leader (Brimley et al., 2020). These two processes must be developed via an integrated approach to achieve the maximum benefits for schools and students (refer back to Chapter 3).

As previously noted, a school budget must have as its foundation the action or improvement plan that details the educational programs and initiatives of a school. Such a plan must be consistent with the school's vision or mission (Mungal & Sorenson, 2020; Sorenson, 2024). Each program, initiative, and/or activity within an action or improvement plan dictates how appropriate budgetary decision making—as related to funding appropriations—will occur and how such decision making ultimately impacts student achievement.

Breaking the Budgeting Myths

Many school leaders begin their careers with several mythical notions related to the budgetary process. Interestingly, several come to mind. These myths frequently serve to complicate the budgeting process and can, in fact, disengage a school leader from monitoring and managing an important, if not critical, aspect of the education business: the school budget. Listed below are five myths often experienced by and associated with school leaders and school-based budgeting. These myths will be dispelled throughout these final seven chapters.

1. School leaders must have an analytical mindset.
2. Budgeting, like any fiscal accounting procedure, is difficult.
3. Instruction and curriculum are more important; budgeting not so much.
4. The school budget is for the campus business office clerk to maintain.
5. School leaders simply do not have the time to meet the demands and dictates associated with managing the school budget.

Few factors pose a greater obstacle to the school leader than untrue, unsubstantiated, and self-limiting budgetary beliefs or myths. It must be argued that by acknowledging and then avoiding these untruths, the school leader is provided with the basis for better understanding, developing, and handling a school budget.

The five budgeting myths are unfortunately prevalent in the world of school administration. However, recognition of these myths provides school leaders—particularly novice administrators—with insights that allow for the development of essential budgeting skills. Mastery of such skills permits the school leader to emerge as an effective manager of a campus budget. Being able to recognize and analyze personal experiences in terms of the budgeting myths may be one of the single greatest contributions this text can provide. Remember, a budget will not work unless you do!

Delineating Between School Finance and School Budgeting

School business is big business. Many school districts across the nation are by far the largest enterprises in their communities in terms of revenues, expenditures, employment, and capital assets. Unfortunately, school leaders often fail to understand the basis for funding public schools. As a result, they become victims of their own demise, failing to recognize the financial challenges that are frequently associated with being a fiscal leader in a big business. School leaders often fail to understand the fundamentals associated with school budgeting. In far too many instances, school leaders possess limited experience or expertise with the budgeting process. This dilemma is further complicated by the fact school leaders have an inadequate understanding of the basic delineation between school finance and school budgeting.

School finance is regulated by state and federal legislation as well as the courts. Each governmental entity has initiated, by law, stringent policies and procedures to infuse greater accountability through the development of financial plans and reports. Such reporting is related to a process that records, classifies, and summarizes fiscal transactions and provides for an accounting of the monetary operations and activities of a school district. School finance is most assuredly a concern for superintendents, district chief financial officers, comptrollers, and/or business managers. The reason? The adequacy, equity, and equality (or the lack thereof) of state and federal funding is the fiscal lifeline of a school district. However, this book is not directly about school finance. This read is from the perspective of the school-site leader who must be dedicated to better understanding and appreciating the interrelationship of school funding, school-based budgeting, and the academic visioning and planning process.

While many school leaders are focused on augmenting revenue for their schools in an era of increased mandates, state funding constraints, and political intrusions, other school leaders are focused on a much more timely and relevant question: Are schools allocating, budgeting, and spending their funding dollars strategically, especially during these times of fiscal restraint, conservative funding, and political polarization?

Budgeting in Troublesome Times

The funding of schools has always been a difficult prospect. Untimely inflation rates from the 1970s to the present day have only aggravated the funding of public schools. During the Great Recession (2008–2010), inflation actually became deflationary, with the economy becoming terribly depressed. By mid-2009, inflation leveled, but only to a low of −2.10 percent (Stokes, 2011). For several years following the Great Recession, school districts unfortunately found that drops in housing prices and property valuations, lingering decreases in property tax revenues, and community job losses—frequently associated with the reduction in crude oil prices—only increased the need for drastic budgetary measures. Additionally, school districts found the politicizing of public school education to be a detriment to securing necessary federal and state funds.

In the recent past, however, most schools have seen an unprecedented infusion of federal funding in numerous incantations, including the Rethink K-12 School Models competitive grant program (criticized as a backdoor approach to providing vouchers for homeschooling and private schooling); the Coronavirus Aid, Relief, and Economic Security Act (CARES; March 2020); the Coronavirus Response and Relief Supplemental Appropriations Act (CRRSA; December 2020); the American Rescue Plan (ARP; March 2021); the Higher Education Relief Opportunities for Students Act (HEROES; May/October, 2022); and, more specifically, in the form of Elementary and Secondary School Emergency Relief (ESSER-I, March, 2020; ESSER-II, December, 2020; and ESSER-III, March, 2021) formula grant dollars (National Center for Education Statistics [NCES], 2022).

For decades, school district financial dollars have depended heavily on individual state funding. During 2020–2024, that so-called center of gravity shifted to the districts with the ESSER monies. Districts were able to tap into the federal public education funds to the tune of some $700 billion. That monumental federal relief funding served to aid school systems, notably by bridging achievement gaps resulting from the pandemic period, especially among students of color and white students in high poverty areas.

Yet even with the infusion of federal funds, the issue of equity and equality in districts utilizing ESSER funds as well as weighted student formulas remain a serious and long-going concern. That noted, seven significant spending trends were identified as relative to ESSER funding: (1) the expansion of staff, (2) a reduction in class sizes, (3) the hiring of new teachers and instructional specialists, (4) the retention of faculty and staff, (5) the earmarking of stipends to pay for increased work loads (aiding students relative to academic recovery), (6) the improvement of working conditions (more planning and collaboration time), and (7) the increase of professional development to equip teachers with additional skills and knowledge (training of teachers relative to evidence-based instructional approaches, family engagement strategies, and new technology platforms).

School Funding Considerations and Concerns

WARNING: The educational funding highway curves ahead are dangerous! Be cautious for there may be no guardrails! As early as 2020, school district financial leaders across the nation, when polled, were responding with a get ready, we're hell-bent and headed for a wild ride as there are serious financial problems down the road (Roza, 2021). At the time of this writing, leading educational researchers and experts predicted that beginning with the 2024–2025 school year, school districts would experience negative impacts on finances due to five funding shocks: (1) federal COVID relief would expire and thus negatively affect school spending; (2) enrollment declines, already occurring, would lead to fewer revenues; (3) any economic slowdown would continue to harm district budgets; (4) labor scarcity, new hirings, step increases (permanent pay raises), and expanded staff rolls would create budget woe vulnerabilities; and (5) voucher programs would reduce state government funding to schools (Modan, 2022; Roza, 2021). Hopefully, these prognoses turned out to be completely inaccurate!

The U.S. Census Bureau (2022), in their annual report, *2021 Public Elementary-Secondary Education Finance Data*, revealed the average per-pupil spending in the United States was $14,330, which was up from 2018 when per-pupil spending was $10,700. The increase in per-pupil funding must be relegated to the district infusion of ESSER dollars. In the report *States That Spend the Most on Education*, Brown (2022) revealed Alaska, Michigan, Hawaii, New Mexico, and Oregon were spending the most funding per pupil. States spending the least per pupil were, in this order, Idaho, Arizona, Florida, Tennessee, and the District of Columbia.

Consider the research conducted by Allegretto et al. (2022), which revealed school finance metrics (equity, equality, adequacy, effort, and sufficiency), even with ESSER funding, continued to fall short of providing an effective education for all students. School districts nationwide are simply not receiving necessary funding to this day. This inadequacy reveals a grave concern: Many states are failing to sufficiently fund education. Far too many school districts across the nation continue to face budget challenges.

There are no easy funding solutions. However, state legislatures could very well provide either short-term or long-term (or even both) stabilization funds if politicians would work together and choose to do so! Obviously, school funding in the United States requires a serious revamping, and reforms are needed that would insert both federal and state government funding at a greater capacity to help overcome the district financial shortfalls.

Listed here are five school finance knowns that must be addressed: (1) Public school funding is inadequate, specifically for low-income students; (2) school funding is even further exasperated during and following recessions; (3) increased federal funding could aid state and local inequities; (4) increased school funding actually benefits the economy and thus everyone; and (5) both state and federal governments must assume a greater responsibility for reforming current school finance systems (Allegretto et al., 2022).

Moreover, Barnum (2022) noted that as the ESSER funding is depleted, the United States, sadly and to the detriment of all school-age children, is set to return to a broken school funding system. Southern states in particular are falling behind the remainder of the nation when it comes to school funding. A Southern Poverty Law Center (SPLC) report, *Inequity in School Funding: Southern States Must Prioritize Fair Public School Spending* (2021), asserts that without adequate, equitable, and equal funding, pervasive racial and economic injustices perpetuate and exacerbate an already flawed system.

Identified below are seven barriers, as reported by Allegretto et al. (2022), that are negatively influencing the education of all students.

1. As previously noted, funding is inadequate, with more than 90 percent of school funding being received from less-than-adequate state and local funding sources.
2. Funding is inequitable. More funding must be disseminated to schools serving high-poverty communities.

3. Too many states are failing to invest in public education relative to their capacity to do so. Consider the following as detailed by the Education Law Center (2022):
   - Alaska, Connecticut, New York, and Wyoming are examples of high-effort, high-capacity funding states, each earning a grade of *A* relative to funding efforts.
   - Arkansas, South Carolina, and West Virginia are examples of high-effort, low-capacity funding states.
   - California, Delaware, and Washington are examples of low-effort, high-capacity funding states.
   - Arizona, Florida, and Idaho are examples of low-effort, low-capacity funding states.
   - States such as Arizona, Colorado, Delaware, Florida, Nevada, North Carolina, Oklahoma, South Dakota, Tennessee, Texas, Utah, Washington, and the District of Columbia each earned a grade of *F* relative to school funding efforts.
4. School funding is overreliant on local taxation efforts. This shortfall readily relates to politics, state legislative decisions, insufficient tax rates, and citizens who oppose additional taxation.
5. State and federal school funding efforts fall short of compensating for local inequities. Federal funds actually better fund schools in wealthier school systems compared to those with higher rates of poverty.
6. As previously noted, economic downturns impair school funding efforts.
7. Inadequate, inequitable, and unequal funding continues to underresource schools serving low-income students of color.

To further exacerbate the problems of funding public education, many state lawmakers continue to push for and in some cases actually attain voucher programs that pull dollars from school systems, therefore harming public schools (especially those that are strapped for cash, such as rural schools) and negatively impacting student achievement across the board.

A Look to the Future of Public Education Funding

The National Conference of State Legislatures (2016) revealed years ago that states were facing fiscal barriers with fewer funding options for public schools. Even with the unprecedented COVID-era federal funding, this remains true to this day. This readily relates to the fact that state legislatures have signaled a continued squeezing of state pocketbooks when it comes to funding schools. To further complicate fiscal matters, a fifty-year overview of K-12 public education funding finds an almost continuous funding decrease since the mid-1960s (NCES, 2020). Will such a trend of inadequate, inequitable, and unequal funding reemerge after the COVID-relief measures have been suspended? The answer to this query is frightening: Probably yes!

Inadequate, inequitable, and unequal public school funding has serious consequences for the future of public education, including but not limited to the following:

- Insufficient educational services are available for schools.
- Local school districts, especially property-poor districts and districts with a disproportionate percentage of students of color, find it particularly difficult to raise additional revenue through taxation increases, which are politically challenging even in times of economic upswings. This is especially true when many states are passing bills that actually cut property taxes at the expense of public schools and educational funding.
- According to the American Society of Civil Engineers (2022) in its *2021 Infrastructure Report Card*, schools received a grade of *D+* as districts are not receiving the necessary funding to maintain campus buildings. At least one-fourth of school facilities are in poor condition. The United States continues to underinvest in school facilities, leaving a more than $40 billion annual funding gap. The grade of *D+* has not changed since 2017—a sad commentary.
- Inequitable and unequal funding cuts to public schools impede priority educational reforms such as improving teacher quality, reducing class sizes, reducing learning gaps, enhancing attendance rates, and increasing student academic achievement.

Such trends reveal a poignant fact: As state funding in particular fails to increase adequately, local funding continues to be unable to bridge the gap, and voucher programs deplete public education funds. The economic health of schools, let alone the nation, is at risk. If schools are neglected fiscally, the creativity and intellectual capacity of our society diminishes and our democracy weakens.

Politicizing Education and the Funding Impact

There is deeply drawn criticism from both ends of the political spectrum regarding state and federal education funding. The push to provide more educational choice to parents and thus to privatize education can very well seem alarming. Partisans on both sides of the aisle have described the privatization agenda and the slashing of public school funding as being more than alarming, in fact, using terms such as *difficult to defend*, *all but impossible*, *abysmal*, and *discriminatory*. Many educators see the strong impetus for voucher funding initiatives to be anything but reforming.

Such initiatives have been described as nothing more than a means of slashing funding for public schools and placing state and federal education dollars in the pockets of those business interests who advocate and lobby for an extreme privatization agenda. School leaders must serve not only as student advocates on the school grounds, they must also advocate publicly. They must politically promote a critical realization: Our democracy, since the January 6, 2021, insurrection, has been proven fragile. A strong democracy is built upon a free and public education for each student, no matter race, color, national origin, religion, sex, sexual orientation, disability, or economic advantage or disadvantage.

Pause and Consider

Public School Funding and Privatization:

New and Improved? Or Is There a Cost? And Does It Really Matter?

School leaders must be keenly aware of this era of contention in which we are living and working. An era in which issues and ideas of expanding alternatives to traditional public school funding are a top priority in both federal and state houses. What is required in such an era of new and improved funding? Is there a cost, and does it really matter? The authors recently came across a product that read on the front of the package "New and improved." Wondering how the product was new and improved, the authors read more carefully and determined the product was *new* simply because it had a revamped package design. The *improved* aspect of the product was more fruit colors; however, the product now containted fewer ounces per package, at an increased cost to the consumer. Quite a scheme!

School leaders recognize educational change is inevitable and can be beneficial in many instances. However, change must be meaningful as well as beneficial—most notably to students and stakeholders. Is any potential change to public school funding new and improved and, if so, at what cost? Or is such change doomed by political interference or indifference? And does it really matter? Listed below are four critical

(Continued)

(Continued)

considerations, subject to study and debate, as related to school funding, public and private education, and essential change.

1. **Publicly funded vouchers and privatization: Push back or pull forward?** At the time of publication (2024), thirty-two states offered some type of school choice plan and thus had in place voucher programs. This number was up from fifteen states in 2017 and then sixteen states in 2021. The 2024 number of thirty-two reveals a 50 percent increase in voucher funding over a very short five-year period. Utilizing Texas as an example, recent polling revealed 46 percent of respondents supported school choice (a voucher system), 43 percent opposed the idea, and 11 percent were not certain. However, 82 percent said they were concerned that any proposed voucher plan would take vital funds from public schools, leading 57 percent to express worry that a voucher system in Texas would equate to higher property taxes (Donaldson et al., 2023; Durrani, 2023).

Vouchers do not increase student achievement, do not improve academic outcomes, do not make schools safer, and do not provide fair pay for educators.

Basically, voucher plans promise to provide parents with enough funding to make a different choice other than public schooling and, further, provide a variety of private school options, including religious schools. But, as in the Texas example above, voucher proposals may face a difficult path through state legislatures. Why? Rural superintendents generally oppose any voucher initiative because students in their areas frequently lack alternatives to public schools and thus rural school districts could very well lose critical school funding (Donaldson, 2022; Graham, 2022).

Nevertheless, nationwide polling conducted in December 2022 found 67 percent of parents support school vouchers, indicating voucher plans remain of high interest among both public school parents and the general public (edCHOICE & Morning Consult, 2022). Both voucher proponents and opponents agree that voucher systems are growing state by state. To what degree public school funding is hurt by voucher systems remains debatable.

- What does the research reveal? Vouchers do not increase student achievement, do not improve academic outcomes, do not make schools safer, and do not provide fair pay for educators (ACERCA, 2022; Boser et al., 2018; Center on Education Policy, 2016). However, there is strong empirically based research evidence that vouchers *do* promote discriminatory public policy, especially against students with disabilities; hurt rural schools; and take funding from public education (Boser et al., 2018; Carnoy, 2017; Center on Education Policy, 2016; Farrie et al., 2019; Weiner & Green, 2018).

- Voucher opponents, citing significant research, stipulate vouchers are a political distraction from real education problems such as funding inequities, teacher shortages, charter school fraud, and school safety (gun violence). Vouchers have been labeled as a taxpayer swindle conceived by ideologues and politicians. Opponents further state vouchers will cause teacher cuts, create serious inequities, and result in public school closures (Knight, 2023; Ravitch, 2021a, 2021b).

- Superintendents regularly note school choice is already available and vouchers are completely unwarranted—other than in benefiting those wanting to avoid public schools and integration and those who have their hands in nonpublic school monetary ventures. They point out that parents and students can already attend other schools of choice as a result of open enrollment. For example, Christie Whitbeck, superintendent in Ford Bend ISD in Houston, Texas, stated, "It just sounds good to say that a parent should have choice. Well, yes they should, and they already do, because we have charter schools everywhere" (Self-Walbrick & Walsh, 2023).

- Proponents, however, postulate vouchers allow parents to choose their child's education and actually improve education by making public schools compete with private schools in a free market. Proponents also claim public education is in crisis and vouchers allow students to escape bad schools. Proponents report voucher students are considered less likely to repeat a grade, score higher on achievement tests, are more likely to take the college entrance exam, and are more likely to earn higher wages.

(Continued)

(Continued)

- One idea for vouchers frequently espoused was for states to subsidize tuition at private schools for parents who did not want their child attending integrated schools. However, proponents have flipped such rhetoric, noting school choice actually empowers poor and minority families to remove their children from underperforming public schools and move them into charter and private schools that are presumed to deliver a better education (Wilder, 2022).
- Educators and many parents see the voucher system as nothing more than a scheme designed to benefit anyone but students. But benefit who, exactly? Definitely ideologues, political operatives, and political action committees. Certainly wealthy families already sending their children to private schools would benefit. Who else might benefit?
- Speculation abounds that certain hands somehow and some way are in the till, engaging in financial chicanery—billionaires, multimillionaires, silent partners, politicians, political operatives, politically connected charter school executives, and potentially even retired public school officials, education agency officials, and school board members (Wilder, 2022). One superintendent noted, "I'm not accusing anyone of laundering money, by the legal definition, but there sure are a lot of hands touching a lot of money in [voucher system plans]" (Wilder, 2022, p.3).
- What is true is that public schools continue to remain the choice of parents but not of all politicians. On the other hand, vouchers are by no means a choice for *all* parents, especially low-income families and peoples of color (Fiddiman & Yin, 2019; Mead & Eckes, 2018; Potter, 2017). Therefore, a question that begs an answer is, why do politicians wish to pass pro-voucher legislation and whom do those politicians really represent? The question certainly provides, at the very least, food for thought, if not debate.
- Finally, the future issue of state voucher systems may very well be tied to court cases such as the ruling in *Carson v. Makin* (June 2022), which requires the state of Maine to fund private religious schools as part of the state's public school funding system. This ruling permits tuition for students to attend private schools if their community does not have a public high school. The ruling, however, does not require the state to fund private schools, but once the state does so, Maine cannot exclude religious schools (Hutchinson, 2022).

- All told, the initial question remains: Do publicly funded vouchers and privatization push education back or pull it forward? The debate continues.What are your thoughts?

2. **Title I dollars and privatization**. Proponents of privatization have readily recommended using at least $1 billion in Title I funding for a school-of-choice portability program—in other words, less money for traditional public schools serving those students most at risk. Congress has previously rejected this funding procedure, but the plan remains highly publicized and politically pressed.
3. **Accreditation, accountability, and privatization**. Proponents of privatization hedge on whether the traditional public school concepts of accreditation and accountability should apply to private and/or parochial schools. Strauss (2017) and Zhou (2022) reveal two familiar privatization lines. The first notes that when proponents of school privatization have been pushed on the issues of accreditation and accountability, a well-known response is, "Students could learn to read by simply putting a hand on a book" (Strauss, 2017, p. 5). Second, in terms of accountability standards, another oft-repeated line is, "States can determine what kind of flexibility they are going to allow" (Strauss, 2017, p. 5).
4. **Outdated, inefficient, inferior, inept, noncompetitive, and unchallenging**. Strong words to describe public education, but in fairness to the privatization agenda, proponents of for-profit schools claim these terms are most representative of traditional public schools, which are all too often described by school privatization proponents as inherently ineffective, existing to survive, and only interested in meeting their own needs.

   Proponents of school privatization believe their system of education provides a more competitive and challenging education as well as quality service to students. Proponents further claim teachers in private institutions are free from bureaucratic norms, regulations, and outdated top-down expectations. Thus, they claim private education is much more apt to monetarily reward high-performance teaching and instruction.

   Public schools are moreover described by privatization proponents as simply enhancing and rewarding mediocrity and ineptitude. However, a recent study reveals private schools are no better than public schools (Barrington, 2022).

(Continued)

(Continued)

Again, are the proposed changes new and improved or is there a cost—and does it really matter? Put another way, do the pros of school privatization outweigh the cons?

- Why is the privatization of schooling such a popular trend in many states? Do vouchers offer a push-back or pull-forward effect on public schools?
- How does underfunding affect your school—your students, faculty, staff, and administration?
- After examining the four above-noted considerations, debate the pros and cons of school funding relative to public and private education.
- Utilize an Internet search engine to determine the yearly cost of tuition at a parochial or for-profit school in your area. Does a proposed or current voucher fund in your state equate to the tuition rate? Compare the per-pupil public school allocation in your state to the voucher allotment and the noted tuition rate. Your thoughts?
- Should a school leader have a vested interest in educational politics? Why or why not? How might the political process impact school-based budgeting?
- Also consider this question: Who is reaping the rewards of privatization and why?

The Effects of Inadequate, Inequitable, and Unequal Funding: A "Must-Understand" Listing for Every Principal

The contentious state of politicizing public school funding brings to the attention of campus leadership a simple yet compelling question: What are the potential effects of insufficient, unfair, and disproportionate funding? Answer: Unless states begin to seriously reform antiquated and unjust school finance funding formulas, budget cuts will become commonplace and directly affect principals, faculty, staff, and, more importantly, students and student achievement. These cuts might include the following:

- laying off teachers
- initiating hiring freezes
- increasing class size
- cutting extracurricular programs or limiting activities
- eliminating summer school

- cutting instructional programs such as the arts and fine arts
- eliminating field trips
- reducing or eliminating teacher and staff stipends and/or bonuses
- closing older/economically burdensome schools
- implementing changes in teacher benefits (for example, higher health care premiums and deductibles)
- cutting professional development for teachers and staff
- revoking contracts, thus requiring teachers and administrators to accept an "at-will" employment status

Following the confrontation of cutbacks such as those in the list above, school leaders would be forced to live with budgetary reductions. In many instances, school leaders would be required to address certain key budgetary considerations and do the following:

> Unless states begin to seriously reform antiquated and unjust school finance funding formulas, budget cuts will become commonplace and directly affect principals, faculty, staff, and, more importantly, students and student achievement.

- Communicate with faculty and staff about how inadequate, inequitable, and unequal funding affects schools, most notably the budgetary process, and discuss how this could be reasonably and effectively addressed.
- Establish budget advisory teams and develop site-based guidelines and practices, including regularly scheduled budget and campus decision-making meetings.
- Conduct needs assessments with an intensive data analysis process.
- Develop a priority-setting process and fund strictly the greatest of instructional priorities.
- Accumulate an expenditure history—examine how campus funding, over a period of three to five years, has been expended, on what, and why.
- Address, most importantly, student achievement by asking pressing questions such as the below:
    - What are the most efficient methods of organizing our instructional programs and student-centered initiatives?
    - How can classes be better scheduled to save funds but not at the expense of students?
    - What are specific and effective, yet inexpensive, methods of presenting instruction in the different subject areas?
    - What classes are crucial for all graduates? Which courses can be eliminated?

  - What is the value of programs such as prekindergarten, dropout prevention initiatives, and support for late graduates? Can any of these programs be eliminated as a cost-cutting measure?
  - What class size capacity can be reached without negatively impacting teaching and learning?
  - How can teacher quality, student learning, and instructional methodology be inexpensively redefined in an era of technological norms and advancements?
  - What are the short-term and long-term impacts of inadequate, inequitable, and unequal budgetary funding on student achievement?
  - What does the research reveal regarding current instructional programs and initiatives, and are schools still doing the same old things the same old ways? Can cost-efficient improvements come with potential fiscal inadequacies?
  - What are other school districts and other schools doing to be more instructionally innovative yet cost effective?
  - What additional or innovative fundraising efforts can be implemented?
  - How can a school team communicate with state and federal legislators and provide them with a clear understanding of local conditions and the need for funding reforms?

- Carefully monitor enrollment trends and conduct at the campus level the cohort survival method process (see Chapter 9).
- Reevaluate student attendance plans and initiatives. Today, in the aftermath of COVID/digital instruction, major research asserts some of the best-spent school dollars can enhance student attendance if school leaders acknowledge and implement strategies that serve to reduce systemic absenteeism. However, if funding is limited, consider other measures, such as the following:
  - developing an open school culture and positive climate
  - ensuring purposeful student–teacher interactions and professional relationships
  - creating an innovative and engaging instructional program
  - creating strong mentoring programs
  - ensuring meaningful engagement and relevant student-oriented instruction
  - recognizing and rewarding rolemodels, such as those teachers who model excellent attendance (Jordan, 2023; Learning Policy Institute, 2022).

Schools might also seek to overcome barriers to attendance. Barriers might include student and/or family health or financial concerns, limited transportation, school safety issues (see the Chapter 6 scenario titled "Budgeted Dollars and School Safety"), student instructional disengagement and aversion to learning, childcare issues, daily start and stop times, and four-day student school weeks as examples.

- Monitor copier and paper usage.
- Sensibly oversee and limit overtime.
- Reduce energy consumption.
- Limit travel expenses, especially out-of-state trips.
- Seek grant and foundation funding.
- Permit district personnel and campus experts to provide quality staff development.
- Utilize district- or campus-developed benchmarking procedures as a method of identifying and monitoring student progress and achievement, thus reducing the purchase of unnecessary materials as well as tutorial expenditures for students not in need of academic interventions.
- Develop community partnerships (Adopt-A-School, Friends of Education, etc.).
- Develop a materials resource center where teaching and learning materials are stored for teacher/student use. Material centers reduce cost duplications, create material check-out systems, serve as inventory depositories, better facilitate the sharing of materials, and reduce pilferage.
- Every "nonnegotiable" must become "negotiable" whereby evaluative measures are initiated at least once a year.
- Abraham Lincoln, often considered the most popular United States president of all time, experienced a troubled presidency. He endured a lifelong struggle with depression and had a nervous breakdown. During his youth, neighbors from time to time held suicide watches over him.

  Yet he had hope, especially during his presidency. On the night Lincoln was assassinated, his emptied pockets revealed newspaper clippings that praised him, his leadership as president, and the positive and hopeful impact he was having over a divided nation. President Lincoln held on unfailingly to hope and encouragement. He was intentional in his hope for a better and united nation, even to the end.

- School leaders must maintain hope and exhibit a positive attitude and create an optimistic work environment whereby a culture of confident determination and expectation—one of constancy of purpose—is the norm. This environment allows for continual improvement in all areas: services, products, and resource allocations. Here's how to do this:
    - Recognize hope is not based on circumstances. A hopeful spirit is contagious and is a leader's gift to others. Pass on hope by speaking the language of hope. That means stop speaking in terms of negativity. Here's an example: Don't say, "Funds are tight." Instead, state, "Let's find the funds. I have a few ideas as to where we can get additional dollars. Do you?"
    - Eliminate despairing thoughts, depressive mindsets, and negative responses. As Cover (2023) said, "Put hope on repeat and turn up the volume!" Stay positive in every discussion, budgetary meeting, strategy seminar, instructional planning session, and school-related event. Cover (2023) also shared how people are tired of being tired. They're tired of postpandemic anxieties, false promises, political lies and deceptions, unexpected outcomes, uncertainty in the workplace, artificial leadership, and constant reminders that things aren't getting better. They want hope and they want leaders who will deliver it in a most positive manner. So, school leader, deliver!
    - Recognize hope is the belief that everything is possible and actually probable, even in the direst of straits! Recall the old adage, "Show me the money!" A school principal that turns this phrase into a positive response, especially when funding is limited, will state, "I'll find the money" or "Let's find the money!"
    - Understand people want something or someone to believe in, something or someone to solve their issues or problems, and something or someone to bring on a brighter future. When a school leader recognizes students, faculty, and staff need more, that leader develops a team of believers—a team that is responsible enough to not only believe in the principal but also in each other. This type of team effort creates a vibrant energy of endless possibilities—a "Let's do it together" mentality.
    - Hope requires a school leader to make good choices with his or her team in order to sustain a positive work environment. Hope definitely does two things: It renews faith and builds confidence. When fiscal times are tough, the best school leaders develop a sense of security for students and the team, a feeling that the worries and concerns will soon be eliminated. It's pretty simple: Individuals want to recapture that moment in time when they felt their best, when the school had minimal fiscal issues and other workplace problems.

- The best school leaders live by and readily share a constant thought: "We are either solving a problem or dwelling on a problem." Why waste time and energy within the quagmire of a problem when a solution is just an idea away? Remember, hope and a positive attitude will alleviate any negativity! Place this quote on your desk: "Your success will be determined by how well you overcome hardship!"

Inadequate, inequitable, and unequal school funding and even fiscal constraint and budgetary conservativism in schools are nothing new! The authors of this text have witnessed, over the years, numerous economic downturns and their effects on schools—from the high-inflation era of the 1970s to the oil industry collapse in the 1980s to the disintegration of tax bases in the 1990s to the Great Recession in the first decade of the 21st century to the serious drop in crude oil prices and to the politics of inequitable, unequal, and inadequate funding in the second and third decades of the 21st century.

Remember, there is and always will be hope! However, it is important to keep in mind that until funding reforms are initiated and fulfilled, effective school leaders must maintain a single and most essential visionary perspective: Students first and foremost, no matter the type of funding. Does this mean school leaders are to sit back and accept the status quo? Absolutely not! School leaders have a voice, and those voices must be heard, heard by parents, business community members, and state and federal legislators. Recall the old adage, "When everyone else is silent, even one voice becomes powerful!" Your voice matters. Use it!

Allocation: The Key to the Budgetary Process

School budgeting is directly related to the allocation of those specified—and, far too often, scarce—sources of state and federal funding. To borrow a financial term, the bottom line to adequately and effectively delineating between school finance and school budgeting can be summed up with one simple word: *allocation*. Allocation is the key to understanding the school budgeting process. Allocation is not only important to state public education systems (school districts) but to the amount of money schools receive for budgetary purposes. It is critical to continued student success and achievement.

Nevertheless, school leaders must realize and understand the school budgeting process is much more than the technical skill associated with the term *allocation*. Exceptional school leaders recognize effective budgeting must be an integrated approach incorporating team planning, visionary leadership, efficient time management, data analysis, and the campus allocation of funds to establish instructional priorities for budgetary funding. This integrated approach to school budgeting was previously explored in Chapter 3 and will be examined in greater detail in Chapter 6.

Final Thoughts

School leaders must invest the necessary time and energy to deal with appropriated funds and the school budget. Wise budgeting brings a sense of accomplishment, even fulfillment—most notably when the instructional program improves and student achievement increases. However, before budgeting, school leaders must plan.

Planning is defined in this context as the development of a vision, the establishment of goals, the determination of objectives, and the initiation of strategies for school implementation. This is critical if a leader expects a continuing effort to increase student achievement. Each of these planning indicators is an essential element in the development of an effective budget using an integrated and collaborative approach to budgeting. Remember, failing to plan is nothing more than planning to fail!

A budget is not a once-a-year event, something developed and never examined again. A budget must be abided by, reviewed, and amended on a regular (monthly) basis as the needs of its academic counterpart change. This requires ongoing evaluation and revision. Nothing in life is perfect, and the same holds true for school budgets. Academic goals—while imperative to the budgeting process—must, from time to time, be reorganized and adjusted. Action planning and goal development, academic improvement, and budget management must be integrated if school leaders intend to bring about educational excellence and increased student achievement.

School budgeting has aways been a difficult prospect. Today, budgeting at the campus level is much more susceptible to troublesome and continuously emerging issues, often political in nature. A current look as well as a glimpse into the future of public education reveals an additional squeezing of the school pocketbook. This compression of district and campus funds readily comes from local, state, and even federal funding sources. As previously noted, added to this confounding fiscal quandary facing public education is the agenda-driven privatization of schooling.

Fueled by special interest groups and other individuals, including certain state and federal legislators, public education continues to be undermined, threatened, and regularly attacked. One way to destroy one of the most essential pillars of a democracy—a free and public education for all students—is to begin defunding schools. Again, as previously stipulated but worth repeating: The privatization agenda often pushes the proposition that Title I and other state and federal dollars be diverted from the public schools and transferred to voucher plans or systems.

Finally, certain standards as analyzed in Chapter 1 must be emphasized and incorporated by the school leader if the budgeting process is to meet with success. Abide by the budget, implement necessary changes, and always follow up with an ongoing evaluation process. School leaders must allow self-discipline, trustworthiness, transparency, integrity, and collaboration to serve as guiding beacons in budgetary decision making. And always remember: An integrated budget and academic action plan will not work unless you do!

Discussion Questions

1. Debate the pros and cons of school privatization and state voucher systems. Explain how vouchers can pull back or push forward public schools. Why, in your opinion, are vouchers so popular with a good percentage of the American public?
2. Why is it important to integrate the school budget and the academic or action plan? How can the budget and academic planning processes be integrated?
3. Which of the budgeting myths pose(s) a more fundamental obstacle to the school administrator in relation to the development of a campus budget? Why?
4. Which two of the seven barriers to adequate, equitable, and equal school funding are critically handicapping student achievement? Be detailed in your answer.
5. "Without adequate, equitable, and equal school funding, pervasive racial and economic injustices perpetuate and exacerbate an already flawed system." Explain the reasoning associated with this chapter statement.
6. Examine the chapter section titled "The Effects of Inadequate, Inequitable, and Unequal Funding—A 'Must-Understand' for Every Principal." Which five of the twelve budget acts are most detrimental to student achievement when contemplating adequacy, equity, and equality? Explain your answer.
7. Review each of the required school leader methods for publicly addressing campus funding cutbacks. Which have you personally experienced during times of inadequate funding? How does each relate to inequity and inequality in not only school funding but also in student academic success?
8. Explain the relationship between hope and a culture of confident determination. Why is hope a critical component of leading during times of funding difficulties?
9. How does this chapter relate to the PSEL as documented in Chapter 1? Which standard(s) are specifically relevant and why?

Case Study

Fiscal Issues and the New Principal

"Boy, Do I Have a Lot to Learn!"

Dr. Ryan Paulson, new principal at Mountain View School, arrived at the Vista Ridge Independent School District from a neighboring state. While Dr. Paulson certainly understood certain aspects of the fiscal and budgetary processes in his former state, he recognized the need for a refresher course in budgeting, especially as it related to the fiscal issues he might face in his new state and school district.

Dr. Paulson decided to stop by the administrative offices of the school district to visit with the superintendent, Dr. Nataly Arom, as well as the associate superintendent for school finance, Dr. Gene Corley. Certainly these two could bring him up to speed on the fiscal expectations of his new state and school district. As good fortune would have it, the first two individuals he encountered as he stepped into the main offices were Dr.Arom and Dr. Corley. Dr. Corley, a most gregarious individual, was the first to see the new principal and hollered at him, "Hey, hotshot, were you able to eat some of that good barbeque I told you about?" Dr. Paulson responded he had not yet had the opportunity, but he was looking forward to a tasty plate of sausage and ribs. Dr. Arom then asked what was on the young man's mind.

"Well, since you inquired," replied Dr. Paulson, "I need some guidance about the state's fiscal policies and the district's budgeting practices." Dr. Arom suggested all three step into Dr. Corley's office for, as she put it, "a quick review of School Budgeting 101."

"School budgeting and finance in this era of accountability, change, inadequate funding, fiscal restraint, and political intrusion can be a real juggling act," noted Dr. Arom. "However, let's start with the basics and get you on the right track before school starts."

Thus began an afternoon of one learning experience after another. By the conclusion of the meeting, Dr. Paulson had come to realize political bickering, a sluggish economy, federal infusion of COVID-relief dollars and the subsequent loss of those dollars, federal and state accountability standards, mandates, and inequitable and unequal state funding, as well as numerous other conditions, had negatively influenced the ability of the school district to raise tax revenues to meet the demands of educating itsstudents. These challenges most notably and negatively reflected on every school's list of priorities and the ability to finance them.

The key takeaway of the first meeting among the three parties was the realization that education must be viewed as an investment in human capital. Resource allocations to public schools are the responsibility not only of the federal and state governments but also of the local school district. Moreover, funding the rapidly increasing costs of education is an ongoing challenge for schools, and such funding is continuously associated with accountability expectations and standards at all levels—local, state, and federal.

A most interesting point made by Dr. Arom related to the proposition that educational services and funding must be provided with equity and equality, but could they be provided for both? *Wow*, thought Dr. Paulson to himself. *Does anyone have an answer to that question?*

Furthermore, Dr. Paulson recognized that even though the cost of education was continuing to increase annually, this burden was eased when one realized that while the cost of public schooling involves money, mostly in salaries, much of the cost is readily returned to the marketplace, thus benefiting the economy, consumers, local households, individual citizens, and, most importantly, local students. This meeting reminded Dr. Paulson of a fact that had been drilled into his head by a former professor in his principal certification program at Southeastern Union State University: "While the cost of education may be high, the defining and measuring result must always be quality in learning."

Finally, Dr. Paulson had been directed to the state's website to review operating accounting codes and structures. It was essential he quickly learn the proper budgetary coding procedures as dictated by the state's education agency. He had already added the website to his favorites. Now he was ready to adapt to the new coding structure and fiscal practices associated with his new school system and campus budget. As he left the district's administrative offices, he could not help but think, *Boy, do I have a lot to learn!*

Case Study Application

1. What is meant by the following terms: *adequacy*, *equality*, *equitable*, *human capital*, and *quality*? How do these terms apply to a campus budget, teaching, and learning?
2. How is the theoretical concept "Education must be viewed as an investment in human capital" realized in your community? Provide concrete examples.
3. How is the process of school budgeting related to integrity, fairness, and ethics? (Recall this trio from Chapter 1.) How about equity, equality, and adequacy?
4. A serious question worthy of serious contemplation: Can educational services and school and district funding be provided with equity, equality, and adequacy? Debate the issue with defensible responses.
5. What is meant by the quote, "While the cost of education may be high, the defining and measuring result must always be quality in learning"? How does this proposition relate to the concept of vision development?
6. Should Principal Ryan Paulson, from a public education and campus budgetary perspective, be concerned about publicly funded vouchers? Explain why or why not.

School Funding and Steps to Budgeting Success

5

> *The secret to successful budgeting is to follow a series of steps. Remember, a budget controls the future, and the future controls results!*
>
> —Anonymous

The Funding of Schools

The key to understanding sources of school funding is realizing that expenditures correlated with student educational needs are affected by whether or not federal, state, and local governments appropriately share in the responsibility of supporting schools (Brimley et al., 2020). As previously addressed in Chapter 4 but worthy of repeating, adequate and equitable funding during any fiscal era (upswing or downturn) becomes a critical issue not only for educators but with politicians and taxpayers as well.

The reason appropriate, adequate, equal, and equitable funding is a contested issue in public education is related to the fact our Founding Fathers failed to provide any arrangements for education in the federal constitution. As a result, the funding of schools has become the responsibility of individual states, whether by design or by default, and not by choice in most instances. By placing the responsibility for public education funding in the hands of individual states, our nation has become, in reality, fifty-one systems of education and, more notably, fifty-one sources of school funding.

Education is the largest single budgetary component of state and local governments. School districts receive nearly all of their funding for instruction, either directly or indirectly, from federal, state, and local governments, although the majority of this funding comes from local and state revenues. While school districts depend on, and most certainly place special emphasis on, the amount of federal funds received, the percentage of federal support for schools is relatively insignificant in relation to state and local funding. For example, many states provide well over 50 percent of school district funding. Federal funding typically amounts to less than 10 to 15 percent (COVID relief dollars being an exception) of a district's funding, with local revenue coming close to or exceeding that of the state funding allotments (National Education Association, 2022).

Naturally, a prerequisite for understanding the budgetary process is a keen realization of where the money comes from—the sources of money received to operate school districts. In financial circles, the appropriate terms are *revenue, income,* and *fiduciary funding*. The flip side of the "money received" coin is *expenditure,* or money spent. Income sources will be examined in greater detail later in this chapter.

A prerequisite for understanding the budgetary process is a keen realization of where the money comes from.

Revenue figures are based on a funding starting point, an allocation simply known, from a school finance perspective, as the *basic allotment*. The basic allotment to school districts can be further adjusted incrementally with adjustment allotments, such as the following:

- **Cost of education index.** A funding "multiplier" designed to compensate districts for geographic (rural schools) and cost (the percentage of economically disadvantaged students) differences beyond the control of the local school system.
- **Small district adjustment.** Small school systems are more expensive to operate due to diseconomies of scale. For example, districts with 1,600 or fewer students in average daily attendance could receive an increase in funding.
- **Impact aid.** Districts can receive additional funding for each student who has a parent serving in the military on active duty.
- **Other weighted allotments.** For example, special education (districts could possibly be entitled to up to five times more funding for a student with special needs); bilingual education (possibly an additional 10 percent for English language learners); compensatory education (potential funding of 20 percent or more to pay for intensive or accelerated instructional services—tutoring, for example—for students who are performing below grade level or are at risk of dropping out of school); and so on.

Revenue is obtained primarily from tax collection and the sale of bonds. The tax collection funds provide the majority of money received and money expended for the instructional and operational aspects of a school district. Bond sales provide, as an example, revenue for the construction of new school facilities.

Income is a particular funding category that is representative of funds received from the sale of goods and services. A perfect example of income funding is the district food services program. Since income can be generated from the sale of food items in the school cafeteria, district administrators must develop budgets that project sales and anticipate expenditures, and then they must implement and monitor a budget.

The *fiduciary* category refers to funds received from donations that thus must be managed by or entrusted to a school district in a most legal and ethical manner. While these dollars are important, such funds are generally not critical to the instructional operation of a school district. However, these same dollars may be very significant to a school that needs additional dollars to finance school-related initiatives and activities not normally funded by a school district. A perfect example of fiduciary receipts are monies generated from fundraisers and collected by student clubs, campus organizations, graduating classes, or booster clubs; the school district must agree to be the depository of these funds and must ensure the funds are expended appropriately.

Expenditures are exactly that—money spent. Whenever money is spent, the expenditure must be charged against a revenue account and source. School leaders will invariably note that within their budget software listings or on their budget spreadsheets, the accounting term *encumbered* appears. *Encumbered* or *encumbrance*, by definition, is by no means the same as *expenditure*. However, both terms maintain a compelling correlation in terms of the budgetary process.

For example, when a specified school account is used to initiate a purchase order, the funds are immediately set aside or *encumbered*, indicating the dollars for products or services ordered have been committed, held back, or set aside. At this point, a school leader can expect the purchase order to be processed, and when the goods are received, a payment will be submitted. When the payment has been issued, an *expenditure* of district dollars has occurred.

The expenditure of funds must always be accounted for, and thus a school leader may complain from time to time about the numerous business department forms that have to be completed, such as purchase orders, requisitions, travel reimbursements, amendments and/or transfers, and vouchers, all of which are examples of the paperwork commonly associated with district expenditures. Completing these forms may seem a nuisance, but they ensure fiscal accountability, and each may very well be the necessary documentation to keep a school leader out of a legal entanglement.

School Funding Sources

State and local governments provide the vast majority of funding for public schools— approximately 90 percent of all school funds. Recently, on average, local governments have provided approximately 44 percent of school funding; state governments contribute 45 percent; and the federal government distributes 11 percent. Most recently, the federal government's contribution to funding schools has dramatically increased to 23 percent, nearly doubling that of previous years, due in great measure to the influx of COVID-related grant dollars.

State governments rely on state aid formulas to distribute funding to school districts. School districts, in turn, use the state dollars and additional revenue from federal funding of education and local sources (generally property taxation) to fund schools. While the intent is to apply these school dollars equitably, equally, and adequately, disparities exist. State aid formulas are the result of legislative choice and, frequently, litigation force, all in an attempt to apply monetary remedies. To date, equitable, equal, and adequate school funding remains inconsistent, if not unjustifiable, from state to state and certainly from district to district.

Federal Sources of Income

Federal revenue comes in the form of different and distinct sources of transfer payments known as *general, categorical,* and *block grants* aid. General and categorical aid, the major sources of federal income for education, significantly impact and expand the capabilities of school districts to enhance student achievement.

General aid flows from federal and state governments with few limitations to local school districts. General aid provides the largest proportion of financial support for school operations. Local school boards and district administrators largely determine how such income will be allocated to educational programs and other related expenditures.

Categorical aid is a source of funding to school districts that links funding to specific objectives of the government in support of specified programs, such as special education, gifted and talented education, career and technology education (formerly vocational education), and compensatory education. Unlike general aid, categorical aid must be utilized for certain groups of students (e.g., those with disabilities); a specific purpose (e.g., pupil transportation); or a particular project (e.g., construction of a school facility).

Most often, categorical aid calls for annual applications, documentation of expenditures, and frequent program evaluations and audits. Categorical aid was once the predominant form of federal income to states and school districts. However, other forms of federal aid now serve as district income supplements, with fewer restrictions at the local level. In recent years, much of the categorical aid has been absorbed into block grants to reduce the local paperwork and personnel productivity burdens associated with federal funds to education.

Block grants provide funding for a wide range of services, with federal requirements for planning, implementing, and assessing programs being much less stringent than those associated with categorical aid. Block grants provide for local funding based on the number of students rather than through a competitive application process that identifies particular educational needs. Local school districts appreciate the greater latitude provided by block grants. This source of federal funding provides district administrators with more discretion in programmatic designs.

The Elementary and Secondary Education for the Disadvantaged (ESED) Block Grant is the largest education block grant program. This program includes all activities authorized under Title I, Title II-A (Supporting Effective Instruction), Title III-A (English Language Acquisition), and Title IV-A (Student Support and Academic Enrichment). Title I funding, for example, reaches thirty million disadvantaged students, with minority students accounting for more than two-thirds of the Title I participants (National Center for Education Statistics [NCES], 2019; U.S. Department of Education, 2023).

Title monies, as part of the ESED Block Grant, go directly to school districts and schools where they are most needed and fund, for example, extra teachers and innovative programs—all of which help students master reading, writing, and mathematics. Over the years, ESED Block Grant funding has served to focus on and improve proven programs that have turned around entire schools and even school districts. Federal aid has certainly served to promote equity and equality in education over the last sixty years and has generally improved the quality of education for all students.

Additionally, in recent years, federal funding in the form of COVID relief dollars was infused into school systems across the nation. These monies, as noted in Chapter 4, have aided school district administrators and onsite school leaders by supporting the bridging of achievement gaps, aiding issues associated with school equity and equality funding, expanding staff, reducing class sizes, retaining faculty and staff, improving working conditions, and increasing professional development opportunities.

Growing Into Equity, Equality, and Excellence

Title I Schools With High-Achieving Students and Teachers

Title I schools in which learning and personalization have combined to form high-achieving learning communities are often exemplified as part of the National ESEA Distinguished Schools program associated with the ESEA Network (2022). Distinguished Title I schools are recognized under the following categories of excellence: Category 1—exceptional student performance and academic growth, Category 2—closing the achievement gap between student groups, and Category 3—excellence in serving special populations of students (homeless, migrant, English language learners, etc.).

Such schools serve a significantly high percentage of economically disadvantaged students, many of whom are students of color. Each Title I school

(Continued)

(Continued)

exemplifies how personalized learning will not only improve academic achievement but also provide an equal, equitable, and high-quality education for all students. These schools focus on the whole child, engaging every student, addressing social justice and injustice, and incorporating equity-driven practices. In doing so, Title I learning communities better ensure the raising of the academic bar and, moreover, narrow the achievement gap among student populations that, tragically, are all too often left behind in other schools. Federal funds well spent!

State Sources of Income

Most states have property taxes, sales taxes, or income taxes as their source of income. These income sources determine the amount of state funding for school districts. This revenue allotment, as previously noted, is then typically distributed to the differing school districts across a state by means of a *state aid formula*. These funding formulas are generally driven by student enrollment and, again, this aid comes primarily from assessed taxes. While property taxation remains the major source of local revenue for many schools across the nation, the local tax base is typically insufficient to support a school district.

To further muddy the waters, some states have recently considered, if not proposed, the elimination of property taxation altogether. One such proposal suggests local property taxes be eliminated by means of pushing exclusively for rate compression,the practice of driving down school property tax rates and sending more state dollars to local districts to replace the lost revenue. The compression approach has long been championed in certain political circles as a means of permanently eliminating school property taxes altogether.

Opponents believe such a funding process is a less than adequate method of infusing state funds into schools. Opponents of rate compression postulate such a process is yet another attempt to diminish public school systems and thus support educational privatization. Until such state legislation is, if ever, enacted, most property-taxing states have developed state aid formulas as the basis for infusing some basic element of funding equity from district to district within a state.

State Aid Formulas

As described, the purpose of state aid formulas is to fiscally counterbalance disparities in educational equity and opportunity that would most certainly be present if school districts depended solely on the local tax base. An example of such a disparity is illustrated below.

Pause and Consider

Port Gregory vs. Nuecestown: A Case of Educational Disparity?

The Port Gregory school system is located along a state coastline near a major seaport. This school system is the recipient of tax dollars generated by several major petrochemical corporations. These taxable entities generate significant per-pupil wealth on the basis of taxable property. A second school system, Nuecestown Public Schools, similar in size and population but located further inland, is solely dependent on the agribusiness industry, and thus this district receives only limited revenue from its economically depressed tax base.

- What type of funding mechanism might help alleviate the disparity between the two school systems identified in the scenario above?
- How is the financing of school systems in your state equalized?
- What has historically been the result of funding inequities relative to public schools in your state?
- Do public school inequities exist or continue in your state? If so, how, and by what means? How could the issue of equity be resolved?

Another example is often evident in states with large urban centers that face vast disparities in their tax base due to ever-growing suburbs and the related citizenry and corporation flight to nearby bedroom communities.

Most states develop foundation programs to facilitate the state aid formulas. These programs are the mechanism by which the equalization of resources from district to district can occur. Foundation programs allow for the difference in the cost of a school program and the amount each school district must contribute from local taxation.

Today, very complex state aid formulas advance the foundation programs, and such formulas are generally related to a fictitious "weighted student" consideration. After the foundation program cost is determined by formula, financing is potentially equalized by determining the local share for each district, and then the remainder is funded by state aid. State aid for individual school districts equals the foundation program cost minus the local share. However, it is worth noting state aid formulas have come under intense scrutiny in recent years, and, again, legal challenges related to formula funding continue.

For example, the issue of equity in relation to educational opportunities for all students regardless of socioeconomic background and/or ethnicity continues to be a critical concern before the courts, both state and federal, as well as state legislatures. Inequities have long plagued public schools, especially in the of funding schools of poverty and students of color, and particularly in the area of financing educational facilities. Minimal funding reforms and inadequate state-led funding efforts have all too frequently been long-lasting and ineffectual norms.

This is not to say the courts have completely ignored equity and equality in public school financing. Consideration by the courts is most certainly revealed in several cases in which lawsuits have demanded states provide adequate and equitable educational facilities, for example. Unfortunately, the operative term and process utilized in response to these legal entanglements has most often been nothing more than *adequate*, which is typically inadequate!

Two excellent sources relative to school finance reform—or the lack thereof—and associated court cases are *Educational Law: Equity, Fairness, and Reform* by Black (2021), specifically Chapter 3, "Poverty," and Chapter 13, "School Finance," in *School Law and the Public Schools: A Practical Guide for Educational Leaders* by Essex (2015).

Voucher Systems—A Point of State Funding Contention

As discussed in Chapter 4, an additional point of contention between school district administrators and far too many politicians is the issue of the privatization of schooling (voucher systems). To conceptualize, public education is the great equalizer of American society and a deep-rooted aspect of a democratic nation. Public schools are the bedrock of a strong, vibrant, and true democracy. How? By what means? Public schools provide a free and appropriate education for *all* students (J. Walsh & Orman, 2022). Voucher systems are deeply flawed, often discriminatory, typically lack accountability, generally favor the wealthy, and harm public education, as well as negatively impact the livelihood of public school teachers and staff (Lopez, 2022; D. A. Walsh & Self-Walbrick, 2023).

Equity can only be achieved when politicians realize the creation of a diverse, inclusive, and welcoming learning community must be ensured. This can be aided by legislative actions that never segregate a child on the basis of color, disability, poverty, sexual orientation, or a differing language. Learning outcomes must be based on the guarantee of education being both equal and equitable, and to date no voucher system has been able to ensure this.

Politically motivated attacks on public education, emerging concerns about fraud in the charter school sector, and book bans are just a few of the current events researchers can speak to given their training, experience, and expertise. A flurry of school choice initiatives continues to emerge. As noted in Chapter 4, as of 2024 thirty-two states had adopted some form of school choice/voucher plans. School leaders—and all educators—must remember: Voice matters! Researchers and administrators must both be encouraged to be more publicly engaged and speak out against the unrelenting attack on public education and democracy itself.

Equity can only be achieved when politicians realize the creation of a diverse, inclusive, and welcoming learning community must be ensured. This can be aided by legislative actions that never segregate a child on the basis of color, disability, poverty, sexual orientation, or a differing language.

DiMarco and Cohen (2023) examined eighty-seven school choice bills with their legislative tracker, with the Florida, Oklahoma, and Texas state legislative bills standing out. Parents of students in these states can potentially obtain state aid for private schooling if their public school districts teach about climate change, social-emotional learning, LGTBQ+ issues, defunding the police, animal rights activism, and a slew of other issues. Additionally, DiMarco and Cohen (2023) found far too many states pushing to expand access to public school funds for private school tuition and other expenses. Some of these states are calling for the dismantling of certain public school instructional programs.

The push for voucher systems across the nation has been described as a corrosive ideological attack on both public schooling and democracy itself. Many public school advocates are asking one simple question: Why are public schools held accountable for academic gains and achievement but private schools receiving voucher (state public school) dollars are not? For example, in 2023, Texas developed a thirty-three-page proposed voucher bill that failed to include the word *accountability*.

Opponents of vouchers frequently refer to them as a taxpayer swindle and claim vouchers continue to be a false choice that amounts to nothing more than handouts to private school parents with taxpayers paying the bill.

Local Sources of Income

Recall, as previously noted, the majority of school districts in the United States obtain their locally generated income from at least one of the following sources: ad valorem (property) taxes, sales taxes, income taxes, or sumptuary (sin) taxes.

The majority of school districts in the United States obtain their locally generated income from at least one of the following sources: ad valorem (property) taxes, sales taxes, income taxes, or sumptuary (sin) taxes.

Property taxation, as previously noted, is the most common source of income for school districts. Typically, a tax is levied on property such as land or buildings owned by individuals and businesses. A property tax is generally determined on the basis of a percentage of the true market value of each piece of property assessed. These assessments are rarely accurate since local assessors either over- or underassess the value of the property. Typically, the assessed value of the property is adjusted to an agreed-upon percentage of the market value when it is sold (Brimley et al., 2020).

Property taxation remains a largely complicated and particularly controversial source of local income for school districts because numerous complexities are associated with the assessment process. Homestead exemptions, tax abatements, legal entanglements, taxpayer associations, and underassessments of property all serve to erode the true tax base for individual school districts. However, property taxation continues to be the most stable income base as well as a dependable source of income for school districts.

Another form of taxation that serves as a revenue source for many school districts is the sales tax, which is quite popular in many states. This tax is assessed on the price of a good or service when it is purchased by a consumer. The seller of the merchandise or service collects the sales tax dollars, which are included in the purchase price, and transfers the amount of the sales tax to the state comptroller office. Since this tax is based on sales, its yield is quite elastic. As a result, a sales tax as a form of revenue for school districts is only as stable as the economy.

Some school districts acquire their local source of income from a state income tax that is levied on corporations and/or individuals. Income taxation is the most widely accepted form of taxation for schools, and it is considered the most equitable of any source of taxation. Over the years, several states have initiated income taxation as a source of funding education. The taxing of income is considered the most appropriate mechanism for property tax relief. In addition, income taxation provides a high revenue yield and creates minimal social and economic disruption (Brimley et al., 2020).

Very few school districts derive income from sumptuary taxes on items such as tobacco, alcohol, and gambling. This type of taxation is somewhat different than income and property taxes because it is based on "sin" sales. Due to this dependency, the tax yield is quite elastic, and thus it—much like a sales tax—is only as stable as the economy. Also, the tobacco and alcohol industries extensively lobby state legislators, and, as a result, this type of taxation has not necessarily served as a viable taxing alternative (Owings & Kaplan, 2020).

Another source of educational revenue can be dollars received from a lottery—an assessment on legalized gambling. State-run lotteries were adopted under explicit marketing campaigns purporting to raise funds for education, either K-12 or college, or both. A few states use their lottery revenue for roads and parks maintenance, but overwhelmingly state lotteries claim a "core mission of maximizing funds for education." Even if lottery proceeds did measurably improve local schools, that improvement still comes at the expense of those who can least afford to contribute to the communal project.

The individuals most susceptible to the promises of a lottery are those in the lower income bracket, which further makes the proceeds from this form of state income regressive (Brimley et al., 2020). There is no evidence any state lottery has significantly supported or benefited any school district or, for that matter, public education in general (Brady & Pijanowski, 2007; Chen, 2022; Erekson et al., 2002; Garrett, 2001; Jones & Amalfitano, 1994; Strauss, 2012; L. Williams, 2022).

Finally, even if lottery proceeds did measurably improve education (student learning), which all evidence proves otherwise, such an improvement would come, as already noted, at the expense of those who can least afford to invest (play the lottery).

Now that several of the possible sources of income for school districts have been explored, it becomes apparent that wherever the funding is derived from, allocations to individual schools at the district level are made, and thus school leaders have as one of their many responsibilities the task of developing a budget. Developing a school budget can be an arduous undertaking, but it can be completed with some sense of ease and satisfaction when a school leader is able to utilize specific steps or methods to collaboratively, effectively, and efficiently plan for a successful school budget.

Ten Steps to Budgeting Success

There are ten important steps to successful budgeting. These steps are identified with brief descriptors explaining why each step is critical to a school leader's success in developing, implementing, and evaluating a budget.

1. Determine the Allotment

Before deciding what educationally related expenditures to budget for, it is important to know the specified funding allotment that has been appropriated within each budgetary category. Furthermore, certain budgetary allotments can only be used for specified services and expenditures at the school level. As a result, some funds are more restrictive than others. These restricted funds, for example, are often associated with Title I, bilingual education, and special education programs. Restricted funds are further examined in Chapter 9.

2. Review, Identify, and Predict Fixed Expenditures

Recognize and note fixed expenditures are typically a budgetary constant from year to year. Set aside the necessary funds in the amount of the fixed expenditures before building the school budget. Such expenditures might include the renting or leasing of equipment (e.g., copiers).

3. Involve All Stakeholders

By involving as many stakeholders as possible in the budgetary decision-making process, a school leader can more effectively ensure ultimate buy-in as related to the school budget and funded programs and initiatives. Stakeholders include, for example, faculty and staff, parents, students, community members, and any other interested individuals.

When all stakeholders are provided with the opportunity for input, with their particular issues being given noteworthy consideration, buy-in is more likely and any plans, preparations, or budgetary considerations are less susceptible to interference or possible resistance or sabotage by a disgruntled member of the learning community. The collaborative involvement process as related to stakeholders is examined in Chapters 6 and 8.

4. Identify Potential Expenditures

The effective school leader reviews past budgetary records to better identify and predict future expenditures. Knowing which expenditures are necessary and imperative will help faculty and staff avoid making impulsive purchases.

5. Cut Back

Most newly created school budgets are overbudgeted. A school leader is responsible for examining all potential expenditures and must determine where cutbacks can occur. Remember, cutting back too severely can build discontent among faculty. School budgets that are continually out of balance lead to greater fiscal sacrifices and may very well lead to a financial point of no return. Cut back as necessary and be aware budgeting is an exercise in self-discipline for all parties.

A simple yet effective way to cut back involves implementing a thorough physical inventory. School administrators should do more than just go through the motions when completing a physical inventory. Such an inventory will identify areas where unnecessary purchases can be avoided. Consider the following: Why continue to purchase supplies such as dry-erase markers, staples, paper clips, and the like when these items may very well be found in abundance in a campus administrative office closet?

While cutting back is important in the school business, the creative school administrator is always seeking windfalls. Additional funding sources are available to those administrators who are willing to put forth the time and effort to seek financial assistance. For example, one school in a property-poor district utilized the campus leaders, site-based team members, and the parent–teacher organization to canvas the community seeking Adopt-A-School partners. A partnership with a large retail corporation proved extremely successful. The school was able to acquire essential supplies and merchandise for student use and consumption, and the corporation also provided funding for laptops and other important resources that otherwise would not have been available to either students or staff. An excellent source of information on finding, raising, and attracting extra dollars for a school or school system is *Achieving Excellence in Fundraising* by Shaker et al. (2022).

6. Avoid Continued Debts

The effective budget manager knows exactly what funds are out of balance and where debt has accumulated. Many school leaders fail to list and total their debts during the course of the fiscal year and wait until the end of the school year to make necessary budget revisions to amend for such shortsighted calculations. This is a poor practice. Most states and school districts do not allow individual school sites to acquire debts on a monthly or annual basis. Avoiding continued debts as a policy is not only worthwhile but wise.

Debt reduction is readily achieved by avoiding unnecessary purchases. Recall the sage advice that was shared with you and your spouse when you first married: "Most marital unhappiness is caused by giving up what you want most for what you want at the moment!" Life as a school leader is stressful enough without further complicating matters by overspending at the expense of the school budget, if not the student population. Remember, the most important word to use as a school administrator, specifically in connection with the school budget, could very well be *no*—especially when it comes to unwise or inappropriate spending!

7. Develop a Plan

Any budget—school, home, or business—should be based on a plan. From a school perspective, an educationally centered action or improvement plan must be developed to target and prioritize instructional goals and objectives, along with school programs and activities. In addition, a second plan of action (a school budget plan) is designed to identify budgetary priorities, focusing on appropriations and expenditures. Such a plan is designed to determine what programs and activities match the budgetary allotments for the school. Campus improvement planning and budget plan development were previously examined in Chapter 3 and will be further developed and enhanced in Chapter 6.

8. Set Goals and Manage Time Efficiently

Many would insist setting goals should be first and foremost on any list of budgetary considerations. No argument here. However, it is important for the effective school leader to do all the preliminary work of determining what funding is available before planning to spend the fiscal resources. This process requires the school leader to appropriately manage time. Remember, the way we spend our time defines who we are. Moreover, setting goals (whether management or instructional) and efficiently managing time are two fundamental steps all self-disciplined administrators utilize. Unfortunately, setting goals is frequently the one step many are inclined to skip. Additionally, managing time is another consideration many allow to escape attention.

As the budgetary process is developed and established, it is imperative deliberate thought be given to those two considerations as issues, demands, and dictates can simply overwhelm the school leader and the development and management of the school budget. First, involving all stakeholders is a most reliable and effective method of ensuring goals are identified and established. Second, setting goals takes time, effort, determination, and considerable thought and preparation. How does a school leader, working in collaboration with a learning community, set goals? Listed below are five essential contemplations.

1. Establish priorities—ascertain what is instructionally important—and recognize instructional leadership in this digital age requires the instructional leader to effectively and efficiently manage time.
2. Decide, in a timely manner, what can wait until later in the budget cycle or until the next school year.
3. Assess what is important today but will not be tomorrow.
4. Determine what priorities are timely and meaningful as compared to those that are mandated or simply unwarranted.
5. Submit various proposed budgets (by department, grade level, etc.) on a timely basis to the site-based committee that serves in part to determine if the allocated dollars within each budget correlate with the established goals of the school.

Finally, remember goals can and will change. Therefore, as the school leader and budget manager, it is imperative that you, in collaboration with the school's decision-making team, regularly assess and evaluate each budgetary goal and make any necessary changes as the school year progresses.

9. Evaluate the Budget

After a plan has been developed, it must be put into action. Take time to meet at least once a month with the decision-making team to evaluate the budget process and to better determine if the established goals and the budgeted dollars are equitable and compatible.

Planned budgeting and goal evaluation go hand in hand. Always seek answers to the following questions:

- Is the budget within the allotted limits, or do adjustments (transfers and amendments) need to be made on the basis of alternative needs or vision changes?
- Is timely progress being made toward the established goals?
- Are purchases coinciding with planned goals?
- Has the budget process been successful when compared with the established plan and goals?
- What improvements can be made in the future?

10. Abide by the Budget

Abiding by the budget means living by the budget. A school leader must set the example in all areas of instructional leadership for others to follow. This is most certainly true in relation to the campus budget. "Time on task" is an old adage in the school business, but nothing rings truer in terms of the school budget and the necessity for the instructional leader to monitor, evaluate, and abide by the budget and the accompanying action or improvement plan.

Abiding by the budget means living by the budget.

Final Thoughts

Education is the largest single budgetary component of state and local governments. School districts receive all of their funding from federal, state, and local governing entities. Many states provide well over 50 percent of school district funding, followed by local tax dollars, and then federal monies. Four terms are closely related to campus budgeting: *income, fiduciary, encumbered,* and *expenditures*. All must be accounted for in a budget. When fiscal accountability is ignored, funding safeguards are very much at risk.

One funding source for school districts is federal dollars in the form of general, categorical, and block grants aid. One critical block grant that represents a fiscal lifeline to school systems is Title I funding, which serves to support instructionally disadvantaged students with a focus on equity, equality, and excellence.

A second source of school funding comes from individual states by means of a state aid formula. The purpose of state aid formulas is to counterbalance disparities in educational equity, equality, and opportunity, though the validity of this is frequently argued in courtrooms across the nation. Voucher systems continue to be a source of funding contention for school district administrators, school-site leaders, and school board members.

Disputes run high relative to voucher programs across the nation. Vouchers have been decried as deeply flawed, discriminatory, lacking in accountability, and favoring the wealthy, and they are said to harm students, public education, democracy itself, and the livelihood of public school teachers and staff.

Local sources of income are derived most commonly in the form of property taxes. Sales taxation, income taxation, sumptuary taxation, and assessments on legalized gambling (state lotteries) may very well serve as other sources of educational income.

Finally, recognize the importance of the ten steps to successful budgeting. These steps aid school leaders in developing, implementing, and evaluating a budget.

Discussion Questions

1. What might be considered a serious risk factor a school administrator could face in relation to fiduciary receipts?
2. Consider each of the local sources of income that support school districts. What are the advantages and disadvantages of each in relation to equity, equality, yield, and taxpayer acceptance?
3. What are the commonalities and differences of the three federal sources of district income?
4. How do voucher systems relate to school funding? Examine the research literature and discuss the pros and cons of state voucher programs.
5. Should any one of the ten steps to budgeting success be considered more important than the others? Is so, which one and why?
6. How does this chapter relate to the Professional Standards for Educational Leaders (PSEL) as documented in Chapter 1?

Case Study

Upturns and Downfalls—What's a Principal to Do?

Dr. Kate Bradley, principal at Homer Bedlow School, sat in her office and thought to herself, *Inequitable, unequal, and inadequate educational funding all started during the Great Recession, and it continues to this day. And who would have ever imagined the state taking dollars from public schools and students to finance voucher systems? What is happening to public education and democracy itself?* Then she mused out loud, "What's with this stinkin' thinkin'? It doesn't solve the problems we face, now does it, Kate?" Dr. Bradley pushed her chair back from the desk that late afternoon, stood up, and walked over to her secretary's office.

Kate asked her secretary and budget clerk, Jo Carson, to print out current enrollment figures and a current budget report. The school secretary handed the reports to Dr. Bradley and watched her walk down the hallway back to her office. Jo knew exactly what was taking a toll on Dr. Bradley this day. It was something no principal ever wished to address: budgetary cuts not only fiscal but material and human as well.

It was obvious to Dr. Bradley that the necessary budgetary cuts most regrettably had to focus on the reduction of certain personnel. She sat down at her desk, placed the budget report in front of her, and with a deep sigh of regret tossed her pencil down onto the report, knowing serious and most difficult decisions had to be made.

It had all begun with a continual decline in student enrollment because of population shifts, along with an ever-eroding tax base and a state legislature playing politics with public school finance and funding. The unprecedented fiscal upturn with the infusion of federal monies during the years of COVID relief packages had also factored in the budget development process, but those essential funds had readily been depleted. The result of all these issues was to be expected: Deep budget cuts!

Federal dollars had done much good over the last few years, bringing to campus a second counseling position, three floating substitutes, two additional instructional specialists, four more paraprofessionals, a second assistant principal, and a second social services caseworker,

(Continued)

(Continued)

as well as new laptops for every student and additional instructional resources and materials for every classroom, among other things. The list went on and on! The federal funding had been much like a late rich uncle having left a niece or nephew a very sizable inheritance!

A week ago, however, word had come to the principal that she and her site-based team would have to potentially make deep budget cuts in the amount of $370,610.00. The amount to be trimmed was staggering, but similar cuts were also necessary at the district level and on other campuses. Little further federal funding was anticipated, and state and local funds would never come close to making up the difference.

The current budget for Homer Bedlow (presented in an abbreviated form for this particular exercise) revealed a total allocation of $736,013.00. Now this budget had to be reduced by $370,610.00. Dr. Bradley and her team had already done their best to trim all nonessential expenditures, but even this didn't bring them close to the required funding reductions. Her only hope was that the federal Department of Education would continue to invest heavily in education, but both she and the district chief financial officer feared this would not occur considering the two congressional political parties and their constant infighting and opposition.

Dr. Bradley closely examined the month of May budget report. She then leaned back in her chair and gloomily thought that cutting personnel had to be a serious if not compulsory consideration to meet the required budget reductions.

Budget Code	Description	Allocation	Expended	Total
199-11-6112.00-102-FY-11	Payroll – salaries or wages for substitute teachers	$32,489.00	$24,366.75	$8,122.25
199-11-6129.00-102-FY-11	Payroll – salaries for support personnel (paraprofessionals)	$35,740.00	$26,805.00	$8,935.00
199-21-6110.00-102-FY-11	Payroll – instructional leadership (instructional specialist/district office directors)	$72,663.00	$54,497.25	$18,165.75

Budget Code	Description	Allocation	Expended	Total
199-23-6110.00-102-FY-11	Payroll – school leadership (administration)	$90,000.00	$67,500.00	$22,500.00
199-23-6110.00-102-FY-25	Payroll – school leadership (administration)	$90,000.00	$67,500.00	$22,500.00
199-31-6110.00-102-FY-11	Payroll – teachers and other professional personnel	$64,000.00	$48,000.00	$16,000.00
199-32-6110.00-102-FY-11	Payroll – teachers and other professional personnel	$39,000.00	$29,250.00	$9,750.00
211-11-6112.00-102-FY-30	Payroll – salaries or wages for substitute teachers	$32,489.00	$24,366.75	$8,122.25
211-11-6129.00-102-FY-30	Payroll – salaries for support personnel (paraprofessionals)	$35,740.00	$26,805.00	$8,935.00
211-31-6110.00-102-FY-30	Payroll – teachers and other professional personnel	$64,000.00	$48,000.00	$16,000.00
211-32-6110.00-102-FY-30	Payroll – teachers and other professional personnel	$39,000.00	$29,250.00	$9,750.00
219-11-6112.00-102-FY-25	Payroll – salaries or wages for substitute teachers	$32,489.00	$24,366.75	$8,122.25
219-11-6129.00-102-FY-25	Payroll – salaries for support personnel (paraprofessionals)	$35,740.00	$26,805.00	$8,935.00
219-21-6110.00-102-FY-25	Instructional leadership (instructional specialists/district office directors)	$72,663.00	$54,497.25	$18,165.75

Important note: Remember, *allocation* relates to the dollar amount allotted at the beginning of the budget cycle, *expended* to the dollar amount spent to date, and *total* to the amount remaining to consume until the conclusion of the budget cycle.

Case Study Application

Examine the abbreviated budget report above. Place yourself in the shoes of Dr. Kate Bradley. How would you handle this potential downfall in funding? Serious, if not extreme, budget reductions would be required. What's a principal to do?

Turn to Resource C in this text and the Accounting Codes Reference Sheet within. Use this resource as a guide in delineating between personnel and allocations, expenditures, and total amount remaining to consume at the conclusion of the budget cycle.

1. Using the Accounting Codes Reference Sheet, determine what personnel position each line item represents. For example, looking at budget code 211-31-6110.00-102-FY-30, Function 31 corresponds to guidance counseling and evaluation services (school counselor). Fund 211 is representative of Title I. Object code 6110 represents teachers and other professional personnel. 102 is an organization code for an elementary school campus. FY = fiscal year code. Finally, 30 is the program intent code (Title I for a schoolwide project/program).

   Therefore, this particular position represents a school counselor being paid with Title I funds. Dr. Bradley has to determine if this campus position is one that could be or should be eliminated. A most difficult decision. What might Dr. Bradley decide?

2. Imagine you are the principal of another school in the same system as Dr. Bradley. Regrettably, word has come to you from your district office that plans for potential mandatory reductions must be made at your school as well. The superintendent of schools, Dr. Sam Drucker, has often stated, "Better to plan to fail, than fail to plan." Therefore, you must plan to balance the budget now. Determine how and by what means reductions would be made if required. Remember, the school budget must be reduced by $370,610.00.

3. Finally, relate your decisions to the ten steps to budgeting success noted within this chapter and to the Professional Standards for Educational Leaders (PSEL) identified in Chapter 1. Which one or more of the ten steps and of the PSEL apply? Explain.

4. Hint: There may be multiple ways in which the accounts can be amended to reduce the budget to the required funding downfall. A principal often has funding flexibility when budgeting. Like a puzzle, a school budget has numerous pieces, and when they are

properly placed together, a complete, satisfactory picture is often the outcome. Is it easy? Sometimes. Other times, as would be the case in this particular scenario, no, it is not so easy, especially when human lives are involved!

5. Good luck and good budgeting!

Effective, Efficient, and Essential Budgeting Practices

6

> *Money is a great servant but a bad master!*
>
> —Sir Francis Bacon, English Statesman (Zeitlin, 2021, p. 207)

The Budget Plan

English statesman Francis Bacon once wrote, "Money is a great servant but a bad master." Consider this quote and then reflect upon the old adage, "Either we can control money or it can control us." Each statement reveals an element of truth that can be applied to the effective, efficient, and essential management of a school budget. Many find the school budgeting process to be complex, problematic, or even traumatic, but in fact school budgeting is far less complicated than one might assume. With this in mind, let's turn to the threefold guide to successful budgeting: (1) visionary demonstration, (2) consistency in planning, and (3) an interwoven relationship among school goals, objectives, action or improvement planning, and the school budget.

Theoretically—and most certainly appropriate in practice—the school academic action or improvement plan should be developed in tandem with the budget plan, as this serves to identify the costs necessary to support the academic plan and instructional program. The budget plan is then converted into fund-oriented accounts (a school budget) as associated with the fiscal allotment provided to the school by the local district.

The rationale for such planning makes sense because the obligation of any school administrator is to, first and foremost, plan for the specified needs of the students and not permit the available funds to dictate or confine any aspect of a school's instructional program (Brimley et al., 2020). Unfortunately, and all too often, a lack of integrated budget and academic planning at the school or district level results in the selection and application of programs and services that are shortsighted, insufficient, and ineffective in meeting the varied needs of the students served. This results in wasted revenue and poor academic performance.

The purpose of the budget plan is to not only support the school's action or improvement plan but also to consolidate it into dollar appropriations.

Basically, an action or improvement plan must be worth more than the paper it is written on if it is to be integrated with the budget plan. Table 6.1 specifies the necessary steps a school administrator and decision-making team should follow in relation to the budgetary process, including training, planning, and development.

The budget plan must be developed with the following eight questions in mind:

1. Prior to any budget planning and development process, has the school leader provided professional development training that is essential to understanding how visioning and planning impact programmatic considerations and the school budget?

> The purpose of the budget plan is to not only support the school's action or improvement plan but also to consolidate it into dollar appropriations.

2. Has a needs assessment been conducted to address what impact programmatic initiatives—federal, state, and local—have on student achievement? Levin (2011) suggests school leaders want to know which particular interventions are most promising for increasing student achievement and cost the least, because monetary resources are far too often in short supply. In other words, it is essential to ensure the effectiveness of school resources by incorporating methods that will promote an age-old adage, "Get the biggest bang for the buck!" This is what a needs assessment is all about.

3. Have student needs and academic achievement been addressed in the form of a school action or improvement plan that emphasizes goal development?

TABLE 6.1 The Budgetary Process—Training, Assessing, Prioritizing, Goal Setting, Objective Development, Monitoring, and Evaluation

1	2	3	4	5	6	7
Professional Development	Planning and Needs Assessment	Causal Barriers Identification	Prioritizing School-Based Needs	Goal Setting and Objective Development	Budget Development and Implementation	Budget Monitoring and Evaluation
8 ◀ Question: Have all stakeholders been actively engaged and involved? ▶						
The budgetary process, from training to planning to goal setting and objective development to actual budget implementation, is a constant course of action that requires a principal to engage the decision-making team in a collaborative and problem-solving effort. This table illustrates how a principal can transform the budgetary process through a series of step-by-step essential elements that clarify the complexities associated with budget development, specifically as correlated with goal alignment and attainment.						

4. Following the needs assessment and goal-development process, have specific instructional as well as nonacademic programs been identified for implementation, improvement, or exclusion?
5. Have learning community representatives been provided with forms and figures that are indicative of previous budgetary allotments and expenditures for at least one prior year, and preferably three to five years?
6. Has the learning community (specifically the teaching staff) been asked by school administration to submit requests for supplies, equipment, and facilities that are essential, if not critical, in meeting the academic needs of the students and that are necessary in relation to the dictates imposed on the school or district academic programs by state and federal mandates?
7. Have budgeted dollars been allocated to support the action plan, and have the budget manager and team regularly and collaboratively monitored and evaluated budgetary expenditures in relation to programmatic effectiveness and student academic gains? This is more than a "wish list" approach to instruction and school budgeting; this is an integrated visionary process, through a needs-assessment process, that readily identifies priorities necessary for programmatic and student success.
8. Finally, have faculty, staff, students, parents, and community members been actively involved in the decision-making process leading to the development of the school action or improvement plan and the campus budget?

These eight components represent essential budgeting theory-to-practice, which better serves to ensure the ideas and recommendations of the learning community are actively sought and incorporated into budgeting practice via the budgetary process.

Analyzing the School Action and Budget Plans

The school action or improvement plan, as previously examined in Chapter 3, serves as the vehicle that drives not only the instructional program but also the budget development process. Effective budgetary planning must allow for the school budget to be based upon the educational programs designated within the confines of an action or improvement plan. In other words, funding should be allocated to the educational programs as identified in priority order in the school action or improvement plan.

There are numerous aspects or designators often associated with an action plan. For example, commonly utilized are thirteen components to be addressed within the action plan. These thirteen designators are identified as (1) student performance, (2) special education, (3) a safe and healthy learning environment (well-being as well as violence prevention), (4) family and community engagement (parental involvement), (5) professional development (human capital), (6) suicide prevention, (7) conflict resolution, (8) dyslexia treatment programs, (9) dropout reduction, (10) technology, (11) discipline management, (12) accelerated instruction (such as tutoring), and (13) career education. All of these components are quite representative of school planning issues that any state, district, or school might encounter.

Budget plans must be developed in tandem with an action or improvement plan. The budget plan serves effectively to (1) project all anticipated income, (2) identify all needed programs, and (3) project current and future average daily attendance or membership for the purpose of seeking a district allocation that will serve to meet the needs of all the students enrolled.

The purpose of the budget plan is to anticipate, project, and predict potential sources of income, program development, any financial deficit, and possible areas for budgetary reduction or additions. The development of the budget plan, much like that of the action plan, should be made in collaboration with a school's site-based decision-making (SBDM) team. This team, following the guidance of the school leader, is most often involved in decisions related to educational planning, curriculum development, instructional issues, staffing patterns, professional development, school organization, and, of course, budgeting.

Prior to developing the budget plan, the effective school administrator must insist on and ensure a professional development program has been initiated to train the learning community in the methods of generating and completing a needs assessment (see Table 6.2). A needs assessment and an information or quality analysis both effectively correlate with campus action or improvement-planning procedures as well as with the budget development processes. When utilized appropriately, a needs assessment instrument and a quality analysis can do exactly what their names imply. Furthermore, each—working in tandem—can be the essential impetus for prioritizing school-based needs with the following caveat: Students and the academic program are always at the forefront of any budgetary consideration.

Performing an Information Analysis

An information analysis, sometimes identified as a *quality analysis*, is a thorough examination of a campus action or improvement plan with implications associated with the campus budget–development process. Information analysis is a four-step process whereby certain

TABLE 6.2 Conducting a Needs Assessment

PHASE	WORK TO ACCOMPLISH
I. Initiating the inquiry process 1. What needs improvement? 2. Why is improvement needed? 3. What data support the need to improve? 4. Do additional data need to be gathered to support areas in need of improvement?	1. Review the district's and school's visionary statement to determine if the campus vision meets the written vision as well as the district's vision. 2. Analyze the current campus action or improvement plan. 3. Identify sources of data such as previously conducted studies and district and statewide test results, along with teacher, student, and parent surveys. 4. Identify other needed sources of data that may not be readily available, such as a longitudinal analysis of state and district indicator systems reports. This is a relevant approach to identifying instructional area(s) in need of improvement. Then determine what methods or procedures are needed to collect any particular data.
II. Deriving consensus 1. Can consensus or agreement be reached regarding the needs or problems that must be addressed? 2. Does the needs assessment process find areas that are important to bringing about organizational change and improvement? 3. Consider the following: Have the principal and SBDM team overlooked any programmatic concerns, issues, or problems?	1. Review all pertinent sources of data in a transparent manner whereby all parties are collaboratively involved in the consensus-building process. Such a procedure better ensures buy-in within the site-based team and across the learning community. 2. Consider all instructional and curricular concerns, problems, and targeted needs that have been identified. 3. Arrive at a high level of consensus and then narrow down the list of needs. This is a priority-driven process.
III. Organizing and analyzing the data 1. What data need collecting and why? 2. From where will the data be collected? 3. What do the data reveal?	1. Following any analysis of data and the initial prioritization of perceived needs, the principal and team must discuss each area of concern, note problems, and then outline specific actions to be initiated. This particular phase is all about answering the question, "Why do we do this?" 2. Principals must be prepared to share action or initiation proposals of data collection with members of the learning community. 3. Never avoid or ignore initiating a careful review of the research literature. Do not consider, and never implement, any organizational initiative that cannot be validated in the research literature, specifically by empirical studies.

(Continued)

(Continued)

PHASE	WORK TO ACCOMPLISH
IV. Focusing on priorities 1. What is the greatest priority? The second greatest? The third greatest, and so on? 2. Priorities must be determined in accordance with the following criteria: What human, fiscal, and/or material resources (including release time) are required? Are internal or external (or both) levels of expertise available and/or required? By what means will the priorities be addressed, solved, and/or resolved? 3. Is there a sound research base in the professional literature for addressing each prioritized concern/ problem/need and for supporting the proposed actions and/or implementations?	1. Conduct a full examination of instructional priorities and hold open, collaborative, and transparent discussions with the SBDM team. These discussions must address each priority consideration proposed. 2. Present team-determined recommendations to the district administrative leader (superintendent or designee) along with the priority rankings of each identified need. 3. Most importantly, work together as a team in a most transparent and collaborative manner, reaching a fair and equitable consensus. Always remember: Students come first!

campus underlying or problematic factors can be identified via a three-point assessment:

1. Establish performance objectives.
2. Conduct a needs assessment.
3. Scrutinize an instructional problem.

Information analysis must focus on a review and analysis of data, followed by the implementation of best-practice strategies. This is a principal-oriented and practice-based method of data scrutiny that guides a school leader and team in determining the problems or factors that are contributing to low student performance in particular subject areas for specific student populations (Sorenson et al., 2011). Information analysis requires a principal, prior to developing a school budget, to seek qualitative data and quantitative data. Such data come from inside and outside the school or district. Now, as a means of determining how to solve an issue or problem, reflect upon the following four-step information analysis.

Steps to Performing an Information Analysis

Step 1: Qualitative/Outside Data and Information

Principals and SBDM teams must examine qualitative/outside data sources by

- reviewing the research literature;
- enlisting the support of district and professional facilitators who understand the problem at hand;
- consulting educational research laboratories;

- determining which best practices, when implemented, will solve the instructional problem;
- providing teachers with release time to participate in essential and relatable professional development; and
- permitting teachers the opportunity to make site visits to schools (local and distant) that are effectively implementing the required best practices.

Step 2: Quantitative/Outside Data and Information

Principals and SBDM teams must examine quantitative/outside data sources by deriving information from state and federal agencies in the form of statutes and reports, including

- the state education agency codes, statutes, or official rulings;
- the United States Department of Education regulations;
- the Office of Civil Rights directives;
- academic performance reports or other state education agency assessment reports; and
- Individuals with Disabilities Education Improvement Act (IDEIA) parameters.

Step 3: Qualitative/Inside Data and Information

Principals and SBDM teams must examine qualitative/inside data sources by doing the following:

- analyzing survey results
- initiating focus groups and gathering relevant information
- conducting interviews of teachers, parents, and students
- initiating observations of effective teaching practices
- surveying organizational climate and culture by listening to teachers (they will report any disconnect between administrative dictates/mandates and teaching and learning capacity), nurturing self-care (school leaders must protect teacher well-being and conference and planning times, as examples), and offering instructional leadership (initiative implementation and effectiveness strongly correlates with campus enabling collaboration);
- examining student profiles
- seeking teacher opinions
- conducting brainstorming sessions with members of the learning community

Step 4: Quantitative/Inside Data and Information

Principals and SBDM teams must examine quantitative/inside data sources by reviewing records, such as

- student academic records (to include cumulative folders),
- state assessment and accountability records,
- Fiscal Education and Information Management System (FEIMS) records,
- school board policies,
- administrative regulations and procedures,
- school district attorney opinions,
- attendance records of school meetings, and
- classroom assessments and other benchmarking reports.

Conducting a Needs Assessment

A needs assessment must be initiated relative to the development of a campus action or improvement plan and the development of a school budget (see Table 6.2 and Table 6.3) for programmatic and student success to occur. Such an assessment requires a principal and team to ultimately prioritize school needs to positively impact the instructional program. To do so, the authors of this text—as former principals—strongly recommend four essential phases be addressed in the assessment process. These phases are identified and explained in Table 6.3.

Generated Income Sources

"If you can conceive it, you can achieve it!" Do you recall this old adage? School leaders are designated many responsibilities, the budgetary process being one, and, as a result, they are often called upon to put this adage to work. The effective school administrator quickly learns to generate additional sources of income for the school beyond those funds already allocated by district administration. The district allocation is just one of numerous income sources that must be generated if a school is to establish a comprehensive, high-quality, and cost-effective program. Such income-generating sources include but are not limited to the ones listed below.

Grants

Grants often provide an additional source of income for schools but are typically obtained on a competitive basis. This practice becomes even more intense and competitive during periods of fiscal constraint. Grant funds are generally tied to a request for application (RFA) process

TABLE 6.3 A Step-by-Step Guide to Effective, Efficient, and Essential Budgetary Funding

1. Examine! The Thirteen Components +   Determine which of the thirteen components are not a basic part of the campus action or improvement plan.
2. Identify! Sources of Data +   As a beginning point in the needs assessment process, ascertain which data sources will be required for analysis.
3. Review! The Campus Action or Improvement Plan +   Pinpoint instructional gaps, holes, missing goals, objectives, and/or actions that must be addressed and resolved when analyzing the campus action or improvement plan.
4. Conduct! A Campus Instructional Needs Assessment +   Perform an assessment examining all state- and/or district-mandated curricular components and data sources to determine what instructional needs must be addressed.
5. Prioritize! The Campus Instructional Needs   Rank the campus instructional needs in order of most significance to best improve student achievement. Calculate each step of the five steps and the resulting answer =   effective, efficient, and essential funding!

whereby a great deal of time and effort, not to mention tedious research and data collection, must occur for an application to be seriously considered. Most grants are categorical in nature. As a reminder, *categorical* refers to funds that are restricted to certain categories or activities, such as technology, science, mathematics, or accelerated instruction.

Finally, one of the best sources for locating grant funding is the Internet. The Internet provides numerous sites containing excellent information regarding grant application processes. Such information includes daily announcements, useful statistics, tips and techniques for writing grants, and current programs that are funded by grant dollars.

Fundraising and Crowdfunding—Always Be Attentive, School Leader!

Additional school income is frequently generated through the fundraising efforts of school-sponsored groups such as parent–teacher organizations (PTOs) and booster clubs, to name a couple. Parental involvement is essential for most school fundraising efforts. Parent groups and organizations provide a wide range of valuable services and activities, both inside and outside the school. However, the role of parents and PTOs must be specifically defined. If not, be advised and attentive, school leaders, as problems—especially in the fundraising and crowdfunding arena—often arise.

Fundraising events typically involve raffles or the sale of merchandise ranging from consumable items (candy, cookies, pizzas, or Thanksgiving turkeys, for example) to nonperishable items such as Christmas gift wrap, T-shirts, candles, senior rings, yearbooks, school pictures, and just about anything else the fertile mind can imagine.

Crowdfunding is an alternative method of raising dollars in schools and enjoyed popular support and use in past years. Today, however, many school districts have banned crowdfunding. What districts learned was that they had to promptly develop guidelines (board policies and campus regulations) due to unwanted situations and legal liabilities with crowdfunding. Proper oversight, monitoring, and strongly defined guidelines and regulations are keys to successful crowdfunding, if crowdfunding is permitted.

Fundraising and crowdfunding can generate significant income for a school—income above and beyond the standard district allocation. They can also serve as monetary sources for purchasing items such as stage curtains, playground equipment, instructional supplies, and even air conditioning for the school gym. However, if fundraising and crowdfunding efforts are not properly planned and organized with keen oversight and associated policies, schools can be faced with numerous financial pitfalls (DeSchryver, 2021; FasterCapital, 2023; Mutter & Parker, 2012).

For example, fundraising and crowdfunding—while financially compelling and potentially rewarding—can quickly turn sour due to lost, missing, or stolen merchandise and/or generated funds, and they also carry the potential for legal entanglements. This can publicly tarnish a school or embarrass an administrator in the eyes of the community, not to mention the district superintendent or school board. As a result, more and more schools and districts are turning to digital fundraising. Consider this old axiom, "Fewer hands, fewer problems!"

Digital fundraising is definitely the future of generating income for schools. Digital fundraising is online outreach using websites, e-mails, and social media. This mode of fundraising permits anyone, anywhere with Internet access to join schools in raising needed dollars. Digital fundraising provides schools the opportunity to expand their donor base with easy giving experiences, competent support, and safe and secure payment methods. Today, schools are no longer confined to students engaging in door-to-door and face-to-face solicitations. The digital process ensures student privacy and safety. But, once again, as safe, sound, and secure as the new and improved may seem, school leaders, always be attentive!

Accountability and Accounting Procedures

One of the most important aspects of the school budgetary process is the accounting for and control of school expenditures. While expenditure accountability and control vary from state to state and from district to district, three closely related activities must be carried out with strict and complete propriety: appropriate visionary planning, careful budgeting, and effective expenditure of school funds. Each is crucial to ensuring students benefit from a school's instructional program. However, let's focus on accountability and accounting procedures.

The responsibility for wisely spending school funds to provide for a high-quality education for each student is further challenged by the precept that school dollars must also be actively and accurately accounted for and protected. The term *accounting* can be readily described as the process by which the effectiveness, legality, quality, and efficiency of budgeting procedures must be measured by the documented stewardship of all public funds. While such a notion may have once been considered simply good business practice by schools and school districts, this same consideration, by today's budgetary standards, is a practical and essential—if not critical—fiscal imperative.

Three closely related activities must be carried out with strict and complete propriety: appropriate visionary planning, careful budgeting, and effective expenditure of school funds.

Accounting procedures are defined as the *fiscal* method of determining whether a school has provided a fiscally valued and educationally valuable service to its clientele. To make this determination, school accounting procedures must do the following:

- monitor all incoming funds and outgoing expenditures in relation to the attainment of the school's vision, goals, and objectives
- protect public dollars from any potential loss attributable to irresponsibility, wrongful utilization, theft, and/or embezzlement by any individual associated with the school or school district
- provide an assurance public funds are being used to better ensure the academic achievement of each student
- ensure all legal requirements are followed
- inform the general community of any and all facts and information regarding the fiscal solvency of the school site and district

In an effort to meet these standards, MIP Fund Accounting (2023) and the *Comprehensive Guide to Accounting for School Administration* as reported by Curacubby Team (2020) submit that accountability is the paramount objective of any budgetary process and, as such, all fiscal accountability reports must include information that (1) compares actual financial results with the legally adopted budget; (2) assesses the financial condition of a school or system; (3) complies with finance-related laws, rules, and regulations; and (4) assists in evaluating the efficiency and effectiveness of a school's or district's fiscal budget and educational program.

Finally, the National Center for Education Statistics (NCES, 2016) and Sorenson (2024) have identified five standard accounting practices that must guide schools and districts in their common goal of accounting for public funds in relation to the budgetary process:

1. Define and utilize account classifications and codes that provide meaningful financial management information.
2. Comply with the Generally Accepted Accounting Principals (GAAP) as established by the Governmental Accounting Standards Board (GASB).
3. Recognize and utilize accounting technology and safety and security procedures.
4. Comply with all state and federal laws and fiscal accountability reporting requirements.
5. Scrutinize and monetarily enhance/fund school safety and security procedures (see the scenario titled "Budgeted Dollars and School Safety" below).

By adopting and following these standards, school leaders allow for the continuous monitoring of expenditures as well as accountability and control of budgeting procedures—all of which are most definitely considered to be best practices for further ensuring students are benefiting from school appropriations. Equally important, all school personnel are protected from any potential legal entanglements that are often associated with the mishandling of district funds.

Budgeted Dollars and School Safety

Not too many years back, a prominent school law textbook noted, for the first time, that murder had to be included within the text as a reason for student expulsion. At the time, it was (and still is today) a sad commentary on society. So for the first time since the first edition publication of this book in 2006, this reason must be included. Why? Read the local, state, and national headlines, or turn on the digital or televised news, and you will see that today gunmen in schools and community mass shootings are recurring issues.

Every reader knows the names and places: Uvalde, Texas; Newtown, Connecticut; Santa Fe, Texas; Parkland, Florida; Virginia Tech University;

El Paso, Texas; Allen, Texas; Lewiston, Maine; Orlando, Florida; Monterey Park, California; Pittsburgh, Pennsylvania; Sutherland Springs, Texas; Las Vegas, Nevada. With deep regret the list goes on and on with no identifiable timeline for a cease and desist. Since 2010, school shootings have resulted in 207 deaths. (NCES, 2023). Since 2018, there have been more than 2,800 deaths as a result of mass shootings in the United States (Statista Inc., 2023).

Budgeting for school safety has become an absolute fact of everyday life in school systems across the United States and thus a resolute inclusion within this book. First, how and by what means are these funds acquired? School safety funding must be secured before more school shootings occur. Second, what's a school leader to do? Take the initiative and lead! School safety funding is a moral obligation of every principal, school superintendent, board member, community leader, parent, and, perhaps most importantly, state and national politician, no matter party affiliation. Our students and teachers cannot be depended upon to secure campus safety! To begin with, it is not their responsibility. It is ours—as the leaders of today and tomorrow!

The solution, in simplified terms, seems quite straightforward: Every state legislator and governor, every federal congressperson and senator, every state and federal Department of Education officer, and the president of the United States must demand the appropriate funding for schools across the nation to financially bolster and support the prioritization of school safety. Everyone must work together to bring an end to the senseless loss of too many lives—lives of students, teachers, campus leaders, parents, and community members! Today, every school leader must *lead* by using your voice and your vote to demand more state and federal safe school funding!

Collection and Deposit Structures

The school leader, as budget manager, will quickly realize that the basis for effective budgeting is not only the planning aspect of the budgetary process but also the proper accounting of revenue collected and deposited. Good budgeting must be based on a structure of collections and deposits that further establishes an accounting control mechanism to preclude any monetary mistakes and possible theft or embezzlement.

Such a structure is imperative since most schools have activity accounts based on the collection of funds from school clubs, booster organizations, general fees, and numerous other dollar-generating initiatives.

The School Activity Account

The school activity account is one important area of the budgetary process in which sound financial practice must be exercised. Many administrators will confide there are two problematic areas that can get a school leader in serious trouble: sex is one, and money is the other—romance and finance (see Chapter 7's "Case Study: Sex, Money, and a Tangled Web Woven"). This is especially true when an activity account is involved (Sorenson, 2007; Sorenson, 2024). An exceptional read as related to inappropriate romance and finance school leader behaviors is *Essentials for New Principals: Seven Steps to Becoming Successful—Key Expectations and Skills* (Sorenson, 2024).

The school activity account is the budgetary area that can pose the most serious financial complications and implications. For example, the activity account at many schools (high schools in particular) can generate significant income from revenue sources such as fundraisers, crowdfunding, vending machines, school pictures, athletic receipts, library and textbook fines, student clubs and organizations, numerous student fees, school store operations, field trip receipts, and appropriated district funds—the list can go on and on. In most states, thousands of dollars flow through a school's activity account. Administrators have the primary fiscal responsibility of not only managing this account but also complying with federal and state laws and district policies and procedures (Brimley et al., 2020).

School activity funds must be safeguarded, and prudent verification of all accounts within the activity fund must be monitored and audited for the purpose of ensuring such monies are appropriately utilized for student benefit. Now, let's return to bookkeeping practices and the development of an income collection and deposit structure.

Components of the Collection and Deposit Structure

The purpose of any collection and deposit structure is to establish budgetary controls to prevent general accounting mistakes, blatant theft, and/or embezzlement of funds. This structure is composed of several components that identify key personnel who should be bonded prior to collecting, accounting for, and depositing funds. The term *bonded* relates to a legal process known as surety bonding, which is frequently defined as a guarantee of performance. In other words, a bonding agency will reimburse a school district for any financial loss related to fraud, theft, or embezzlement that might occur as a result of an individual who has been entrusted with the handling of funds (Brimley et al., 2020).

Returning to the components of collection and deposit, a carefully crafted budgetary structure should include and ensure the following:

- **Cash receipts collections.** When generated dollars, typically in small denominations, are brought into the school office by an activity sponsor, at least two bonded individuals should collect, count, and account for the funds. The total amount of cash and checks submitted should accurately match the receipts presented and also match the amount listed on the receipt given to the sponsor.

- **Activity account postings.** Following the cash receipts collection, the monetary amount should be counted and double counted, again by bonded personnel, and then entered into the bookkeeping system. A summary cash receipts report is electronically and automatically generated and provides the bookkeeping staff and school leader with a listing of the receipt entries, as designated by date, along with the dollar amount of said receipts and the specified activity account (athletics, school pictures, or library fund, for example) into which the collected receipts are to be entered.
- **Bank deposit procedures.** Following any account posting, a bank deposit slip must be prepared immediately. Then, a third bonded individual (someone different than the two individuals who are collecting, accounting, and preparing the deposit slip) should be selected to place the funds in a deposit bag and promptly make the bank deposit. Many school districts require two individuals take any deposits to the bank. Today, school districts can also contract the bank depositing process with an armored collection and transport service. Additionally, many school districts utilize electronic banking to reduce human error and the potential for theft or embezzlement, and most certainly for convenience. Proper bank depository procedures help ensure the amount of money received totals the daily deposit.
- **Bank reconciliation processes.** The bank reconciliation process reveals much about the management of a school's budgetary practices. Proper reconciliation of bank statements and records is considered one of the most important fiscal safeguards available to a school leader. Bank reconciliation is nothing more than a check-and-balance system that ensures the school's bank statement matches the data recorded in the school's financial records. This process, while tedious and time consuming, provides an opportunity for the school leader to identify differences that may exist between bank records and school records.

All of the above serve as wise practices. Additionally, the process should also include a monthly analysis of the school's financial records. School leaders should be cognizant of the possibility that problems associated with the school's bank statement could very well signal financial problems elsewhere—in other school accounts, for example, or with the school's accounting procedures.

Irreconcilable differences between a bank statement and campus fiscal accounting books may reveal either incompetence or fraud. Every school leader must recognize such possibilities can and do exist in schools, and, as a result, the administrator, as the budgetary manager, should be ever vigilant.

Applicable to today's school budgetary accounting process—and a motto every principal should adopt—is a quote attributed to President Ronald Reagan when speaking about the U.S. relationship with the Soviet Union and intermediate-range nuclear missiles during the 1980s: "Trust but verify" (Reagan, 1987). Exactly! The authors highly recommend a principal must trust but verify all accounting procedures. Another truism: "Inspect what you expect" (Miranda, 2012). Both quotes make good business sense!

Understanding each of the specified components of the budgetary process as well as the need for income collection and deposit is essential and must be mastered by the school administrator to prevent fiscal problems that could lead to the end of what may have been a most successful and satisfying administrative career.

It's a New Day!

Coming to a school near you (if they have not already arrived) are digital advances including but not limited to pupil facial biometric recognition for financial services (in the lunchroom, for example); fingerprint recognition as a component of digital fiscal transactions (applicable for business department personnel at district and campus levels); the use of cellphones to make deposits and other budgeting-related activities simpler; e-balancing; and the transfer and amendment of budgetary line items done electronically—all fairly effortlessly and quite seamlessly. And to think this is just a start!

Consider how new technologies such as virtual reality (VR), augmented reality (AR), artificial intelligence (AI), and intelligent assistance (IA) devices will, if they are not already in use, impact school systems and personnel, particularly business departments and campus administrators, when it comes to fiscal and budgetary considerations. Teachers and students will also see their effects on instruction. Even the swiping of campus employee identification cards is becoming past history as it is being replaced by facial and fingerprint recognition (Sorenson, 2021). Yes, it's a new day in the world of school budget management and day-to-day instruction. Are you there already? If not, you will soon be!

The Advantages and Disadvantages of Cashless Schools

Listed here are the benefits and drawbacks of cashless schools as detailed by PaySchools (2016). First, the benefits:

- **Convenience.** There is no need for bank deposits and no waiting in line inside the bank or in the drive-thru or spending countless business hours inputting data.

- **Crime prevention.** Theft protection from fraud and potential embezzlers is provided.
- **Stability.** Mobile money may very well replace all banking systems. The potential for a banking collapse thus becomes minimal.

Next, the drawbacks:

- **Less privacy.** Transactions leave histories, enabling the government and/or corporations to track, monitor, and possibly intimidate businesses, including schools and individuals.
- **Decreased security.** While mobile money has distinct advantages, potential power outages or network problems could make it difficult, if not impossible, to retrieve mobile monies. System malfunctions are also a possibility as is the inevitable presence of hackers.
    - One of the authors of this text recently received correspondence from a highly regarded national life and annuity company that read, "We are writing to inform you of an incident that may have affected your personal information. We were alerted to the existence of sophisticated ransomware. We determined that an unauthorized malicious actor accessed and acquired certain files from our systems and your personal information may be at risk." This meant the hackers could potentially access bank accounts, savings, and other investments. Now, that's a wake-up call that exemplifies one of the disadvantages of cashless schools.
- However, while a cash-based system may offer greater security, this is always accompanied by greater inconvenience. Who hasn't become inpatient with the district's cash-handling and check-writing procedures when purchasing, for example, supplies and materials and/or furniture and equipment under $5,000?

The advantages of cashless schools are causing school district administrators to proceed in quick fashion to adopt these methods in order improve cash flow (without cash), increase employee productivity, decrease personnel responsibilities, and better negate theft and embezzlement. At the same time, the associated disadvantages of cashless schools must not be ignored. "Ever vigilant" must be the mantra of every school leader and, of course, all individuals. When actual cash dollars are not in human hands, the temptation to steal and/or embezzle is more readily avoided. As one principal recently stated, "You can't steal what you can't touch!" Generally, this is true, but the possibility of theft is always there. However, that will be addressed in the next chapter!

Technology Today: Effective, Efficient, and Essential Budgeting Required

Budgeting funds for technology continues to be a hot topic in schools, yet nearly 40 percent of principals and 43 percent of teachers indicate allocations for technology lag behind digital innovations and remain most insufficient (Promethean, 2022). Shrinking school budgets equate to shrinking technology funds. Educators also believe strategic technology visioning is failing both teachers and students as the digital world continues to pass schools by. Below are selected findings from *The State of Technology in Education—2022* (Promethean, 2022) report relative to technology incorporation, budgeting, and implementation in schools.

- Seventy-seven percent of educators believe technology is a highly effective yet costly method of engaging students.
- Eighty-three percent believe technology must be integrated within lessons, yet implementation remains stagnant due to insufficient funding.
- Seventy-six percent agree technology improves teaching and learning, yet 66 percent of teachers continue to utilize copiers and paper as opposed to digital technology.
- Nearly one-third of teachers lack confidence when implementing technology in classroom teaching and learning.
- Nearly 50 percent of educators lack technology training.
- Both teachers and principals agree with the following:
    - Technology is indispensable in schools, yet schools continue to lack critical funding for proper training and implementation.
    - Students today are technology driven and live in a digitally oriented world, but far too many teachers and principals are not and do not.
    - Technology gaps in schools equate to insufficient budgetary funds.
    - Most teachers continue to use the same technology their teachers used.
    - Technology is a crucial attribute to effective and essential schooling.

Gray and Lewis (2021) presented additional findings often related to funding for technology, or the lack thereof.

- Fifteen percent of schools permit students to take home school-provided laptops.
- Only one-third of students have laptops to carry throughout the instructional day.

- Only 31 percent of teachers rate the overall quality of their teaching and learning software as very good and up to date.
- More than 50 percent of educators report having inadequate Internet connections or speed, despite a growing number of students needing to work online.
- Forty-two percent of principals report they have moderate funding flexibility in selecting learning and teaching technology.
- Time, training, and hands-on interactive learning are challenges facing teachers and principals when it comes to using technology in teaching, leading, and learning.
- Twenty-two percent of teachers report the difficulties of using outdated computers and software. Twelve percent indicate this is a major challenge.

Make no mistake, while the educational landscape is always changing, traditional instructional methods and strategies as well as face-to-face learning will continue, often due to insufficient funding, even when the use of technology can make for better and more effective learning. Such is a sad fact as students are coming to school more and more digitally wired!

According to Gray and Lewis (2021), the issue of technology in schools in this digital age suggests the following:

- Principals must make every effort to expand funding for technology in schools to keep up with ever-changing digitalization as well as workforce demands.
- An insufficient number of students are engaged in high-quality, digitally oriented coursework.
- Principals must lead curriculum reform efforts to better ensure more digital instruction.
- School systems must continue to fund and increase the number of qualified technology teachers.
- Technology coursework in schools most underrepresents female and minority students.
- Instructional models using technology must be funded in early literacy learning.
- Seventy percent of students surveyed stipulate that campus technology needs a major overhaul. It's important to note that of everyone who might see the need to overhaul technology in schools, students are likely to have an edge! In this increasingly high-tech world, students are often more advanced in the use of digital devices than educators and able to communicate with them more effectively. Meaning that educators can easily be left lagging, if not way behind, when it

comes to digitalization (Asif, 2013; Husarevich, 2023). Scary when considering the facts presented within this chapter section!

- Teachers continue to fail in keeping up with using mobile and other digital devices as instructional tools in schools.
- Technologically reconfigured, redesigned, and repurposed school facilities must be funded and become the norm.
- Of the top ten skills that need to be taught in schools to ensure students are hired in the real world, nine of those skills are technology related and digitally based.

A Final Technology Tidbit

Social media, including school budgetary and other school data platforms, continue to be threatened by not only account hacking but account *cloning* as well. Unlike hacking, where a bad actor (a hacker) acquires a real account, cloning involves utilizing school data and/or personal information such as photos, instructional materials, budgetary data, and often other school-related information to simply copy or clone an account and thus create a duplicate (fake) account. Cloning is commonly associated with an individual growing followers, all of which leads to real followers getting scammed, often monetarily. Many times the victim is completely unaware a crime is occurring. Be aware anything that looks even remotely suspicious on school-related data storage platforms or on school or personal social media platforms is probably worthy of investigation. All too frequently a scam may be in play—criminal activity at work! For additional information, see Chapter 7 and the section titled "Frequent Types of Fraud in Schools #3: Phishing Scams."

Budget Amendments

Flexibility is an operative term associated with school budgeting. Those administrators who carefully manage and monitor the school budget realize all purposeful planning, even when combined with the best of intentions, can go by the wayside when academic goals and objectives change for the betterment of the students served. For example, consider the following scenario.

Pause and Consider

The Above-Basic Allotment Arrives at Clark Andrews School and Creates a Principal Dilemma

Just a few days into the second semester of the school year at Clark Andrews School, Principal Teresa Méndez was appreciating the fact additional funds were being allocated to the school due to a significant increase in unexpected first-semester student enrollment. An above-basic allotment of $50,000 was transferred to the school by district administration at the conclusion of the first semester to make up for the financial strain the increased enrollment was imposing on the educational program, most notably in the area of technology enhancement.

Dr. Méndez had only recently learned from an administrative colleague in an adjacent school district about an exciting digital initiative—one in which active-learning technological tools were being utilized to enhance student achievement. These tools, with average pricing per student, included laptops ($500.00), a robotic telepresence for virtual learning ($3599.00), virtual reality headsets ($138.99), smartphones ($615.00 per phone + a one-time plan billing fee of 127.27), and even app-enabled wrist bands ($140.00). Additionally, two large locked storage cabinets would be required ($680.00 each) All excited now, and being a techno-geek herself, Dr. Méndez was determined to bring to life a digital vision at her school.

As the first of several planned digital steps, each student was to be issued a long overdue laptop in order to be better instructionally supported. Because of the increased student enrollment, funding for the virtual reality headsets, smartphones, and app-enabled wristbands fell short by about thirty-three students. Moreover, funding was inadequate for all students by thirty-five laptops. Additionally, funding needed to be secured for the two essential locked storage cabinets. Dr. Méndez began calculating all identified items, as noted below:

• Laptop computers – 35 x $500.00 =	$17,500.00
• Robotic telepresence – 1 x $3,599.00 =	$3,599.00
• Virtual reality headsets – 33 x $138.99 =	$4,586.67
• Smartphones – 33 x $615.00 =	$20,295.00
• One-time phone billing fee – 12 × $127.27 =	$1,527.24
• Locked storage cabinet – 2 x $680.00 =	$1,360.00
• App-enabled wrist bands – 33 x $140.00 =	$4,620.00
• GRAND TOTAL =	$53,487.91

Immediately Dr. Méndez recognized there was a digital funding shortfall that equated to approximately $4,000.00. She exclaimed, "Oh, wouldn't you know it, I'm already over budget! This happens every time

(Continued)

(Continued)

I try to balance the school budget! Where can I make the necessary budget cuts?"

Dr. Méndez had been ecstatic when she realized she could use the above-basic allotment to supplement the school's technology account to purchase the digital equipment, but her excitement was snuffed out with the realization the technological costs were more than the allotment. Technology budget cuts had to be made. But where to cut the approximately $4,000.00? Dr. Méndez soon decided she would have to forego a portion of the planned purchase.

Subsequently, Dr. Méndez completed the proper school district form and made an amendment or transfer within the school budget. This decision facilitated the purchase of technology-related items with the incoming above-basic dollars. Dr. Méndez kept in mind the need to reduce the overbudgeting as necessary and, therefore, account for the distribution of the new funds.

1. First, think carefully! What is absolutely missing relative to this scenario from a school leadership perspective? What must be applied by Dr. Méndez, as an instructional leader, if she is to expect buy-in from the learning community? Need a hint? Think, "All of us are smarter than any one of us!"
2. Next, knowing that the school's above-basic allocation of $50,000.00 must be reduced by close to $4,000.00, where might such a reduction be found? Explain your reasoning for your choice selection.
3. Consider the digital equipment being purchased for Clark Andrews School. Now reflect, as would an effective instructional leader, as to how the robotic telepresence for virtual learning and virtual reality headsets might be instructionally incorporated within each of the different subject areas—English, mathematics, science, computing, design technology, and history. Explain.
4. Now, as a follow-up to the previous question, provide a few instructional strategies as examples. How might these strategies better assist a school leader to support the amendment/transfer justification?
5. Reflect back to the text box titled "Technology Today: Effective, Efficient, and Essential Budgeting Required." How does this scenario relate/compare? Explain.

6. To conclude this activity, consider the following questions:

- In your estimation, could the above-basic funding at Clark Andrews School be better utilized elsewhere on campus? Explain.
- From a budgetary perspective, is this expenditure achieving the biggest bang for the buck? Provide a thorough explanation.
- Is the proposed transfer of funds for digital purposes a real "go for it" project or simply a principal's "pie in the sky" figment of the imagination?
- How would the identified technological equipment and proposed transfer of funds be received at your school or in your district?

7. **Finally, recognize and remember budgetary dilemmas confront every school leader!**

Budget amendments are an essential part of the budgetary process and are utilized in an effort to move funds from one account to another and, at times, to correct an accounting error that has been made. It is recommended the school leader follow district budget amendment instructions and procedures by making wise and appropriate decisions regarding income and expenditure adjustments and transfers. Such decision-making will always be accompanied by appropriate e-form completion.

Budget amendments are an essential part of the budgetary process and are utilized in an effort to move funds from one account to another and, at times, to correct an accounting error that has been made.

While budget amendments are sometimes necessary, the effective school administrator readily understands the overuse of the adjustment and transfer process can send questionable signals and raise serious inquiries from business department personnel, district-level administrators, and even school board members, who in most systems have final approval over budgetary changes.

When amendments or transfers are necessary, the school administrator must move funds from one account to another to correct a previous posting by transferring a portion, if not all, of a balance from one account to another. Reflect on the previous technology-oriented scenario and note an above-basic allotment had been provided to the school to adjust for an unexpected increase in student enrollment. This allotment (over $10,000) could very well be transferred from the district level to the school and placed in the technology line item account.

Therefore, an adjustment or amendment would need to be submitted, with the funds being transferred to the proper account: technology equipment/software over $10,000. To facilitate the transfer of any funds and to further amend the school budget, administrators utilize standardized e-forms that have been approved by the school district. The e-form serves as a method of budgetary accountability and provides the necessary documentation, ensuring the adjustment and/or transfer will occur.

Final Thoughts

The budget development process, with its numerous components, is a legal mandate in most states. Effective, efficient, and essential budgeting practices are dependent upon skillful school leaders who know more than budgetary management. School leaders must not only understand fiscal accountability and control, they must also be aware of collection and deposit structures and budgetary systems. Moreover, school leaders must realize how the visionary component of school-based planning integrates with the budget development process and how they collaboratively function to build a stronger academic program that, in turn, positively impacts student achievement.

The budget development process is more than implementing and utilizing effective, efficient, and essential fiscal practices. The budget development process is an integral part of visioning and planning in which all members of the learning community have a voice, a stake, and a right to impact the academic success of students. Many decades ago, long before the concept of school-based budgeting gained popular acceptance in schools, Roe (1961) revealed the school budget is the translating of "educational needs into a financial plan which is interpreted to the public in such a way that when formally adopted, it expresses the kind of educational program the community is willing to support, financially and morally, for a one-year period" (p. 81).

Such a sentiment still couldn't be expressed any better more than sixty years later, other than to say it is hoped educational leaders find allocating money to support academic goals and student achievement to be a worthy investment—a great service to all members of the learning community!

Discussion Questions

1. How can a principal and instructional team utilize the sections "Steps to Performing an Information Analysis" and "Conducting a Needs Assessment" and Tables 6.2 and 6.3 to ensure a stronger technologically centered instructional program?

2. Most principals recognize their campus budget is limited relative to increased funding for technological reforms and enhancements. What can a principal and instructional team do to find additional, if not essential, funding sources? (Hint: Read the "Generated Income Sources" section). Be specific in your answer.
3. What is the purpose of a budget plan and how does it interact with the school action or improvement plan?
4. Examine the chapter section "Steps to Performing an Information Analysis." Explain how the steps integrate campus improvement planning with school-based budgeting.
5. Which components of the collection and deposit structure are essential to the budgetary handling of the school activity account? Support your answer. Are the noted procedures currently implemented within your school or simply out of date based on technological and digital advances? Check with your school principal and/or district chief financial officer.
6. Consider the purposes of accounting procedures and explain how such practices can assist school leaders in their quest of accounting for the expenditure of public funds.
7. Examine the "Technology Today: Effective, Efficient, and Essential Budgeting Required" section of the chapter and identify which of the section listings apply to your school. Explain how and by what means generated sources of income could aid in further enhancing technological development and innovation at your school. Be specific in your response.
8. How does this chapter relate to the Professional Standards for Educational Leaders (PSEL) as documented in Chapter 1? Which standard(s) are specifically relevant and why?

Case Study

Love That Principal!

The principal at Maynard G. Krebs School, Dr. Margaret MacDonald, spent the morning hours of a cold, snowy, wintry day thinking about how the school funds continued to be limited. Additional dollars were

(Continued)

(Continued)

needed for instructional supplies and materials dedicated to projects related to science, technology, engineering, and mathematics. She called her assistant principal, Bob Collins, into the office along with Zelda Gilroy (her budget clerk), Charmaine Schultz (the school's parent–teacher association president), and Thalia Menninger (the school's academic booster club president). Dr. MacDonald hoped these individuals would be able to generate ideas for funding the following science, technology, engineering, and mathematics (STEM) needs:

- manipulatives and teaching/learning kits
- cooperative learning centers
- digital readers and e-tablets
- virtual and augmented reality products
- simulation activities
- professional development for teacher training/support
- technology/digital-driven supplies, materials, and/or resources
- artificial intelligence
- use of hands-on robotics kits
- development of cybersecurity projects
- drones and high-altitude balloons for designated payloads
- telescopes to study planetary systems
- field trips to the NASA space flight center
- rockets constructed to complete a variety of space-inspired missions
- gamification

Dr. MacDonald and her team were excited to begin the work at hand. In fact, Charmaine Schultz whispered to Bob Collins, "Love that principal!". Bob grinned and said right back, "You bet! She means business and we'll find the money to help our students and teachers!"

Case Study Application

Utilize the "Generated Income Sources" section of this chapter and the specific segments regarding grants, fundraising, and crowdfunding to respond to the following queries.

1. Consider the circumstances at Maynard G. Krebs School and determine what potential grants available today (via an Internet search) might help alleviate the financial burden Dr. MacDonald and her team face when it comes to funding the STEM efforts on campus. Be specific in support of your answer.
2. Determine potential funding endeavors to help bolster the school's STEM efforts. How might differing funding be of benefit? Be specific and determine a funding example/process to incorporate at Maynard G. Krebs School. Then, detail the advantages and disadvantages of using said funding method in this particular example.
3. Both Charmaine Shultz and Thalia Menninger are determined to raise funds for the STEM projects at Maynard G. Krebs School. Generate ideas of potential fundraisers. Identify the pros and cons of your identified fundraising example(s) as related to this situation.
4. What does your district's school board policy stipulate regarding fundraising and crowdfunding? Be specific.
5. From the perspective of the budget clerk, Zelda Gilroy, think about what is right with potentially using fundraising, crowdfunding, and/or other approaches to the STEM-related project. What is wrong?
6. What technological and/or digitally driven resources, materials, and/or supplies are available today that could best assist with the school's STEM-oriented approach beyond those identified within this chapter and case study? How might these resources be funded?

7 Accounting, Auditing, Risk Factors, and Leadership Behaviors

Leadership is all about the right kind of behaviors—those that positively influence, gain followers' respect, make others successful, and pursue results!

—Anonymous

Accounting and Auditing Procedures

Proper accounting and auditing procedures serve as a protective process for school district administrators and personnel. These two processes, accounting and auditing, go hand in hand and serve as the critical elements in best safeguarding individuals and organizations from financial wrongdoing, suspicion, accusation, or even just innuendo (Sorenson, 2024; Sorenson & Goldsmith, 2006). Auditing serves four functions:

1. Auditing makes good business sense. Audit investigations are essential to determining if appropriate and legal expenditure of funds has occurred.
2. Auditing and the accompanying regular investigations provide written documentation to school administrators, superintendents, and board members who must be kept abreast of the financial dealings of the district and schools. Such documentation provides proof to the educational constituency (parents, taxpayers, state and federal governmental agencies) that the fiscal integrity of a school or district is sound, intact, and follows the dictates of law.
3. Auditing helps to detect human and technical error in the accounting process. In any school system, large or small, errors will occur, and the audit investigations delineate between accidental and intentional errors.
4. Auditing can be the guiding force that brings about necessary change to accounting procedures and financial operations in need of improvement.

Several types of auditing procedures have been developed to provide a system of checks and balances to an educational organization. The two most common are internal and external auditing.

Internal auditing is a self-checking process that typically provides monthly reports to the school board. These reports detail the financial status of the school district and, in most instances, reveal expenditures of the different schools within a district. Internal auditing is generally a continuous examination of a school's and district's accounting system in which a multiple-approval process is incorporated to safeguard against error or fraudulent practices.

External auditing is the formal accounting process by which a school's financial records are examined by a qualified and independent accountant—typically a certified public accountant. External audits are generally ordered on an annual basis, with an accounting firm spending anywhere from three to nine weeks conducting an extensive and exhaustive investigation that checks revenues and expenditures and further compares cash balances against encumbrances.

External auditing ensures all statutory and legal requirements are in good order. External audits provide reports and findings in written and presentation formats as well as fiscal and accounting recommendations to superintendents and school boards. Audits serve as a measurement of the trust factor in any educational organization by validating the fiscal management (good or bad) of a school system. The auditing process is more than good business; it is money well spent to better ensure the sound fiscal stewardship of a school and school system.

Fraudulent Practices

Fraudulent practice in the education business may not be an everyday occurrence. However, newspaper accounts regularly reveal that dishonest and unethical employees manage to divert thousands of dollars from school accounts into the pockets of the unscrupulous embezzler. School personnel may hear gossip about such capers but realize these types of dealings are not making the local newspaper or evening newscast. This is usually associated with the fact school systems do not want to provide unsolicited attention and unsettling fodder for community consumption. However, if you are a school leader of any tenure, you quickly recognize embezzling can very well happen during your watch. Therefore, the possible advent of such fraudulent actions makes it worthwhile to learn about the subject. School leaders would be well advised to examine the school's recordkeeping and auditing procedures to best negate any tempting prospects and looming loopholes.

Fraudulent practices are closely akin to an individual's ethical decision-making process, as revealed in Chapter 1 and Chapter 2. Hoban et al. (2018), for example, examined the topic of responsibility and two related considerations: discretion and accountability.

C. E. Johnson (2020) examined character and integrity. Both note a school leader must exhibit discretion and accountability by exemplifying high levels of honesty, trustworthiness, and responsibility that appropriately and discretely follow school policies and procedures.

What is the fraud triangle? The triangle visually represents a framework for identifying high-risk fraudulent situations or circumstances. The three corners of the triangle represent pressure, opportunity, and rationalizing. Each is described as follows:

1. **Pressure.** A financial need exists and serves as the catalyst that motivates an individual to commit a fraudulent act. For a school employee, for example, pressure to commit an illegal act may be related to a family member losing their job, having his or her house in foreclosure, medical bills that are continuously increasing due to a sick family member, gambling, or credit card abuse.
2. **Opportunity**. Opportunity serves as the open door or ability to commit an act of fraud. Opportunity increases with a lack of oversight or accountability. Opportunity occurs when fewer steps are necessary to commit the crime or when there are limited or no restrictions on access, oversight, and/or accountability. Simply, opportunity is viewed by the employee as the ability to execute a devious plan without being caught.
3. **Rationalizing**. Rationalizing occurs when a school employee recognizes committing a fraud can be justified—in his or her mind, of course. Most individuals who commit fraud consider themselves to be, and are viewed as, honest and trustworthy. However, they also view themselves as being victims of unusual or unjust circumstances and thus rationalize within their own minds that the fraudulent behavior or illegal activity is acceptable. Common rationalizations, verbalized after the fraudulent actor is caught, include the following:
    - "I needed the money."
    - "I deserved it."
    - "I'm only borrowing the funds and intend to pay it all back."
    - "I'm underpaid, overworked, and my principal is at fault because [he/she] doesn't pay any attention."
    - "I have family obligations."
    - "I must take care of my [child, parent, spouse, etc.]."
    - "My spouse is a gambler or can't control [his/her] spending habits."
    - "My medical expenses are astronomical."
    - "Our credit card debt is massive, and creditors are demanding repossession of goods or properties."

Accountability standards exemplifying the highest levels of ethical conduct must also be maintained. A perfect example was unfortunately showcased in a school district in which an associate superintendent for business and financial affairs entertained colleagues at a local men's club and subsequently charged lap-dancing expenses to the tune of $2,000 to the school district's credit card. The expectation for responsible, ethical behavior and personal moral standards quickly went by the wayside. The cost for such a personal indiscretion was serious: the loss of the associate superintendent's position and professional reputation, and the subsequent public humiliation of the individual and his family.

The district also suffered both internal turmoil and external criticism. This, in turn, negatively affected the public's confidence in the school district's leadership team and several school board members. Ultimately, the community outcry resulted in numerous administrative resignations, and several school board members who ran for reelection went down in defeat (Osborne et al., 1999).

Pause and Consider

"It Shouldn't Be a Problem!"—Credit Card Fraud and Accountability Questions

Millicent Lowe, principal of Shermer Boynton School, was perceived by the school community as an outstanding instructional leader. That is, until she was arrested and charged with three counts of theft by embezzlement for using a school credit card for personal expenditures. Principal Lowe used a district credit card for more than $15,000 worth of purchases for personal use, and another $28,200 was, at the time of her arrest, unaccounted for, according to Grace Harper, Cade County police investigator.

Prior to Detective Harper's involvement, a random audit by the Northern Lakes School District turned up a charge on the school district credit card issued to Principal Lowe at a store on the island of Maui, in Hawaii. The auditor continued to examine numerous charges over a twelve-week period and found other credit card charges that were not school-related expenses. The auditor, in the company of a district business officer, contacted Principal Lowe about the charges and Lowe stated she must have accidentally used the wrong credit card. She then offered to write a personal check to cover the $4,300 in charges found during the period of the school audit.

The auditor and school district business officer both declined to accept the check and returned to the district business offices to uncover other suspicious credit card charges dating over a three-year period. To make the scheme work, Principal Lowe would simply log into the district's budget and fiscal accounting system, upload associated receipts, add a corresponding budget code, and then click the "approve" button.

In addition to the Maui store charge during her trip to Hawaii, Principal Lowe also used the district credit card to purchase gift cards for family members and friends; auto rentals; summer European tours to England, France, and Italy; alcohol; cell phone services; computers and laptops for family members; clothing; and meals at different restaurants within the school district as well as in Hawaii and in cities across the nation as Principal Lowe and husband followed the Grand Lakes University football team, attending games each fall.

When Detective Harper asked Principal Lowe why she committed the credit card fraud, she responded, "I accidently used the district credit card for a purchase of shoes and when I realized nothing happened, it just became an easy thing to do. You know, no one was watching, no one seemed to care. So, I just kept on doing it. I was planning to pay the money back as soon as my husband returned to work following his layoff at the Grand Lakes Steel Mills three years ago; it shouldn't be a problem. I know other principals and teachers are doing the same thing!"

- Examine your school regulations and district board policy to determine how fraud and, more specifically, credit card fraud is addressed. How can this policy be enhanced or improved in the form of school-site regulation(s)?
- How does the fraudulent incident and Principal Lowe's explanation for theft as detailed in this scenario relate to the fraud triangle in Figure 7.1? Explain.
- How does this scenario violate the Professional Standards for Educational Leaders (PSEL) as identified in Chapter 1?
- Principal Lowe stated, "I know other principals and teachers are doing the same thing [committing credit card fraud]!" How might a school principal and/or district ensure fraud is not committed by school employees entrusted with credit cards? Need a few hints? See the forthcoming section titled "Credit Card Fraud."

FIGURE 7.1 The Fraud Triangle

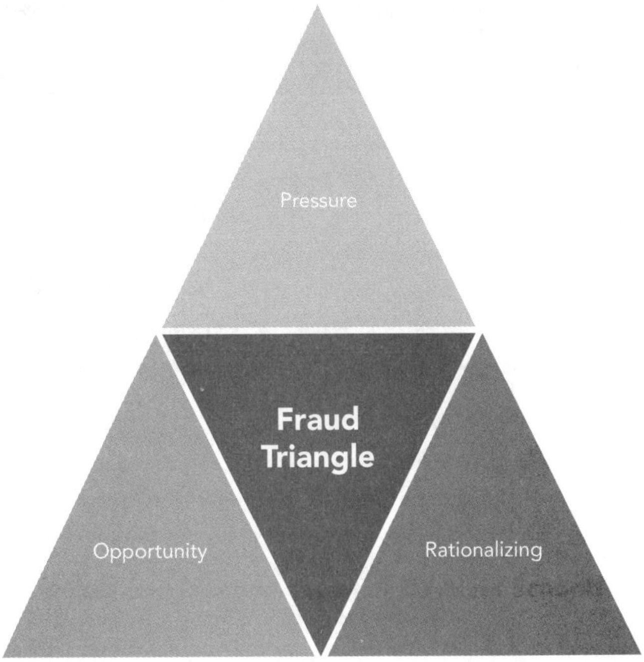

A second example of fraudulent behavior involved the superintendent of an urban southwestern school district. Conspiring to defraud the school district by securing a $450,000 sole-source contract under false pretenses, the superintendent was arrested at his office, handcuffed, and subsequently escorted by Federal Bureau of Investigation (FBI) agents to a federal courthouse where he was charged with conspiracy to commit mail fraud and aiding and abetting theft from instructional programs receiving federal funds. Charges called for up to twenty years in a federal prison. The superintendent resigned in disgrace to await federal prosecution and sentencing.

At the time, the same superintendent was leading numerous school officials in a scheme to fraudulently boost the district's test scores and attendance and graduation rates to meet federal accountability standards. Six years later, an associate superintendent, along with multiple other school leaders—including principals and assistant principals—continued to plead guilty or were facing charges of conspiracy to defraud the United States (Martinez, 2017).

What makes this fraudulent activity so blatantly wrong is the fact the entire scheme was based on pushing students out of school, placing them in wrong grade levels, improperly denying services to English language learners (ELLs), or deliberately and unashamedly denying students credit—all because these school leaders believed certain students would be unable to pass a state accountability exam.

Following an early release from prison, court documents reveal the former superintendent began a new and different career, working for a roofing company in a major metropolitan center on the opposite side of the state. During the former superintendent's career as a school district leader, his annual salary was more than $280,000. The new roofing company career earns him a net income of $5,000 per month, or $60,000 per year.

Additionally, the court ordered restitution in the amount of $1,500 per month from the former superintendent's net monthly income. He must repay the school system $180,000 (Harsha, 2023; KVIA.com, 2011). Truly this represents a loss of personal and professional perspectives, a colossal failure in leadership, and a sad fall from grace because of certain unethical, if not immoral, behaviors!

Three points to recognize and remember:

1. The effects of corrupt and fraudulent behaviors are frequently irreversible and typically long-lasting for both a school system and the fraudulent practitioner.
2. No one is above the law—no matter title or position.
3. School leaders have a moral obligation to ensure students are never placed in harm's way by any unethical, immoral, or illegal means or activity.

Frequent Types of Fraud in Schools

The most common perpetrators of fraud in schools and school systems today are principals, teachers, coaches, and superintendents. The most common reason for fraud relates to individuals having complete or near-complete control over monies, purchases, credit cards, and checks. As noted in Chapter 6, many school districts have become cashless entities, therefore effectively eliminating some theft. However, fraud continues to be widespread and, in far too many cases, easily enacted. Listed below are five commonly recognized types of fraud as identified by Casner (2021) for Weaver and Tidwell, L.L.P, along with information on how such schemes are perfected and, most importantly, how to prevent the ever-present temptation to steal.

Cash and Checks

The easiest and generally most undetectable type of fraud, cash and check fraud, often occurs when individuals such as secretaries or principals manage and have easy access to the campus student activity account. Granted, the average financial impact is often significantly smaller with this type of fraud than with other types, but these particular schemes are often difficult to detect as the unscrupulous can divert funds and alter financial records with some ease. Listed below are a few prevention tips.

- Ensure separate duties are conducted by separate personnel.
- Ensure robust financial accountability along with district policy or campus regulations that dictate allowable and unallowable purchases.
- Provide periodic training for those in charge of writing checks or handling cash.
- Carefully review all purchases by demanding receipts for accountability purposes.
- Dictate that all student activity cash coming into the school office must be deposited on the day of receipt.

Vendor Kickbacks

A frequent means of fraud, vendor kickbacks are generally associated with those in decision-making positions, such as superintendents, principals, department chairpersons, and even school board members. Kickbacks often come in the form of "under the table" cash payments, equipment for personal use or application, and job opportunities. Watch for the following red flags to better detect vendor kickbacks:

- higher costs for services rendered
- payment for no services provided
- sudden and expensive purchases of personal items (furniture, housing fixtures and contractor services, outdoor/farm equipment, fencing, land acreage) that are often far too expensive for the salary of the individual or in very expensive locales, such as on a lake, in the mountains, by the shore, etc.

Ways to prevent vendor fraud include the following:

- Vendor fraud can be prevented by requiring background checks for all vendors to verify and identify, at the very least, potential conflicts of interest or legal entanglements.
- Ensure that the securing of vendors and the payment for the vendor service is the responsibility of more than one individual. These functions should be regularly rotated among different employees, and leaders should confirm the individual ordering supplies or services from vendors is not the same person who approves the vendor invoices.

Phishing Scams

Phishing scams are quite prevalent today and may target homes, businesses, and definitely schools or school systems. Such scams are perpetrated by external parties that electronically divert monies intended for legitimate vendors, contractors, and/or bond payments (Casner, 2021). Casner reports the average loss to phishing scams equates to $2.1 million, the largest fraud amount of any of the five schemes identified.

How do phishing scams work? Generally e-mails, disguised as coming from legitimate vendors, are sent to school personnel requesting changes to payment structures. Often phishing scams will involve the fraudster colluding with school or district personnel who have regular access to payment funds. Furthermore, phishing scams often correlate with district transparency on websites. Such transparency is often required by law, thus making it easier for a fraudster to divert fund payments.

Phishing scams are not only becoming more prevalent, they have definitely become much more sophisticated. By what means? The scammers intercept funds before a school or district even knows the funds were stolen, and sophisticated software can readily mask the scammer's identity and location. To make things even worse, the scammers are often working overseas, which makes it difficult to recover stolen dollars even if the culprit is identified.

To prevent phishing scams, schools and districts must do the following:

- Require dual factor verification. Yes, this a pain in the neck for personnel, but it's an absolute necessity for fraud prevention.
- Always confirm with a vendor any payment differentiations are school or district or vendor authorized.
- Restrict access to vendor payment processes or procedures.
- Implement mandatory personnel training regarding the identification of potential e-mail phishing scams.
- Require personnel to report any suspicious e-mails.
- Invest in technological filtering software that filters phishing scams.
- Develop policies regarding the reporting of phishing threats to IT department personnel as well as to district or local law enforcement agencies.
- Remember, don't get hooked when phishing occurs!

Payroll Checks and Unauthorized School-Site Check Schemes

Payroll schemes are not common at the school-site level but do occur more typically at district offices. A perfect example is a forged payroll check scheme. At the campus level, payroll is generally never a responsibility or expectation of office personnel. However, the writing of unauthorized checks can easily occur if districts permit the writing of checks at the school site. Such a fraudulent activity can occur quite simply. Certain skilled individuals—say an office secretary or clerk with check-writing responsibilities—can forge signatures. The secretary or clerk, who has easy checkbook access, falsifies a principal's signature and makes the check out to cash or to a local merchant who is willing to exchange cash for the check. A check-writing scheme involving checks made out to a fictitious vendor is also not uncommon, especially if a principal never looks at or reconciles the campus bank statements. A few prevention tips to avoid unauthorized checks being written include the following:

- Again, ensure a separation of duties with more than one individual double-checking the other(s) in terms of process and procedure. Divide the responsibilities and conquer the scheme!
- At the district level, the direct deposit of personnel/payroll checks must be the norm.
- At the campus level, regularly (each month) conduct a thorough review of the bank reconciliation statement. Doing so better enables a school leader to detect abnormalities or anomalies in check-writing and deposit procedures.
- Remember, inspect what you expect!

Credit Card Fraud

Credit card fraud in schools continues to be a regular occurrence. Sad, but true! Just six years ago, with the publication of the third edition of this text, credit card fraud was the one and only identified fraudulent activity affecting schools, although we did address cash and check fraud as well. How fast different types of fraud have spread in schools! The rise of so many different fraudulent schemes in so few years between text editions serves as a prime and frightening example.

Recognize that as more school systems move from campus checks and bank reconciliation processes to online automated banking, the number of district credit cards issued to principals—and teachers, too—has increased. With the increase of credit card distributions, an alarming increase in credit card fraud has occurred.

Such fraud has raised not only accountability issues but also problems related to cultural norms—or, in the case of credit card fraud, cultural abnormal behaviors! It would take too much time and space—and consulting with psychiatrists and psychologists—to address the issue of abnormal behaviors in society today. However, what can and must be addressed are methods by which accountability standards and preventions can be put in place to better ensure credit card fraud does not occur. Listed below are a few recommendations.

- Limit the number of credit card users in the school district.
- Ensure district policy and campus regulation changes are made, reviewed with school district credit card holders, and enforced. When said changes fail to make sense or simply work ineffectively in terms of good business sense, reform them.
- Establish a credit card usage code of conduct. Statements related to clearly stipulated rules and procedures—what behaviors will not be tolerated—must be included within any code of conduct.
- Audit regularly (monthly) for purchases that were not approved before payment or not approved at all.
- Monitor employee behaviors. Investigate immediately any behaviors that do not look or feel right. If something doesn't appear appropriate, chances are it is not!
- Have great confidence in the accounting system. Remember, trust but verify! If trust and confidence in the system is not present, make changes in software and implement human detection processes as well.
- Examine spending practices at the district and school levels. Restrict certain credit card purchases, such as food, travel, lodging, and so on, unless preapproved by district business officers.
- Implement districtwide virtual conferences detailing accountability procedures and related consequences for inappropriate credit card usage.
- Ensure credit card purchases are from authorized vendors.
- Establish guidelines for purchases of electronic hardware and software. No items in this category should be made with a district credit card—only by means of approved requisition forms (Halsne & Koeberl, 2016; Worth, 2015).

Embezzlement

Embezzlement has been defined as the fraudulent appropriation of property by an individual to whom it has been entrusted (Sorenson & Goldsmith, 2006; U.S. Department of Justice Archives, 2020). The operative term within this definition is *entrusted*. The embezzler is usually a trusted employee who is taking advantage of a school leader's confidence or their lack of attention to detail. Embezzlers have a method of operation, a thinking process that is frequently thrust upon unsuspecting schools or school systems and school leaders. Embezzlers often believe they are

Embezzlers often believe they are smarter than the school leader, and they generally perceive themselves as being someone who can outwit a less-than-sterling school business department.

smarter than the school leader, and they generally perceive themselves as being someone who can outwit a less-than-sterling school business department.

Embezzlers are more likely to be

- female (64 percent of the time);
- employed as a clerk in a school business, finance, budgeting, bookkeeping, or accounting office or department; a school club (booster) official; a parent–teacher association officer (frequently a treasurer) or a school principal;
- acting alone (84 percent of the time);
- well dressed; and
- hidden in a single office or cubicle (L. Green, 2016; KEVGroup, 2020;).

Fraud and Embezzlement: How the Money Vanishes!

Go to a favorite search engine and type in "embezzlement and the school activity account" and you'll find more than 46.6 million results! Why? This particular act of fraud and theft at the school-site level is rampant across the United States today. Probably not in your state or school system, you think? Think again!

The authors selected the first fifteen postings as a sampling of where the most recent embezzlement of school activity accounts has occurred: Washington, New York, Texas, Wisconsin, California, Connecticut, Ohio, Nebraska, Tennessee, Kentucky, Mississippi, Georgia, Virginia, Michigan, and Oklahoma. That is just fifteen of the fifty states. Is this type of criminal activity occurring in the remaining thirty-five states? Absolutely! Why? And what will stop it? The *why* elicits a simple response: the opportunity is there, financial pressure is a very common incentive, and thieves can readily justify their stealing—even from students!

Recognize that schools across the United States readily collect *billions* of dollars in student activity fees and other money collections. School fees and associated monetary collections continue to be largely paid in cash and are often handled by multiple staff, so there remains to date a great opportunity to embezzle cash on hand. While such misappropriation of school dollars often occurs in small amounts, the frequency of reported cases of embezzlement in schools is one of the highest of all businesses. Now consider the following scenario and pay attention to the recommendations on how to prevent embezzlement of funds from school activity accounts, because your school just might be next!

There's No Right Way to Do Something Wrong!

One principal embezzled from her school's activity accounts more than $700,000 over a period of seven years. This money was taken from the collected funds of students and parents—monies dedicated to benefiting students. The principal also robbed the students, faculty, administration, and families of their self-worth and dignity by falsifying standardized test scores. She was ultimately charged with embezzlement of more than $750,000 in student activity account funds, four charges of fraud, and one count of conspiracy. When the judge's gavel fell, the principal had to pay back $500,000 of the $750,000 embezzled dollars and serve a forty-month sentence in federal prison—a sentence that could have been as much as fifteen years! How did it all happen?

Patty Ann Landers was hired as a teacher by the Cleaver Consolidated School System in the month of June. By August, she was promoted to an assistant principal position. Within two years, she was a principal. Later, before her embezzlement escapades were discovered, Landers was promoted to assistant superintendent.

Landers was admired and respected. She worked diligently—albeit unethically—to turn around a school where test scores were regularly low. She was actively involved in the community where she, her husband, and their adult children were considered to be pillars of a local church. But Landers, using student funds, purchased expensive clothing for herself and her family, took her family and friends to vacations in the Caribbean, remodelled her home as well as the home of one of her sons, and purchased at least two luxurious automobiles. Life was nice for Landers—really nice—especially on a principal's salary!

The nice life began to unravel right after Landers was promoted to assistant superintendent. Due to board policy, a mandated audit of the campus budget and funds occurred. Over the next few months, Landers was investigated, arrested, and charged. Following a total of four years of court appearances, plea bargaining, and verdicts, Landers was sentenced for the criminal acts she committed, all at the expense of the students she was charged to serve and protect.

Prior to the U. S. Marshals taking Landers into custody and transferring her to prison, she broke down and cried out, "My actions are nothing

(Continued)

(Continued)

more than hurtful and shameful. I'm especially shamed that my mother, father, and my husband and family had to witness all of this." Her husband, Charles, cursed the media in an interview and then went on to divorce his wife of forty years.

Landers was ordered to pay 25 percent of her retirement income to recompensate the $500,000 debt as part of the plea agreement. Tragically, the criminal efforts, investigations, and ultimate conviction of Landers also led to criminal convictions of embezzlement for five other individuals who had worked for or with Landers.

The Top Ten Embezzlement Prevention Tips

1. Realize that lax control of the school activity account opens the door to embezzlement.
2. Recognize the warning signs of embezzlement, including
   - continued deficit balances,
   - corrective actions bringing no improvements,
   - a lack of communication with the district business office,
   - a lack of organization at the school-site business office, and
   - failed school leadership oversight.
3. Create annual budgets that are monitored and reconciled by a group of people, especially the inflow and outflow of club (activity account) dollars.
4. As previously noted, school leaders must dictate more than one person maintain the activity accounts and create a division of duties to ensure separate and independent oversight.
5. Regularly rotate club officers responsible for financial control processes.
6. Require all monies collected be immediately deposited.
7. Dictate a two-signature process be implemented relative to all written checks if check-writing remains a campus procedure.
8. Stipulate annual independent audits occur with all outside school-related organizations, such as parent–teacher associations or booster clubs.
9. Ensure appropriate accounting and record-keeping procedures.

10. Demand all individuals who touch school/student monies be bonded to prevent losses from embezzlement. Ensure the school district purchases fidelity bond insurance; $1 million per occurrence and $2 million aggregate are common recommendations.

Cures for the Common Scheme

School administrators must understand the school activity account can quickly become a nightmare if appropriate bookkeeping practices are not in place, followed, and maintained. Funds collected from various school-related activities must be accounted for, as money received and spent, in relation to the different activity accounts in which said dollars have been allocated. For example, money collected from ticket sales related to the school athletic banquet must be placed in the athletic account, and money collected from the sale of school pictures for the purpose of postal services must be placed in the postal account.

Common schemes are typically quite simple to employ because the trusted employee has generally won the confidence of a school or district leader. In fact, the best embezzlers are often the individuals who are given more authority than a position dictates. These individuals have also realized that the ability to embezzle is only limited by their own imagination. Most embezzlement at the school level involves the pocketing of cash received through activity fund–related dollars coming into the school office—especially in relation to differing types of fundraising programs and efforts.

The theft of cash is quick and easy, and it is often difficult to detect. An act of embezzlement is accomplished by a trusted employee who simply doesn't enter the cash receipt in the accounts receivable records. A perfect example involves cash received from a club sponsor who is not interested in the details associated with recordkeeping and thus simply trusts the administrative office clerical staff, stating, "Count this for me, please; I've got to get back to class—my students are taking a test!" To prevent this scenario and the associated monetary temptation, a school principal should insist all cash received be accompanied by a written receipt of the calculated dollar amount, and a cash receipt must be provided by the "trusted" employee to the club or activity sponsor immediately upon receipt of the cash funds.

Another preventive step is a spot-check process instituted by the school leader. This process further assures cash received is cash recorded. In other words, the school leader needs to purposefully check in, on a regular basis, with school activity or club sponsors to determine when funds are coming into the school and, most notably, into the school office. The school leader should also carefully monitor the bookkeeping records, always looking for suspicious signs of fraud and theft. The school leader should also understand that unexpected internal audits by district business office personnel can often prevent employee embezzlement efforts.

Finally, never underestimate the vulnerability of a school or district to an act of embezzlement. An ounce of prevention may very well be the cure for the common scheme. Effective school leaders must recognize that the ten precautionary practices listed below can inhibit and discourage embezzlement.

1. Ensure individuals who expend monies are not custodians of accounting for said monies.
2. Review all bank statement reconciliation procedures.
3. Keep two separate and independently maintained sets of bookkeeping records as related to receipts and expenditures.
4. Provide effective and appropriate reconciliation of receipts and accounts.
5. Never sign blank checks before leaving for a conference or vacation.
6. Develop and utilize bookkeeping policies or regulations.
7. Always utilize bonded employees only.
8. Cross-train office personnel to perform bookkeeping responsibilities.
9. Employ an independent accountant to conduct regular internal and external audits.
10. Review the detailed expectations for appropriate and ethical office bookkeeping standards and procedures with office staff on a regular basis.

Special note: Realize that all ten of these practices may be null and void in today's world of school business transactions. As previously revealed in Chapter 6, many school systems have initiated cashless software systems relative to booster club and other fundraising efforts as a means of combating fraud and embezzlement. Are all cashless software programs free from fraud and/or embezzlement? Absolutely not. Such programs are preventative, not foolproof. Remember, hackers are highly prevalent today and are always scheming when it comes to finding an online opportunity.

Other Risk Factors

While an incident of monetary theft or embezzlement may not be directly tied to the school administrator, a public perception will definitely exist that such a fraudulent practice occurred on the administrator's watch and, therefore, the administrator shares responsibility. Some school leaders take a lax approach to budgeting procedures by delegating all or part of the budget process and accompanying tasks to others. They may simply declare, "Instruction is my bag" and, as a result, neglect important budget details. Such thinking or action can very well be a costly risk factor, if not an ultimate criminal mistake.

Appropriate auditing and accounting procedures, while never completely foolproof in eliminating the potential for fraud and embezzlement, do serve to assure the educational clientele of the fiscal state of a school and district, and such procedures further discourage unethical practices. Effective school leaders understand any misuse or misappropriation of school funds can quickly destroy public trust. Most importantly, the effective school leader acknowledges any and all unethical, immoral, and fraudulent activities can very well derail, if not promptly conclude, a career that was once perceived to be most promising and enduring. Think back to the career-ending fraudulent behaviors of the former school superintendent and Principal Patty Ann Landers.

The Leadership Role: Ethical and Moral Behaviors

We live in an era in which cultural norms are shifting, woefully, from a society built upon genuine respect for one another to one in which far too many individuals are abusive to those who lead our schools and school districts. The latter group often prefers a scorched earth approach to social interaction. Why build people up when it is easier to tear them down? Why offer a simple truth when a disparaging lie is more convenient and, of course, damaging, if not completely damning?

Far too often in this day and age of incivility and a lack of public decorum, stories surface about community members blatantly attacking leaders and working to destroy credibility and character simply because these "concerned" citizens didn't get their way. Civic rage has become a societal norm—often an accepted practice in public interactions. Sadly, school leaders and teachers are not exempt from such mistreatment. Many ethical and moral school leaders become burned out and seek to escape their leadership role not because of more money elsewhere, but because they are tired of the abuse. For school leaders, it is easy to become discouraged by the brokenness and despair observed in society today. The prevailing disrespectful manners and pervasive methods and behaviors all too frequently reveal a callous disregard for the harm done to others.

Donahue (2022) suggests ethics are a type of guide people must use to ensure their behavior is morally correct. Ethical behaviors aid leaders in their actions toward others; these are behaviors intended for the greater good. Donahue also stipulates ethics not only guide behaviors, ethics provide a set of principles that assist leaders in making decisions, solving problems, handling conflict, and performing admirably in daily life.

Ethics not only guide behaviors, ethics provide a set of principles that assist leaders in making decisions, solving problems, handling conflict, and performing admirably in daily life.

Cooper (2012) proclaimed, "Modern society is preoccupied with action, to the exclusion of reflection about values, morals, and principles" (p. xi). Question: What is important about Cooper's statement? Answer: We know Cooper is correct! We also recognize something has to give; something has to change; some cultural normalcy must prevail upon our society and guide individuals in their actions within our schools and school systems. We also know a Biblical truth: "Neither shall you allege the example of the many as an excuse for doing wrong!"

Cooper (2012) further related that "principals must direct the activities of those under their supervision . . . and monitor performance. In turn, principals are accountable for clearly defining the assigned duties and are held accountable for the fulfillment of any assignment" (p. 68). Tschannen-Moran (2014) has asserted it is the principal who is responsible for advancing a school's vision in an ethical, moral, and trustworthy manner. Moreover, think back to Chapter 1 and *PSEL 2: Ethics and Professional Norms*. How does this standard relate to this chapter? Now consider ethical questions that must be raised relative to the different chapter scenarios.

With regard to unethical behaviors, C. E. Johnson (2020) asserts that principals must never be the following:

- deceitful (lying and giving false or misleading information)
- selfish (blaming followers and making them into scapegoats)
- disregarding (ignoring normal standards of responsibility or having an obvious disdain for followers)
- imperious (creating a master–servant relationship in which school leaders believe they can do whatever they desire because they are superior to their followers)

To conclude this chapter section, describe the key principles or values that define your personal vision of good moral and ethical behavior. How does your personal vision relate to the PSEL? Also, reflect upon your own district regulations or school board policies. Which might apply to the situations detailed throughout this chapter?

What's a Principal to Do, or How Must a Principal Behave?

Let's now return to the question that has been posed in previous chapters: What's a principal to do? The authors—who have both been in the education business more than forty-five years—have some recommendations for answering that question. The very best, the most exceptional of school leaders offer a character example based upon exhibiting the following character traits:

- **Genuine and caring.** *Genuine* is much more than just a passing term when it comes to leadership. It is a *we* thing, a statement of what *we* must be as school leaders: *We* make a living by what *we* get. *We* make a life by what *we* give. Are you genuinely giving or duplicitously getting? Being genuine and giving and caring is the right way to lead!

- **Dependable, reliable, and responsible.** *Dependability*, *reliability*, and *responsibility* may very well be three of the most important words in a school leader's tool kit of appropriate actions. School leaders are frequently confronted with issues that demand prompt action. They are depended upon to make decisions that are in the best interest of students and the entire learning community. School leaders must be reliable in identifying a problem, confronting an issue, and deciding on a response. Thus, a school leader defines her or his administrative responsibility by asking themselves a simple question: "Am I dependable and reliable?"

- **Trustworthy**. A trustworthy person is defined as one who is ethical and moral in all aspects of life, both personal and professional. There's an old saying, a most demeaning one, about those of us in education: "There are those who *do*, and then there are those who *teach*." We are much more than that! Our credo must be that of longtime educational leader Wilhour (1998), who said, "I teach, I lead. While students may not always recall what I taught, they will remember what I stood for as a teacher and leader!"

- **Transparent.** Simply defined, a school leader is transparent when his or her actions are clear, obvious, apparent, aboveboard, and/or visible. The authors believe transparency in leadership is key to restoring faith in school principals. When transparency is ignored, a distrust of the school leader develops, as does a critical sense of insecurity among followers.

- **Task and relationship oriented.** Task-oriented school leaders focus on planning, scheduling, coordinating meetings and activities, and providing necessary resources, supplies, and technical assistance. Relationship-oriented principals are supportive and helpful, exhibiting trust, confidence, friendliness, good humor, and consideration. They care, keep faculty and staff informed, and show appreciation. Today, school leaders must be all this and more! Leaders must be sincere in building up and maintaining the personal worth and importance of others without negating realistic task-related goals and expectations.

- **Even-tempered.** Personality affects leadership and followership. School leaders who have a calm disposition and do not belittle others or issue personal attacks are much more likely to receive helpful and timely information from faculty and staff. Authoritative leadership lessens legitimacy and creates in others a decreased sense of psychological identification. An uneven temperament or a narcissistic temperament is much more likely to result in a demand for loyalty and faculty and staff running scared. Instead, what do the best leaders do? They *earn* loyalty by showing respect, care, and interest. If people are working in fear, they will make bad decisions to the detriment of the leader, the organization, and themselves.

- **Student centered and achievement oriented.** Effective school leadership is all about placing students first and foremost in all thinking and decision making. No ifs, ands or buts! The best administrative leaders never overlook their students. The authors repeatedly shared with their faculty members that students always come first, then faculty, and then parents. Being student centered is an absolute. However, school leaders must also be achievement oriented. This means exhibiting leadership behaviors that are demanding yet supportive, setting challenging academic goals, and continually seeking methods to improve performance and achievement.

Mungal and Sorenson (2020) postulate that educational leaders face numerous dilemmas of differing dimensions on a regular basis. The best leaders recognize these dilemmas as opportunities for doing what is right, not necessarily what is expedient. School leaders have an obligation to set ethical and moral examples for the organizations they serve. Those leaders who do not honor integrity, those who fail to establish truth and who further negate moral reasoning, are the same leaders who fail to inspire honesty and ethical practice in others. Such inappropriate behaviors in the education business lead to moral abandonment, pure selfishness, and the ultimate in career derailment.

Those leaders who do not honor integrity, those who fail to establish truth and who further negate moral reasoning, are the same leaders who fail to inspire honesty and ethical practice in others.

Numerous years ago, a Harris Poll reported 89 percent of employees surveyed believed it was important for leaders to be upright, honest, and ethical in their behaviors. However, only 41 percent indicated their current leader had such characteristics (Vamos & Jackson, 1989). Such an indictment serves to this day to underscore the need for strong character and ethical behavior in the school leadership business. Followers place their trust in a leader who models integrity, and when leaders compromise their moral and ethical values, they risk losing the respect they so readily deserve (Sorenson, 2024).

What is known about ethics is striking: "Ethics has to do with what leaders do and who leaders are" (Northouse, 2021, p. 378). "Fast and loose" behaviors frequently lead to devastating professional and personal consequences. While the daily pressures of life and career are often overwhelming, the effective school leader must remain an individual of committed character, integrity, and personal ethics. Leaders can ill afford to ignore strong moral and ethical margins because the aforementioned stresses can compromise the decision-making processes.

When such a compromise occurs, a leader's character is terribly strained, revealing flaws, cracks, and defects that in turn allow the leader to be susceptible to deception (lying and cheating), inappropriate behaviors (sexual affairs), questionable or illegal actions (embezzlement), and a general lack of personal accountability (Goldsmith & Sorenson, 2005; Sorenson, 2007; Sorenson, 2024). See the chapter-concluding case study, "Sex, Money, and a Tangled Web Woven," for a real-life account. Remember, truth is often stranger than fiction!

Professional Behavior, Personal Integrity, and Appropriate Ethical and Moral Conduct

Professional behavior, personal integrity, and appropriate ethical and moral conduct must be the defining qualities of any leader. Nothing less will do. If trust and integrity serve as the paramount bond between school administration and faculty, what guidelines or principles can better ensure ethical conduct and moral leadership? Here are five targeted areas for serious leadership consideration:

1. **Show respect.** True leaders earn respect by showing respect. When leaders fail to respect followers, they fail to understand the main goal of leadership, which is leading! This may seem quaint, but effective leaders provide affirmation, attention, esteem, care, and concern—all inherently related to respect. Respect has been described by Northouse (2021) as granting credibility to the ideas of others and treating others in a way that makes them feel valued and competent.

2. **Demonstrate integrity.** Whatever qualities, skills, or talents a leader may possess, if they lack integrity it is a serious flaw. Yukl and Gardner (2019) advance the theory that leaders who demonstrate high levels of integrity are more credible, more open, more collaborative, more receptive to receiving bad news or negative feedback, and less likely to be consumed with impressing their superiors at the expense of others.

3. **Exhibit honesty.** Honesty is best defined in relation to what it is not, to what an effective leader cannot be: deceitful, untrustworthy, and fraudulent. The leader who exhibits honesty reveals a genuine honorableness in character and action.

4. **Resist temptations.** The moral and ethical strength of any school leader is often tested by the many temptations in life. Resistance is often accompanied by endurance. When a leader is close to temptation, a loss of perspective has occurred. Resisting temptation serves to make a school leader more respected, honest, and endearing to others, who furthermore perceive the leader to be an individual who possesses the highest level of integrity and moral character.

5. **Provide service.** The effective school leader is one who is involved in servant leadership. The servant leader is one who

The best school leaders are always making appropriate decisions by upholding legal, moral, and ethical behaviors.

is willing to empathize and understand by listening to, by observing, and by assisting others within the learning community (Blanchard et al., 2018). The late DePree (2003), in his classic read *Leading Without Power*, asserts servant leadership provides for a level of tolerance by recognizing the strengths and talents of others when their weaknesses and mistakes may be more than obvious (Sorenson, 2024).

LEADERSHIP BEHAVIORS

Now, some serious advice for the educational leader: The best school leaders are always making appropriate decisions by upholding legal, moral, and ethical behaviors. This is true even in an era when a general cynicism exists regarding the integrity of those in leadership positions. Principals who fail to espouse strong personal ethics and appropriate moral values will find it very difficult to be honored and respected as leaders. All school leaders would be wise to consider and remember the following adage, as no words of advice could ring truer:

> *It's important that people know what you stand for. It's equally important that they know what you won't stand for.*
>
> —Mary Waldrop (Hughes et al., 2021)

Final Thoughts

Proper accounting and auditing procedures serve as a protective process for school district administrators and personnel. Fraudulent practices *do* occur, even in education. Such practices typically relate to pressure, opportunity, and/or rationalization on the embezzler's part. The effects of fraudulent activities are often irreversible and long-lasting. School leaders have a moral obligation to ensure students are never placed in harm's way by any unethical, immoral, or illegal means or activity.

Five different types of fraud have become regular occurrences in the school business, as has embezzlement. There are ten embezzlement preventions identified within this chapter that must be initiated at the campus level. School leaders must never underestimate the vulnerability of a school or district to an act of fraud or embezzlement. Proper accounting and auditing is the best medicine for deceitful behaviors and activities.

School leaders must exhibit ethical and moral behaviors at all times. The very best educational leaders are genuine and caring, dependable and reliable, trustworthy, transparent, task and relationship oriented, even-tempered, and student centered and achievement oriented. These leaders must show respect, demonstrate integrity, exhibit honesty, resist temptations, and provide service.

Discussion Questions

1. Reflect back to Chapter 6 and consider which of the components of the collection and deposit structure are essential to the budgetary handling of the school activity account? Support your answer.
2. Consider the purposes of accounting procedures and explain how such practices can assist school leaders in their quest of accounting for the expenditure of public funds.
3. What precautions should a school leader take with regard to the possibility of embezzlement? In what ways is your school vulnerable to this budgetary risk factor and how would you as a school leader address the identified vulnerabilities?
4. Consider the chapter section "Frequent Types of Fraud in Schools" and share which one of the five commonly recognized frauds is most likely to affect schools and school leaders. Have you observed any of the noted types of fraud in your school? Explain.
5. Fraudulent practices have been described as being closely akin to an individual's ethical decision-making process. How does *PSEL 2*, identified in Chapter 1, support this statement?
6. How does this chapter relate to the Professional Standards for Educational Leaders (PSEL) as documented in Chapter 1? Which standard(s) are specifically relevant and why?

Case Study

Sex, Money, and a Tangled Web Woven

Dr. Edgar Buchannen was the principal at Fullerton Peak High School in the suburban community of Gibsonville. He had been in this position of instructional leadership for nearly five years. Previously he had experienced a very successful principalship at Woodson Middle School in a major metropolitan area just north of the state capital. Dr. Buchannen had worked diligently with his new faculty at Fullerton to raise student

(Continued)

(Continued)

academic achievement from low performing to a significantly higher state department standard of accountability. Such a task had not been easy, but Dr. Buchannen was convinced he and his team—along with the students at Fullerton—had cleared a most difficult hurdle.

In the interim, Dr. Buchannen developed a great working relationship with Betsy Emery, the school's bookkeeping and attendance clerk. The two had clicked from their first day together, and they really appreciated each other's work ethic. One Saturday morning, Eddie—as he had asked Betsy to call him—came in early to catch up on a few budgeting issues while Betsy was completing the student demographic information needed for the next scheduled round of statewide testing. Both were pleased to see one another working on the important tasks at hand, and soon they took a break to enjoy a morning doughnut and cup of coffee. Betsy complained of a neck ache from working all morning to enter the demographic data into the computer system, and Eddie quickly offered to massage her neck. Betsy did not object.

Over the next few months, a steamy affair developed, although the two tried to keep any suggestion of impropriety away from the office. Betsy's marriage was falling apart, and although Eddie was married with three children of his own, the two continued their secret romance. With Betsy's failing marriage, she had developed—along with her husband, who had a serious gambling problem—credit card debts to the tune of $225,000.

Betsy was in deep trouble since these financial complications were in her name, and the collection agencies were demanding payment or repossession of tangible assets. What she needed was cash, and she needed it fast. As the romance grew between Eddie and Betsy, so too did a little problem Betsy had at work: She was regularly taking money from the school's different activity accounts, such as athletics, drama, band, choir, and even the "cola wagon," which took in hundreds of dollars at the varsity football game each Friday night.

Eddie had no clue about these embezzlement efforts until one evening when Betsy broke down in tears and told him he needed to help her get out of her financial predicament. He grew furious and yelled, "Help you? Wait a minute, aren't you the one stealing from the district? Don't involve me in your petty theft crimes!" Betsy, with a steely-eyed stare, retorted, "Don't play games with me, Mr. Self-Righteous. You're the one cheating on your wife, you two-faced fraud. You help me or else!"

Thus began a criminal partnership conceived in a mutual distrust of one another and based on some very questionable ethical and moral standards. From that point forward, a dangerous game of "borrowing" money, with every intention of paying back the stolen funds, escalated to a point of no return. The "borrowed" dollars never found their way back into the accounts, and the cover-up only lasted until someone in the district business office caught on to this scheme built on lies, deceit, misjudgement, and unethical practices.

Case Study Application

1. What probable repercussions will Dr. Edgar Buchannen and Betsy Emery face as a result of their actions? Explain the risk factors associated with their behaviors.
2. Cooper (2012) examines two approaches to maintaining responsible conduct in organizations: internal and external controls. *External control* has been described as responding to an unethical situation by developing new rules, rearranging the organizational structure, or establishing more cautious monitoring procedures. *Internal control* is often described as increasing preservice and in-service training programs or placing ethical leadership discussions on local meeting agendas. Which of these two policy perspectives would best be associated with this case study and why?
3. What legal implications are at issue in this case study? Which laws, education codes, or board policies have been broken or infringed upon? Give specific examples and explanations.
4. From the perspective of a school leader, how could the act of embezzlement presented in this case study have been prevented? Identify specific precautionary practices you would incorporate.
5. Northouse (2021) defines *ethics* as a "system of rules or principles that guide us in making decisions about what is 'right or wrong' and 'good or bad' in a particular situation" (p. 424). He further stipulates ethics provide "a basis for understanding what it means to be a morally decent human being" (p. 424). Is Dr. Buchannen a morally decent human being? Support your answer and relate it to the PSEL.
6. What is the possible impact on the school district of the actions described in the case study? Support your response from both a budgetary and political perspective.

Site-Based Decision Making, the Budget Coding Structure and Applications, and Other Budgetary Considerations

8

All of us are smarter than any one of us!

—Japanese proverb attributed to Deming (2000, p. 114)

Site-Based Decision Making

School leaders of the 21st century must know how to work within the political functions of educational organizations and be highly skilled in operating in arenas of competition, conflict, problem solving, and decision making—and all in a timely fashion (Ball, 2022; Bambrick-Santoyo, 2018; Sorenson, 2024). Such thinking exemplifies how school leaders must utilize differing strategies for working with the learning community and readily correlates with the statement attributed to W. Edwards Deming in the introductory quote. Deming identified personnel as the key to program quality. He believed that working collaboratively with employees to help them perform better—making decisions and solving problems as a team—and placing importance on the gathering of data were the essential keys to organizational and individual improvement (Hughes et al., 2021; Sorenson, 2021; Sorenson & Goldsmith, 2009; Sorenson et al., 2011).

One of the most effective strategies to be incorporated by a school leader in the budget development process is the site-based decision-making (SBDM) process, as this approach to school leadership is superior to the autocratic process (in which followers do not play a role in defining the problem or in generating a solution or decision) and likewise exceeds the consultative process (where followers are consulted but the leader makes the decision).

What we do know about decision making relates to the concept that a high-quality decision has a direct and measurable impact on an organization (Hoy & Miskel, 2012; Northouse, 2021; Sorenson, 2024). When the SBDM process is properly implemented, there is a total quality component to a decision—generally one in which the decision made has improved budgeting and positively impacted services to the clientele (the students, parents, faculty and staff, and the overall learning community). Visioning, planning, developing, implementing, and continuously evaluating a school budget must be an extension of the leader–follower collaborative decision-making dimension. Consider the words of Edward L. Bernays: "I must follow the people. Am I not their leader?" (Hughes et al., 2021, p. 389). He might have added, "I must lead the people. Am I not their servant?"

Visioning, planning, developing, implementing, and continuously evaluating a school budget must be an extension of the leader–follower collaborative decision-making dimension.

During the 1980s, public schools began to shift to a business-purpose approach, incorporating business principles into program planning, daily operations, and an overall reform movement in response to concerns about the quality of American education (Urban & Wagoner, 2019). This paradigm shift, as applied to school fiscal matters, was associated with the decentralization of district budgets. During the late 1980s and early 1990s, Deming's total-quality principles were infused into the mainstream of public school reform efforts.

The term *quality*, like integrity, fairness, and ethics—as discussed in Chapter 1—was then and continues to be difficult to define, although everyone claims to know quality when they see it. John M. Loh has stated the definition of quality is quite simple: "It is a leadership philosophy which creates throughout the entire enterprise a working environment which inspires trust, teamwork, and the quest for continuous, measurable improvement" (Hughes et al., 2021, p. 459).

While Loh's definition serves as a starting point for understanding the school budgeting process, a more practical and working definition of quality might be identified as a continuous process that is achieved through a change in organizational culture. In other words, a school leader must ensure the budgeting process, in collaboration with SBDM, is never-ending (continuous) by transforming the shared norms, values, or beliefs (culture) of a school into an environment in which the leader becomes a facilitator and the followers become active participants (SBDM).

Therefore, the school leader, for the betterment of the organization, must place emphasis on total quality through the empowerment of others by utilizing participative decision making, by articulating a vision, and by involving many in the planning and development stages of a school budget. Hence, all of us are smarter than any one of us. This change process makes the work of schools more intrinsically motivating and thus more appealing, rather than one of a controlling nature in which the members of the learning community are extrinsically motivated as a result of a top-down attitude and approach (Hughes et al., 2021).

Why Site-Based Decision Making?

The SBDM process is crucial to building an effective school budget. First, all actions regarding the budgetary process are considered, assessed, evaluated, and approved in a public forum with all stakeholders involved. SBDM is essential in an era of intense scrutiny, transparency, accountability, inadequate funding, and political intrusion. Effective school leaders welcome the opportunity to showcase the sensitive subject of public fund expenditures and the overall school budget in an open forum.

Ensure the budgeting process . . . is never-ending (continuous) by transforming the shared norms, values, or beliefs (culture) of a school into an environment in which the leader becomes a facilitator and the followers become active participants (SBDM).

Second, when utilizing SBDM, the budgetary process is aboveboard or transparent. In other words, there are no hidden funds or secret accounts. Third, all stakeholders are involved, and thus private and personal agendas meet with little merit and have a tendency to go by the wayside. Fourth, decentralizing four key resources (power, information, knowledge, and rewards) enhances organizational effectiveness and productivity (Hadderman, 2002). Hadderman further stipulates that

> highly involved schools need real power over the budget to decide how and where to allocate resources; they need fiscal and performance data for making informed decisions about the budget; their staff needs professional development and training to participate in the budget process; and the school must have control over compensation to reward performance. (p. 27)

For all these reasons it only makes sense to incorporate the SBDM model into the budget development process. Finally, recognize budgetary decision making can occur through the following methods:

- by autocratic method and manner ("My way or the highway!")
- by involving a select group of individuals ("Those who I believe understand best")
- by working in collaboration with a SBDM team ("All of us are smarter than any one of us!")

The latter is the best approach to building a school budget because those who have worked collaboratively in developing an academic action or improvement plan must be responsible, along with the school leader, for determining the budgetary needs of the organization.

Budget Coding: The Nuts and Bolts of Budgeting

199-11-6399.00-102-(20??)-11

Next we turn to an examination of what is often referred to as the nuts and bolts of school budgeting: the prescribed coding structure (see a coding example in the subheading above). A standardized coding structure aids school leaders in budgeting dollars into more than five hundred appropriate, yet diverse, fund categories. Examples of coded categories include the general fund, Title I, bilingual education, special education, and the campus activity account.

Every student at every school deserves the best instruction, and before instruction begins each school year, a campus budget is required by state statute. Budgetary decisions must be made on a student-first basis. The inclusion of funded line items within a school budget begins with a strong site-based mentality, a thoughtful potential plan, and some serious decision making. Where should the dollars be allocated to best generate the biggest bang for the buck? If budgeting practices are not based on a student-first basis, with every dollar assigned to best support pupil learning, the process has been a waste of time.

Before examining the budget coding structure and associated applications, consider the following question and how it provides a school leader or prospective school leader with an easy method of making the coding structure understandable: What *fund* (199) will *function* (11) in providing the most appropriate *object* (6399) within the *organization* (102) this *fiscal year* (20??) to be placed within the *program intended* (11) for student success? That is the numerical coding structure in a single question. The answer: (199) general—(11) instruction—(6399) supplies and materials—(.00) sub-object [high school mathematics department, for example]—(102) elementary school—(20??) fiscal year—(11) instruction (see Table 8.1). Now, let's get started!

Coding Structure and Applications

Today, budgets for public education entities are reported on the basis of a standard operating accounting code structure (see Tables 8.1 through 8.6). The system must meet the minimum requirements prescribed by state boards of education and is subject to review and comment by state auditors. A major purpose of the accounting code structure is to ensure the sequence of codes is uniformly applied to all school districts to further account for the appropriation and expenditure of public funds. The budgetary accounting code system is a labeling method designed to ensure the accuracy and legality of expenditures. School budgets are tracked by state education agencies via the budgetary accounting code system.

School district accounting systems are organized and operated on a fund basis. A fund is an accounting entity with a self-balancing set of accounts

TABLE 8.1 Example of a State's Operating Accounting Code Structure

<table>
<tr><td>199</td><td>—</td><td>11</td><td>—</td><td>6399</td><td>.00</td><td>—</td><td>001</td><td>INSERT CURRENT YEAR</td><td>—</td><td>11</td></tr>
<tr><td>1</td><td></td><td>2</td><td></td><td>3</td><td>4</td><td></td><td>5</td><td>6</td><td></td><td>7</td></tr>
<tr><td colspan="11">#1 Fund code. How will the expenditure be financed? What is being funded?</td></tr>
<tr><td colspan="11">School district accounting systems are organized and operated on a fund basis. A fund is an accounting entity with a self-balancing set of accounts recording financial resources and liabilities. There are more than five hundred different types of fund codes, and examples include general fund, bilingual education, special education (SPED), Title I, vocational education, and so forth.</td></tr>
<tr><td colspan="11">#2 Function code. Why is the expenditure being made? What is the function or purpose of the expenditure?</td></tr>
<tr><td colspan="11">The function code is an accounting entity applied to expenditures and expenses and identifies the purpose or function of any school district transaction. There are at least twenty-seven different types of function codes; examples include instruction, school leadership, guidance counseling, health services, and so forth.</td></tr>
<tr><td colspan="11">#3 Object code. What object is being purchased?</td></tr>
<tr><td colspan="11">The object code is an accounting entity identifying the nature and object of an account, a transaction, or a source. There are more than thirty-five different types of object codes, and examples include instruction, payroll, professional and contracted services, supplies and materials, capital outlay, and so forth.</td></tr>
<tr><td colspan="11">#4 Sub-object code. Which department- or grade-level purchase is being made?</td></tr>
<tr><td colspan="11">The sub-object code is an accounting entity that provides for special or additional accountability and is often utilized to delineate, for example, secondary-level departments.</td></tr>
<tr><td colspan="11">#5 Organization code. What unit or organization within a school system is making the purchase?</td></tr>
<tr><td colspan="11">The organization code is an accounting entity that identifies the organization—the high school, middle school, elementary school, superintendent's office, and so forth. (Note that the activity, not the location, defines the organization within a school district.) There are more than nine hundred organization codes. For example, expenditures for a high school might be classified as 001, as the organization codes for high school campuses are generally identified as 001 through 040. Middle school organization codes are typically stipulated as 041 through 100. Elementary schools fall into the organization code range of 101 through 698. For example, Cypress Fairbanks School District in Texas has fifty-seven elementary schools, nineteen middle schools, twelve high schools, and five special program schools, all with different yet independently identifiable organization codes.</td></tr>
<tr><td colspan="11">#6 Fiscal year code. During what fiscal year is the purchase being made?</td></tr>
<tr><td colspan="11">The fiscal year code identifies the fiscal year of any budgetary transaction. For example, during the 2033–2034 fiscal year of a school district, the numeral 34 would denote the fiscal year.</td></tr>
<tr><td colspan="11">#7 Program intent code. To what student group is the instructional purchase or service being directed or intended?</td></tr>
<tr><td colspan="11">The program intent code is used to designate the rationale of a program that is provided to students. These codes are used to account for the cost of instruction and other services that are directed toward a particular need of a specific set of students. There are approximately a dozen program intent codes; examples include basic educational services, gifted and talented, career and technology, SPED, bilingual education, Title I services, and so forth.</td></tr>
</table>

Note: Individual state budgetary coding requirements/processes may vary. To learn more about individual state coding and budgeting requirements, contact your state education department, which can typically be done via a state website.

recording financial resources and liabilities. A school district designates the fund's financial resources for a distinct purpose. State or federal governments, as well as the local school district, may establish the fund's purpose. Shown in Table 8.1 is an example of a state's operating accounting code structure as well as explanations that describe the specifics of each code. Tables 8.2 through 8.6 provide examples of categories for fund codes, function codes, object codes, organization codes, and program intent codes.

#1-Fund codes are typically mandatory for all financial transactions to identify the specific group or program to be funded (see Tables 8.1 and 8.2). Fund codes contain three digits with the first digit identifying regular, special, and vocational programs. A second digit denotes either the grade level or particular program area or category, such as the local operating fund. The third digit further defines program type in relation to student classifications, type of services, and/or student population. For example, the number 211 identifies the Title I federal fund group.

TABLE 8.2 Categories for Fund Codes

FUND CODES (TEN CATEGORIES)	
100 –	Regular programs
200 –	Special or federal programs (Examples: Title I—211, bilingual education—219, special education—224, school breakfast and lunch program—240, etc.)
300 –	Vocational programs
400 –	Other state and local instructional programs
500 –	Non-public school programs
600 –	Adult and continuing education programs
700 –	Debt service
800 –	Community service programs
900 –	Enterprise programs
000 –	Undistributed expenditures

#2-Function codes are typically mandatory two- to four-digit numbers that identify the function or purpose of the expenditure (instruction = 11, for example). Function codes further designate budget program areas (see Tables 8.1 and 8.3). Function codes represent as many as nine different categories. As noted, the most commonly used function code category within a school budget is instruction, although other areas, including school leadership, guidance counseling, and health services, are frequently incorporated.

TABLE 8.3 Categories for Function Codes

FUNCTION CODES (NINE CATEGORIES)	
10–	Instruction and instructional-related services
20–	Instructional and school leadership
30–	Support services—student (pupil)
40–	Administrative support services
50–	Support services—nonstudent based
60–	Ancillary services
70–	Debt service
80–	Capital outlay
90–	Intergovernmental charges

#3-Object codes are mandatory three- to four-digit numbers (see Tables 8.1 and 8.4) that identify the particular nature or object of an account, a transaction, or a source. Object codes further describe program allocations and expenditures. Object codes represent seven different categories.

TABLE 8.4 Categories for Object Codes

OBJECT CODES (SEVEN CATEGORIES)	
6000–	Expenditure/expense control accounts
6100–	Payroll costs
6200–	Professional and contract services
6300–	Supplies and materials
6400–	Other operating costs
6500–	Debt service
6600–	Capital outlay—land, buildings, and equipment

#4-Sub-object codes are two-digit numbers used as accounting entries by local school districts to delineate, for example, secondary-level departments such as English, mathematics, science, physical education, and history (see Table 8.1). The sub-object code is intended to provide for special or additional accountability. For purposes of this text, the sub-object code will be .00. (No exemplifying sub-object table is necessary.)

#5-Organization codes are mandatory three-digit numbers identifying accounting entries or organizations as being high school, middle school, elementary school, superintendent's office, or school board (see Tables 8.1 and 8.5). This code readily notes which high schools in a district are the oldest or the newest. For example, Elm High School (001) is the first or oldest high school, followed by Birch High School (002), Oak High School (003), and Hickory High School (004), and so forth. The same coding designation is true for middle and elementary schools as well.

TABLE 8.5 Categories for Organization Codes

ORGANIZATION CODES (TWO CATEGORIES)	
001–699	Organization units—schools
700–	Organization units—administrative

#6-The fiscal year is a mandatory single- or double-digit code that identifies the fiscal year of budgetary transactions (see Table 8.1). For example, if the fiscal school year is 2033–2034, the fiscal year code would be 34. The fiscal year code is not exemplified in a table here.

#7-The program intent code is frequently represented by two digits and designates the intent or rationale of a program provided to students (see Table 8.1). This code accounts for the cost of instruction and other services directed toward a particular intent or need of a specific student population. The eleven program intent code categories are identified in Table 8.6.

TABLE 8.6 Categories for Program Intent Codes

PROGRAM INTENT CODES (ELEVEN CATEGORIES)	
11–	Basic educational services
21–	Gifted and talented
22–	Career and technology
23–	Special education
24–	Accelerated instruction (at-risk programs, tutoring, etc.)
25–	Bilingual education
26/27–	Non-disciplinary alternative education programs
28/29–	Disciplinary alternative education programs
30–	Title I

Pause and Consider

It Doesn't Take a Secret Decoder Ring!

Learning how to use budget codes is not a difficult process. In fact, coding can be quite simple, even if the long strand of numbers looks intimidating. Below are four questions related to understanding the code definitions. Beyond that, the reader will find two coding activities. The correct answers are located at the conclusion of the chapter.

1. A principal seeks to purchase a printer for the school during the current fiscal year. Which code would be incorporated to describe a department the purchase is intended for?
   A. Object
   B. Sub-object
   C. Organization
   D. Program intent
2. A teacher wishes to requisition a box of five thousand staples. Which code would best describe the item being requisitioned for purchase?
   A. Fund
   B. Function
   C. Object
   D. Sub-object
3. An instructional coach decides to secure supplies and materials for instructional uses. What code would best serve the instructional coach relative to the purpose of the purchase?
   A. Fund
   B. Function
   C. Object
   D. Sub-object
4. The campus nurse determines a special medical equipment item is needed for a wheelchair-bound SPED student. What code would the nurse use to identify the specific program or type of service required to fiscally support this purchase?
   A. Fund
   B. Function
   C. Object
   D. Program intent

(Continued)

(Continued)

5. A principal determines certain services in the way of a consultant, as related to the Title I program that targets a specific student population, must be budgetarily accounted for. Identify the particular coding required.
   A. Fund
   B. Function
   C. Object
   D. Program intent

Using Tables 8.1 through 8.6 and the Accounting Codes Reference Sheet found in Resource C, carefully read and assess each of the activity scenarios presented and then determine and apply the proper accounting codes. Write your answer in the blanks provided. (Answers to both activity scenarios are provided at the conclusion of the chapter.)

Activity 1: Utilizing Accounting Codes

The special services department has requested additional mathematics manipulatives to be utilized in several classrooms at Maple High School. These needed supplies could very well help to increase the overall mathematic test scores at the second-oldest high school in the Mapletown Independent School District, as the statewide accountability system now holds all schools accountable for the academic achievement of SPED students.

________-______-______________-________-______

Activity 2: Utilizing Accounting Codes

Kit Monami, assistant principal at Eagletown High School, the third-oldest high school in the district, was designated as the budget manager by her principal this school year. Kit is very competent in her new role and finds working with the school budget and budget team to be quite challenging yet most interesting. In her role as budget manager, she interacts with the different high school departments and their many demanding personalities. Most recently, James Sorsby, the head football coach at Eagletown High, has asked Kit if his request for additional athletic supply funds has been included in the budget for the upcoming school year.

The head football coach is particularly concerned about the need for a new digital recording system for filming the defensive line during after-school practice. "How does the district expect us to win if I can't properly video the weekly progress of the team?" the coach inquired. Kit explained she needs Coach Sorsby to calculate the cost of the digital system and complete the necessary requisition form, then she will determine if there are additional funds available in the specified account within the school budget.

In this scenario, as Coach Sorsby completes the budget requisition form, consider the proper coding for each category—fund, function, object, organization code, and program intent code—and then fill in the budget accounting code.

________-______-______________-_________-______

Specialized Electronic School Budget Forms Described

This section of the chapter describes specialized electronic school budget forms and worksheets. Electronic budget worksheets are typically incorporated and utilized as part of a school's budgetary reporting process.

Today, electronic budgetary forms and worksheets are found in the vast majority of school systems throughout the United States. Specialized electronic budget forms and worksheets are beneficial and productive, better ensuring quality management of the campus budget and further safeguarding against fraud and embezzlement.

Allocation Summaries

Sometimes referred to as an allocation statement, this budgetary form or worksheet may come in differing formats that frequently identify discretionary funding distributions that could be consolidated into single revenue lines for the purpose of developing a school-based budget. Utilizing allocation summaries, the school leader and team will create line-item accounts identified by fund, function, object, sub-object, and program intent codes and descriptors.

Such line-item accounting might include the regular or general education allocation, supplemental programs allocation, or indirect allocation (*indirect* meaning those funds for counselor, administrative office staff, or custodians, for example) that cannot be explicitly identified with direct instructional activities, cocurricular or extracurricular allocation, gifted and talented allocation, career and technology education allocation, bilingual education allocation, state compensatory education allocation, Title I allocation, and so on.

Purchase Requisitions

School leaders must be aware of the amount of funds committed yet not approved for the current school year. The use of purchase requisitions allows the price of the item requested to be encumbered against the budget while the requisition proceeds through the workflow approval process. This minimizes the risk of overspending budgeted line-item amounts.

Purchase Orders

Once a requisition has completed the approval process, it is converted to a purchase order, which, in turn, serves as the legal authority for obligating district funds. This allows the school leader or district business office to send the purchase order to the vendor to acquire the goods/services. The vendor now has a legal, binding agreement obligating the district to pay for the ordered goods/services. Much like the requisition, the purchase order encumbers the funds against the budget until the items are paid, again minimizing the risk of overspending budgeted amounts.

Budget Transfers and Amendments

From time to time, a school leader will need to reallocate funds within the campus budget from one area to another. This method is typically referred to as a budget transfer or amendment and as such is a process of conveying or adjusting funds from one function, object, and/or program code to another. Recall that the topic of budget transfers and amendments was previously examined in Chapter 6.

Cash Receipts and Deposits

Proper cash-handling procedures require the issuance of a receipt every time money is collected or received by the school/district. The cash receipts and deposits process ensures proper recording of the transaction and minimizes the risk of theft or fraudulent activities. The cash receipt will indicate how the funds are received (cash, check, credit card, or PayPal® or other online payment systems, for example), the person or company making the payment, the person collecting the payment, the reason for the payment, and the correct organization to receive credit for the payment. Having an electronic cash receipt system provides additional internal controls by automating the receipt-numbering system and by providing reports for bank deposits and reconciliation.

Federal Funding Accountability

School systems typically require all purchases made using federal dollars include a reference to the campus improvement plan (CIP) or campus action plan (CAP). The school leader or campus designee must enter the reference on the requisition form/window. This particular form provides a quick reference for reviewers and auditors to know where to look in the CIP or CAP for the goal and objective that support the purchase. Federal guidelines require all purchases be included/documented in a CIP or CAP and on a federal funding accountability form.

Inventory Management/Fixed Assets

An inventory management/fixed asset form allows the campus/district to maintain a subsidiary ledger detailing specific capital items purchased. This ledger documents the item purchased, date purchased, tag number (if tags are used), serial number, make, model, specific location of the item, acquisition cost, and useful life, and it can be used to systematically calculate depreciation when necessary.

An inventory management/fixed asset e-module can be used to generate reports for the school leader to conduct annual inventories of assets and to ensure the safekeeping of said assets. The school leader and/or campus designee must accurately maintain this list to ensure the safekeeping of fixed assets and to properly record disposition or surplus of inventoried and/or unused items.

Year-to-Date (YTD) Reports

A year-to-date (YTD) budgeting report provides the school leader and team with a line-item analysis of available budgeted dollars, funds expended to date, and what percentage of the line-item fund has been expended. It further identifies any transfers and/or amendments that have been made by the school leader. Additionally, the YTD report identifies the original campus appropriation. This is an important report to share with the site-based team when reviewing budgetary expenditures each month and when preparing to build next year's budget.

Campus Improvement Plan (CIP) Budget Report

A CIP budget report provides the school leader and team with detail regarding purchases made and how said purchases align with district goals and campus objectives. In other words, is the school leader guiding purchases that are aligned with the action or improvement plan as developed during the SBDM process, and, moreover, do said purchases support student achievement?

Important Budget Considerations

American philanthropist Barbara Hutton once stated what is obvious in life and in the practice of effective and efficient budgeting: "So, you want to take it with you—well, I've never seen a Brink's truck follow a hearse to the cemetery" (Lazear, 1992, p. 221). While an individual can save as much money as possible, at some point in time, those saved dollars must be spent, given away, or inherited by someone because, as Hutton implied, you can't take it with you!

The same holds true in school budgeting—spend it or give it back. The authors suggest effective school leaders spend all the campus allocated funds but do so in the most accurate, effective, and efficient manner possible. In other words, spend the money and spend it wisely! With this thought in mind, consider the following top ten school budgeting priorities. At the conclusion of each of the ten statements, the identification (in parentheses) of district or school site responsibility is denoted.

1. **Utilize a budget calendar.** (Reference Chapter 9.) The purpose of the budget calendar is to ensure the budget development process is continuous. The school leader who follows the guidelines and dates associated with a budget calendar maximizes the possibility nothing interferes with budgetary preparation requirements or the best interests of the school and school system. (district)

2. **Identify budgetary allocations and restricted funds.** Know and understand the revenue sources and how they impact the school budgetary allotment. Recognize allotments can be based on an average daily attendance (ADA) formulation and know how critical it is for the school leader to continuously monitor the enrollment of all students, including those students served in special programs such as bilingual education, Title I, SPED, and gifted and talented. Realize certain funds have specified restrictions associated with appropriateness of expenditures and student services. (district and school site)

3. **Project incoming and exiting student populations.** The effective school leader regularly monitors incoming and exiting student populations, as the student enrollment of a school can significantly impact the budget allocation. In addition, accomplished school leaders learn to utilize the cohort survival method (see "Projecting Student Enrollment" in Chapter 9) as a process of projecting student population into the future. (district and school site)

4. **Project faculty and staff increases and reductions.** Any increase or reduction in faculty and staff strongly correlates to student enrollment. By utilizing the cohort survival method to forecast into the future, the school leader can assess how many faculty and staff will be needed to ensure personnel stability and a strong educational program. (district and school site)

5. **Conduct a needs assessment.** Efficient needs assessments allow school leaders to recognize which interventions were most effective in increasing student achievement and cost the least. (school site)

6. **Receive input from all stakeholders.** Effective school leadership incorporates collaborative strategies, which in turn

generate the involvement and input of organizational followers. When collaborative decision making is implemented, visioning, planning, evaluating, and the overall budgeting process generate measurable improvements, all of which ultimately benefit students, faculty, and the organization. (school site)

When collaborative decision making is implemented, visioning, planning, evaluating, and the overall budgeting process generate measurable improvements, all of which ultimately benefit students, faculty, and the organization.

7. **Project and prioritize expenditures.** Consider all line-item accounts within the budget, including supplies and materials, salaries (if applicable), and capital outlay, for example, when analyzing and prioritizing budgetary expenditures. The school leader who actively monitors and regularly evaluates the budget is able to project and prioritize expenditures that focus on specified objectives, which are correlated with the instructional program, the school action or improvement plan, and the overall vision of the learning community. (school site)

8. **Build the budget.** Exceptional budgetary leaders regularly (monthly) meet with the budget development team to create a school vision, develop a plan of action, and build a budget. This level of quality leadership demonstrates the following attributes essential in the budget development process:

   - knowledge of the complete budgetary process
   - knowledge of the amount of funding available and where the budgetary allotment is derived
   - knowledge of collaborative decision-making procedures as well as proper protocols involving the input of all stakeholders
   - knowledge of accounting codes (school site)

9. **Defend the school budget.** (Reference Chapter 9.) Skilled leadership and knowledge of the school budget permit an administrator to exercise ingenuity and competence in addressing questions, suggestions, and criticisms of the school budget at a budget defense hearing. Effectively defending the budget is an act of elucidating clear points and explicating proper justifications for budgetary decisions. Such actions in the formal budget defense hearing reveal leadership traits of credibility, transparency, and expertise. (district and school site)

10. **Amend and adjust the school budget.** Even with all the purposeful budgetary planning and careful monitoring and evaluation, no administrator can expect the school budget to remain on target without certain adjustments being made during the course of a fiscal year. Budget amendments and transfers

are necessary when unexpected circumstances and situations inevitably arise. Having a working knowledge of the amendment and transfer processes will facilitate the need to move funds from one account to another without leaving an impression of budgetary incompetence or mismanagement. (district and school site)

Final Thoughts

The effective school leader, as a means of ensuring program quality, incorporates the SBDM process into school operations. This approach to school leadership is superior to the autocratic approach and also exceeds the consultative process. High-quality decisions have a direct and measurable impact on organizational and student success. The SBDM process works, has long been proven in the research literature, is open and transparent, and encourages school leaders to openly showcase the sensitive subject of public fund expenditures.

The nuts and bolts of school-based budgeting evolves around coding structures and applications, including fund, function, object, sub-object, organization, fiscal year, and program intent codes. The utilization of the school budget coding structure does not take a secret decoder ring to decipher or master! It simply takes a school leader or prospective leader to examine, learn, and incorporate the coding examples and related activities within this chapter.

Specialized electronic school budget forms have been identified and described, including (1) allocation summaries, (2) purchase requisitions, (3) purchase orders, (4) budget transfers and amendments, (5) cash receipts and deposits, (6) federal funding accountability, (7) inventory management/fixed assets, (8) year-to-date reports, and (9) campus improvement plan (CIP) budget report forms.

Finally, ten important budget considerations were identified and explained, thus providing school leaders with a school budgeting priority listing. These budget considerations are (1) utilize a budget calendar, (2) identify budgetary allocations and restricted funds, (3) project incoming and exiting student populations, (4) project faculty and staff increases and reductions, (5) conduct a needs assessment, (6) receive input from all stakeholders, (7) project and prioritize expenditures, (8) build the budget, (9) defend the school budget, and (10) amend and adjust the budget as is necessary.

Discussion Questions

1. Why is site-based decision making (SBDM) an essential aspect of the budget development process?
2. How have the total-quality movement and the SBDM process impacted the development of budgets in public schools?

3. How does the term *quality* interact with and impact integrity, fairness, and ethics as related to leading and budgeting? Explain.
4. What is the purpose of the accounting code system? Why is the coding structure considered the nuts and bolts of school budgeting?
5. Reflect on the chapter section titled "Specialized Electronic School Budget Forms Described." Of the nine identified forms, which one seems to be the most critical to the school principal? Explain your reasoning.
6. Examine the ten important budget considerations and determine which three are absolutely essential to ensuring a school leader expends campus allocated funds in the most accurate, effective, essential, and efficient manner. Be specific in your response.
7. How does this chapter relate to the Professional Standards for Educational Leaders (PSEL) as documented in Chapter 1? Which standard(s) are specifically relevant and why?

Case Study #1

Shifting Paradigms With Changing Times—

A Continuation of the Chapter 3 Case Study

Note: The reader will recognize the characters portrayed in this study and will apply accounting codes to the budgetary allotments designated in Table 3.4 of Chapter 3 in the PBHS Nonprioritized Identified Needs chart.

Part IV: The Budget—Coding the Budgetary Allotments

The Situation

Dr. Hector Avila, principal, and Ms. Abigail Grayson, assistant principal, at Pecan Bay High School sat down with the SBDM committee to review the prioritized needs listing as related to the next fiscal year school budget. It was obvious there were more needs than dollars at PBHS, and funding every need would be impossible based on the $100,000 allotment. Hector thought to himself, *Isn't that always the case!* Nevertheless, the decisions had been made in the best interests of the students. Hector was proud of the committee's efforts. Abigail was more than impressed with the progress that had been made and with how much she had learned from an outstanding instructional leader.

(Continued)

(Continued)

The next step in the visioning, planning, and budgeting process was to integrate the needs with budgetary descriptors and accounting codes. This would be a learning experience for not only Abigail but the entire SBDM committee. What Hector really appreciated about the SBDM initiative was the fact every aspect of the budget was being considered, assessed, evaluated, and approved in a public forum so all stakeholders would recognize there were no hidden agendas or secret principal "slush" funds.

Following a short period of welcoming committee members to the conference room, the business of coding the different needs began in earnest. Jonathan Hedras, one of the initial opponents to the SBDM process and a good friend of Ed Feeney, was present, a smile on his face, excited to be a part of a group who had bought into the concept of "All of us are smarter than any one of us!" Even old Ed was slowly but surely coming along and had sat in on a SBDM meeting for Jonathan a few weeks ago when Jonathan had to take his wife to a doctor's appointment.

Thinking It Through

Now that you have prioritized the different needs at Pecan Bay High School and constructed an abridged action plan, it is time to consider all line-item accounts within the school budget in relation to the fund, function, object, sub-object (utilize .00 for this exercise), organization, fiscal year, and program intent codes. Review the ten steps to budgeting success from Chapter 5 and then determine what the committee has accomplished to (1) determine the allotment, (2) identify any fixed expenditures, (3) involve all parties, (4) identify potential expenditures, (5) cut back as is necessary, (6) avoid any debts, (7) develop a plan of action, (8) set goals, (9) evaluate the budget, and (10) abide by the budget. Question: Where are you and your team in the ten-step process?

Turn to the Accounting Codes Reference Sheet located in Resource C. Use this document to complete the Budget Development Spreadsheet exhibited in Table 8.7 by listing the correct accounting codes as associated with the prioritized needs previously selected. To better assist, an example indicating the proper accounting code for health services (nurse or clinic) has been provided and listed on the first row of the spreadsheet.

Note that the description category of the Budget Development Spreadsheet is associated with the function and object code descriptors. Remember, accounting codes may vary from state to state and from district to district. The process utilized in this text is simply an example. If you prefer, seek out your own state or school district version of the accounting code process to complete this task.

TABLE 8.7 Budget Development Spreadsheet

1. FUND	2. FUNCTION	3./4. OBJECT/ SUB-OBJECT	5. ORGANIZATION	6. FISCAL YEAR	7. PROGRAM INTENT	DESCRIPTION	TOTAL
199	33	6399.00	002	Current date	11	Health services (nurse)	$1,000.00
						Grand Total	$

Note: This form also appears in Resource B.

Case Study #2

Requisition Season at Kay Carter Middle School

Donna Arnold, assistant principal at Kay Carter Middle School, has been given the responsibility of serving as budget manager. Donna has been an assistant principal at Kay Carter for three years. She has really come to like the old school, the first one built in the school district, well over sixty years ago. One of Donna's specified tasks associated with the role of budget manager is to review all campus requisitions and assign the appropriate accounting codes.

This particular evening, after a long day at school, Donna sits down and begins analyzing a stack of requisitions placed on her desk. As she examines each requisition, she realizes how important it is to learn the different accounting codes in order to save time. While Donna thumbs through the stack of requisitions, she notes what is being ordered and then speculates as to the appropriate code for entry in the fund account blank.

Requisition #1: Janice Minsky wants to order the director's cut of the 1957 American courtroom drama *12 Angry Men*, starring Henry Fonda, to show to her Title I government classes.

______-____-__________.____-____-____-______

Requisition #2: Laurie Tallgan needs one grand prize trophy and several ribbons for placing as well as certificates of achievement for the gifted and talented students participating in the annual National Geography Bee.

______-____-__________.____-____-____-______

Requisition #3: Joyce Pringser, librarian, requests several new book titles for the school library, as the bilingual teachers strongly desire books in the native languages of their ELLs.

______-____-__________.____-____-____-______

Requisition #4: Alice Shobb, the school nurse, is requesting she be permitted to attend the National Conference for Wellness Programs to be held in Chicago, Illinois.

______-____-__________.____-____-____-______

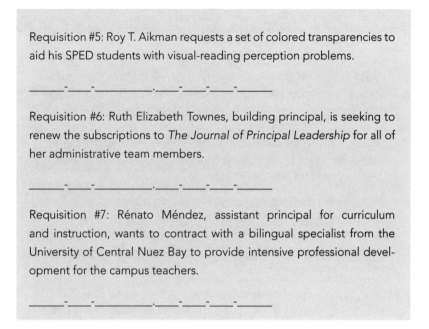

Requisition #5: Roy T. Aikman requests a set of colored transparencies to aid his SPED students with visual-reading perception problems.

______-____-__________.____-____-____-______

Requisition #6: Ruth Elizabeth Townes, building principal, is seeking to renew the subscriptions to *The Journal of Principal Leadership* for all of her administrative team members.

______-____-__________.____-____-____-______

Requisition #7: Rénato Méndez, assistant principal for curriculum and instruction, wants to contract with a bilingual specialist from the University of Central Nuez Bay to provide intensive professional development for the campus teachers.

______-____-__________.____-____-____-______

Case Study Application

1. Using Tables 8.1 through 8.6 within the chapter as well as the Accounting Codes Reference Sheet in Resource C, indicate the fund, function, object, sub-object (utilize 00 for this exercise), fiscal year, program intent, and organization codes for each of the requisition submissions noted above. Place your answer in the blanks below each requisition number. (Answers are provided at the conclusion of this chapter.)

2. Contact your business department administrator or school superintendent or state finance/budget website to obtain a copy of the state's operating accounting code structure. How is this structure similar to or different from the examples incorporated within this chapter?

3. Exceptional school leaders have been described as showing and sharing love, joy, peace, kindness, forbearance, goodness, gentleness, self-control, gratitude, strength, wisdom and knowledge, skill application, high expectations, tenacity, perseverance, and understanding. These descriptors have long been documented in the research literature as attributes of a successful leader and, in fact, a successful life. Which of these five attributes do you believe are most applicable to excellence in budgetary management? Are there other attributes not noted you would suggest? Explain your answers.

Chapter 8 Answers

Below are the answers to the activities in this chapter.

Answers to "It Doesn't Take a Secret Decoder Ring!"

#1: B. Sub-Object

#2: C. Object

#3: B. Function

#4: A. Fund

#5: D. Program Intent

Answers to Activity 1 and Activity 2: Utilizing Accounting Codes

#1: 200-10-6300-002-23

#2: 199-36-6399-003-91

Answers to Case Study Application Questions

Requisition #1: 199-11-6399.00-Current School Year-11-101*

Requisition #2: 461-11-6399.00-Current School Year-21-101

Requisition #3: 219-12-6669.00-Current School Year-25-101

Requisition #4: 199-33-6411.00-Current School Year-11-101

Requisition #5: 199-11-6329.00-Current School Year-23-101

Requisition #6: 199-23-6329.00-Current School Year-11-101

Requisition #7: 219-13-6200.00-Current School Year-25-101

* Note that 101 as an organization code represents an elementary school. Readers are welcome to utilize either elementary school, middle school, or high school as an organization code for the completion of this activity.

Building the School Budget

9

Budgetary Applications and Specialized Forms and Procedures

> *Building a budget doesn't limit freedom, it provides freedom! Do remember, however, never go over budget!*
>
> —Anonymous

School Budget Applications

Ovsiew and Castetter (1960), in their classic text, *Budgeting for Better Schools,* suggest there are several integrating aspects of a school budget that ensure better budgets for better schools. Their book—more than half a century old—may be dated, but their message is not. Let's examine the budgetary components and applications essential to building an effective school-based budget. By following a prescribed step-by-step process, the school leader can experience a sense of security in knowing the proposed budget will meet with appropriate recognition and approval at the district-level budget hearing and defense session.

Below are thirteen budgetary components and applications essential to developing an effective school-based budget. Each of the thirteen will be examined in this chapter and ultimately applied to the development of a school budget as detailed in Resource A.

1. **Descriptive narrative.** A detailed description of the school (years of operation, location, demographic information such as percentage of free and reduced-price lunch population, federal program eligibilities and identifiers, and other important descriptors, such as socioeconomic backgrounds and poverty status of the student population). These descriptors identify, in narrative form, the areas of budgetary need and consideration.
2. **Programmatic identifiers.** Identifiers relating the grades of the school, total students enrolled, ethnic distribution, and other programmatic considerations (special education, gifted and talented, bilingual education, vocational education, etc.),

along with the number of faculty employed—teachers, counselors, nurses, administrators, librarians, paraprofessionals, clerks, secretaries, and so on—are detailed in this narrative.

3. **Mission statement.** This statement of introduction related to the school's goal or philosophy regarding the nature of learners, learning, and the purpose of the school serves to explain the rationale of the organization and how it impacts the decision-making and budgetary process.
4. **Student enrollment projections.** A chart or table utilizing the cohort survival method (see "Projecting Student Enrollment" in this chapter) is used to project student populations and is critical to any school budget as future student enrollment increases or decreases. Increases or decreases in student enrollment are indicative of the funding necessities essential for a school's success. Many school districts, especially in urban areas, will project student enrollment out as much as thirty years. The reason? Districts must know the locations of potential population growth patterns to purchase land for the construction of future schools and/or to make decisions regarding school closures.
5. **Analysis of academic action or improvement plan.** When analyzing the academic action or improvement plan of a school, consider the following questions:
   - What aspects of the instructional program need improvement?
   - What pertinent sources of data verify any areas of improvement?
   - Which of the concerns, problems, or needs are most significant for improving the overall instructional program?
   - Which proposed improvement efforts are within the school's budgetary scope and capability for effective action and implementation?
   - Which concerns, problems, or needs are of the highest priority, and is there a sound research base for addressing each prioritized concern, problem, or need?

Additionally, numerous states identify components to be addressed in campus action or improvement plans. For example, as previously identified in Chapter 6 but important to review, there are thirteen essential campus action or improvement plan components: (1) student performance, (2) special education, (3) violence prevention, (4) parental involvement, (5) staff development, (6) suicide prevention, (7) conflict resolution, (8) dyslexia treatment programs, (9) dropout reduction,

(10) technology, (11) discipline management, (12) accelerated instruction, and (13) career education.

A careful analysis of a campus action or improvement plan should reflect the inclusion of these and/or other important components as identified by a state or school district. Such components are essential to a campus action or improvement plan, which serves as the vehicle that drives the direction of a school's instructional program, thus positively impacting student academic achievement.

6. **Needs assessment.** A needs assessment serves to identify what areas or aspects of the school program need improvement after a review of all pertinent sources of data (e.g., academic action plan, previous studies, local and statewide test results, and surveys of teachers, students, and parents). In addition, a review of the research literature, along with collaborative team discussions regarding each area of instructional and/or programmatic concerns, is particularly useful and beneficial.

7. **Priority analysis.** A priority analysis immediately follows a needs assessment. The principal and team interacting collaboratively determine the campus instructional and student-centered priorities and then ordinate the priorities. In other words, they list in order what is the most important need, followed by the second most important, then third most important, and so forth. The funding of needs must be in priority order. Listed below are several examples of identified priorities from a needs assessment recently conducted at a public school in an urban center located in the southwestern United States.

    - Staff development will be initiated for all faculty, with a concentration in research-based strategies proven to be effective in assisting English language learners (ELLs) to acquire the language and skills needed to be successful in all content areas. Forms of assessment must be empirically researched and utilized to monitor the progress of this particular subgroup in order to best determine if the implementation of instructional strategies is effective relative to increasing student test scores and improving academic achievement. This training will be conducted and facilitated by the Hispanic Educational Learning Program (HELP) initiative.

A priority analysis immediately follows a needs assessment. The principal and team interacting collaboratively determine the campus instructional and student-centered priorities and then ordinate the priorities. . . . The funding of needs must be in priority order.

- Staff development will be initiated for all faculty with a concentration in research-based strategies proven to be effective in assisting and motivating male Hispanic students to best experience academic success in all instructional core areas. Teachers must be provided additional training regarding the analysis of student data to determine the academic progress of this subgroup. Consultants from the Southwestern Regional Research Laboratory (SWRL) will conduct this training.
- To increase special education (SPED) test scores to 85 percent > and ELLs' test scores to 90 percent > in mathematics, specifically seventh- and eighth-grade mathematics, teachers will continue to utilize the Closing the Gap academic initiative to best provide SPED and ELL students with academic achievement–oriented instruction. Teachers will also utilize district-determined best teaching and learning practices and strategies during classroom instruction to target programmatic objectives in which SPED and ELL students are at risk of failing.
- To further increase SPED and ELL student test scores and to improve the teaching and learning of students in these subgroups, teachers will incorporate differentiated instructional techniques utilizing the research-based EdScope-At-Risk Student Analysis program, to be purchased by the school.
- Student attendance rates, most notably of ELL students, must be increased by implementing the empirical, research-based, and more efficient student attendance monitoring system StudentTrak, to be purchased by the school. Research reveals this particular tracking system of student attendance provides for a more efficient collaboration with parents and guardians, community members, assistant principals, attendance clerks, teachers, and counselors.

8. **Teacher/student distribution table.** Table 9.1 indicates the distribution of students by grade level (elementary schools) or subject area (secondary schools) in relation to the number of staff dedicated to serving students from a programmatic consideration (e.g., bilingual classrooms, inclusion-monolingual classrooms, and monolingual-only classrooms). This table provides a visual understanding of why and how an increase or decrease in student enrollment impacts the budgetary allotment for teacher salaries, paraprofessional assistance, and program development.

TABLE 9.1 Teacher/Student Distribution Table

	BILINGUAL	INCLUSION-MONOLINGUAL	MONOLINGUAL ONLY			
PREK	15 t & ta	15 t & ta				
K	22 t	5 + 10 t & ta	21 t	22 t	22 t	22 t
Grade 1	21 t	5 + 10 t & ta	22 t	22 t	20 t	21 t
Grade 2	20 t	5 + 10 t & ta	21 t	22 t	22 t	
Grade 3	22 t	5 + 10 t & ta	22 t	22 t	20 t	21 t
Grade 4	20 t	4 + 10 t & ta	22 t	21 t	22 t	
Grade 5	28 t	5 + 15 t & ta	31 t	35 t	33 t	32 t
SPED			43 2 t & 5 ta			
# Students	148	29 + 65	197	144	139	96
# Staff	7 t 1 ta	6 t 6 ta	9 t 6 ta	6 t	6 t	4 t

Note: t = teacher; ta = teacher aide or assistant.

9. **Faculty apportionment.** See Table 9.2, which reveals the apportionment or distribution of the entire faculty in relation to the number of assigned personnel to a school. This table allows the school leader and team as well as district office and business department administrators to visualize areas of need in relation to the student enrollment projections.

TABLE 9.2 Faculty Apportionment Table

POSITION	# ASSIGNED TO CAMPUS
Principal	1
Assistant principal	1
School secretary	1
Fiscal Education and Information Management System (FEIMS) clerk	1
Instructional facilitator/coach	1
Counselor	1
Nurse	1
Nurse assistant	1
Librarian	1
Total faculty	**9**
Position	# Assigned to Campus
Gifted and talented teacher	½
Speech therapist	½

(Continued)

(Continued)

POSITION	# ASSIGNED TO CAMPUS
Physical education teacher	1
Music teacher	1
Office aides	2
Title VI aides	1
Custodians	4
Food services	5
Total faculty	**15**

10. **Above-basic personnel request and justification.** The above-basic personnel request narrative is another necessary component of the budgetary process as this particular section of the school budget justifies the need for increased faculty and staff. Furthermore, this narrative seeks those critical funds for additional personnel that may be above the basic school allotment.
11. **Allocation statement.** The allocation statement serves to provide in tabular form (see Table 9.3) a brief but descriptive distribution of funds. Within this statement, the total student population count is noted, along with the average daily attendance (ADA) or average daily membership (ADM) rate. In addition, the statement identifies the ADA or ADM funding on a per-pupil basis, along with the SPED, gifted and talented, bilingual/English as a second language (ESL), Title I, and state compensatory funding allocations. Finally, a total allocation is listed. This total allocation is the basis for building the school budget.

TABLE 9.3 Allocation Statement

		STATE ALLOCATION				CAMPUS ALLOTMENT
Student population	=	818				
Average daily attendance (ADA)	=	90%		818 × 0.90	=	736.2 = 736
ADA funding	=	736	×	$2,537.00	=	$1,867,232.00
SPED	=	72	×	$7,125.00	=	$513,000.00
Gifted and talented	=	45	×	$285.00	=	$12,825.00
Bilingual/ESL	=	148	×	$237.50	=	$35,150.00
Title I (82%)	=	671	×	$262.50	=	$176,137.50
State compensatory	=	671	×	$475.00	=	$318,725.00
Total Allocation					=	**$2,923,069.50**

BUILDING THE BUDGET

12. **Salaries for personnel table.** This section of the school budget details in tabular form (see Table 9.4) the exact identification and distribution of salaries for personnel.

TABLE 9.4 Salaries for Personnel

PERSONNEL SALARIES		
Teachers, nurse, librarian	=	$55,000
Principal	=	$101,000
Assistant principal	=	$87,000
Counselor	=	$61,000
Diagnostician	=	$63,000
Instructional facilitator/coach	=	$62,000
Speech therapist	=	$52,000
Testing coordinator	=	$49,000
Security officer	=	$54,000
Secretary	=	$36,000
Instructional/clerical aides	=	$31,000
Nurse assistant	=	$40,000
Custodian (head)	=	$35,000
Custodian	=	$30,000
Food services	=	$19,000
Consultant(s)	=	$1,000 per day
Supplements (Stipends) = $2,000	*Also –*	
Resource (SPED)	Head nurse	
Bilingual	Head counselor	
Math	Head custodian	
Science	Department chairs	
Librarian	Diagnostician	
Home economics		

13. **Salary distribution table.** Table 9.5 reflects salaries and supplements (stipends) of all school personnel, incorporating the appropriate payroll descriptions and budgetary coding. While most school districts across the United States do not require principals to be responsible for payroll budgetary allotments and management of personnel salaries, some smaller districts in fact do so. Payroll is typically a fixed cost and is frequently either removed from the campus budget allocation or simply frozen at the district level. However, the process of compiling a payroll analysis via the Salary Distribution Table does provide for a better understanding of how payroll (personnel salaries) significantly impacts district and campus budgetary costs.

TABLE 9.5 Salary Distribution Table

FUND	FUNCTION	OBJECT/ SUB-OBJECT	ORGANIZATION	CURRENT SCHOOL YEAR (CSY)	PROGRAM	DESCRIPTION	TOTAL
199	11	6119	103	CSY	11	Payroll: regular education teachers (24)	$ 1,320,000.00
199	11	6119	103	CSY	11	Payroll: math/science stipends	$ 24,000.00
199	11	6119	103	CSY	23	Payroll: special education aides (4)	$ 124,000.00
199	11	6129	103	CSY	11	Payroll: secretary	$ 36,000.00
199	11	6129	103	CSY	11	Payroll: support personnel (FEIMS)	$ 31,000.00
199	11	6129	103	CSY	11	Payroll: support personnel (attendance)	$ 31,000.00
199	11	6129	103	CSY	11	Payroll: support personnel (budget)	$ 31,000.00
199	11	6129	103	CSY	11	Payroll: support personnel (receptionist)	$ 31,000.00
199	11	6129	103	CSY	11	Payroll: support personnel (at-risk)	$ 31,000.00
199	11	6129	103	CSY	11	Payroll: support personnel (discipline)	$ 31,000.00
199	11	6129	103	CSY	24	Payroll: tutors (8)	$ 248,000.00

FUND	FUNCTION	OBJECT/ SUB-OBJECT	ORGANIZATION	CURRENT SCHOOL YEAR (CSY)	PROGRAM	DESCRIPTION	TOTAL
						SUBTOTAL FUNCTION 11: INSTRUCTION	$ 1,938,000.00
199	12	6119	103	CSY	11	Payroll: librarian	$ 55,000.00
199	12	6119	103	CSY	11	Payroll: librarian stipend	$ 2,000.00
						SUBTOTAL FUNCTION 12: INSTR. RES. & MEDIA SRVC.	$ 57,000.00
199	23	6119	103	CSY	11	Payroll: principal	$ 101,000.00
199	23	6119	103	CSY	11	Payroll: asst. principal	$ 87,000.00
						SUBTOTAL FUNCTION 23: SCHOOL LEADERSHIP	$ 188,000.00
199	31	6119	103	CSY	11	Payroll: counselor	$ 122,000.00
199	31	6119	103	CSY	11	Payroll: head counselor stipend	$ 2,000.00
199	31	6119	103	CSY	23	Payroll: diagnostician (.5)	$ 31,500.00
199	31	6119	103	CSY	23	Payroll: diagnostician stipend	$ 2,000.00
						SUBTOTAL FUNCTION 31: GUIDANCE, COUNSELING	$ 157,500.00
199	33	6119	103	CSY	11	Payroll: nurse	$ 55,000.00

(Continued)

(Continued)

FUND	FUNCTION	OBJECT/ SUB-OBJECT	ORGANIZATION	CURRENT SCHOOL YEAR (CSY)	PROGRAM	DESCRIPTION	TOTAL
199	33	6119	103	CSY	11	Payroll: nurse stipend	$2,000.00
						SUBTOTAL FUNCT 33: HEALTH SERVICES	$ 57,000.00
199	35	6129	103	CSY	11	Payroll: food services (cafeteria manager)	$ 22,000.00
199	35	6129	103	CSY	11	Payroll: food services (7)	$ 133,000.00
						SUBTOTAL FUNCTION 35: FOOD SERVICES	$ 155,000.00
199	51	6129	103	CSY	11	Payroll: head custodian	$ 35,000.00
199	51	6129	103	CSY	11	Payroll: head custodian stipend	$ 2.000.00
199	51	6129	103	CSY	11	Payroll: custodians (6)	$ 180,000.00
						SUBTOTAL FUNCTION 51: PLANT MAINT. & OPERATION	$ 217,000.00
199	52	6129	103	CSY	11	Payroll: security	$ 49,000.00
199	52	6129	103	CSY	11	Payroll: security clerk	$ 31,000.00
						SUBTOTAL FUNCTION 52: SECURITY SERVICES	$ 80,000.00

FUND	FUNCTION	OBJECT/ SUB-OBJECT	ORGANIZATION	CURRENT SCHOOL YEAR (CSY)	PROGRAM	DESCRIPTION	TOTAL
219	11	6119	103	CSY	25	Payroll: bilingual teachers (5)	$ 275,000.00
219	11	6119	103	CSY	25	Payroll: bilingual stipend	$ 10,000.00
						SUBTOTAL FUNCTION 11: INSTRUCTION (BILINGUAL)	$ 285,000.00
224	11	6119	103	CSY	23	Payroll: special education teachers (5)	$ 275,000.00
224	11	6119	103	CSY	23	Payroll: SPED stipend	$ 10,000.00
224	11	6119	103	CSY	23	Payroll: speech teacher (.5)	$ 26,000.00
						SUBTOTAL FUNCTION 11: INSTRUCTION (SPED)	$ 311,000.00
243	11	6119	103	CSY	22	Payroll: career/ technology teacher	$ 55,000.00
						SUBTOTAL FUNCTION 11: INSTRUCTION (CAREER/ TECHNOLOGY)	$ 55,000.00
						TOTAL PAYROLL COSTS	$ 3,500,500.00
						GRAND TOTAL	$ 3,500,500.00

> It is important to keep in mind that upward of 75 to 85 percent of a school district's revenue is typically required for payroll expenditure. This means the majority of a school's budgetary funding allocation is expended even before a principal and campus SBDM team examine the campus budgetary allotment. This enormous expenditure requires principals to be effective financial stewards of the funding allotment they receive. To coin an old phrase, money does not grow on trees—or in the case of a school, in the principal's office!

The final budget compilation is to be completed in a tabular format as dictated by the school district and on the forms (typically in electronic format) provided by the district business department. If the school district does not specify the format or provide the necessary budget compilation forms, the use of the Microsoft® Excel software program is a recommended method, although other marketed versions are readily available. The final budget compilation must utilize the fund, function, object, sub-object, organization, fiscal year, and program intent codes. Reference "The Budget Development Project" in Resource A, which serves as an experiential activity for the process of building a school budget.

Budget Allocations

Recall from Chapter 5 that budgetary allocations are derived from a variety of revenue sources. These sources—federal, state, and local—provide funding dollars associated with budgetary allocations and are generally identified as governmental fund types with descriptors such as *general, special revenue, capital projects,* and *debt services*. The two most important governmental fund types insofar as the school budget allocation is concerned are general and special revenue. General funds are typically available for school allocations with minimal planned expenditure and purchasing restrictions.

General funds are needed to sustain the normal operations, administration, and counseling expenditures of a school. Special revenue funds are governmental funds used to account for the proceeds of specific revenue sources that are legally restricted to expenditures for specified purposes. Examples include Title I (improving basic programs), vocational education, and food services. Dollars from these funding sources are then utilized as the basis for budgetary allocations at the school level.

School budget allocations are typically based on an ADA or ADM formulation. ADA versus ADM is a school finance issue regarding the relationship between student attendance and financial support. Determining the allocation by ADA benefits school districts with higher attendance and penalizes those with lower levels of attendance. More students in attendance equates to more money for districts. In addition, more students in attendance equates to more learning taking place, a fact supported by test scores. Proponents of ADM as the basis for school funding cite that whether a student is in attendance on any particular day or not, the costs of district operations (salaries, utilities, transportation, other services, etc.) remain constant and thus the allocation of funds should recognize this (Brimley et al., 2020).

Nevertheless, the allotment (based on either of the formulations)—along with additional dollars that may be appropriated as a result of the number of identified ELLs, gifted and talented, SPED, and at-risk students—serves as the initial basis for school allocated funds. Other allotted monies for the school can come from grant dollars, technology funds, maintenance funds, staff development allocations, and other miscellaneous allotments. While most of these allotted dollars allow for administrators to implement and manage activities authorized by the budget, certain limitations or restrictions can be placed on the budget for the following reasons:

- The budget limits the type, quantity, and quality of instruction provided at the school-site level, especially in an era of fiscal conservatism, which is often a result of an economic downturn.
- The public is critically interested in education and, more specifically, instruction.
- School operations are often diverse and broad in scope, and thus important budgetary planning is necessary for effective and efficient expenditure of funds.
- School allocations provide direction for the school's future.
- State politicians exert a vested interest (sometimes good, other times not) in educational policies and programs as well as push their social and philosophical perspectives (read the national headlines for examples).

Restricted Funds

While budget allotments are used for a variety of services and expenditures at the school-site level, some are more restrictive than others. Once basic school allotments are appropriated to particular areas within the budget, function restrictions limit their use unless district approval is obtained in the form of a budget amendment or transfer.

Recall from Chapter 5 that restricted or categorical funds are often associated with Title I, bilingual education, SPED, and other federal dollars and programs. For example, many school districts carefully restrict the expenditure of funds appropriated to these particular programs on the basis of federal and state guidelines that often stipulate funded dollars within these particular budgeted categories can only be utilized for the purpose of student-related instruction. In recent years, ESSER funds (see Chapter 4) serve as an example. Now, consider the following scenario.

Pause and Consider

Hey, I Found the Money!

The office secretary at Somerville School needed a new file cabinet, desk, and carpet but recognized the general funds allocated had already been appropriated and encumbered within the budget. However, Sam Hacnin, the school administrator, thought to himself, *Hey, I found the money!* after noting the Title I accounts had just enough funds to be appropriated for office upgrades. Thus, in an electronic instant, the Title I dollars were encumbered and plans were made for a quick purchase of office items.

No doubt, this was creative thinking on the part of Mr. Hacnin. His actions are a reminder of the old adage, "Necessity is the mother of invention." However, the Title I funds were specifically and categorically designated for Title I–eligible students. Chances are the justification for incorporating Title I funds for the purchase of new office equipment for the school secretary would be a real stretch of the imagination in relation to the budgeted funds utilized.

- Check with administration at your school to determine the specific guidelines regarding the expenditure of Title I funds.
- Can Mr. Hacnin purchase office furniture, equipment, and carpeting for his school secretary? If not, why do you think these stringent guidelines are in place? What do your district guidelines dictate?

Projecting Student Enrollment

Student enrollment information is important to schools and districts relative to declining or increasing enrollments and the corollary revenue generation. Declining enrollments can be detrimental to a school's budget. Consider the following in relation to a decline in a school or district enrollment: reduced state aid; hiring freezes or a reduction in force (RIF); smaller class sizes, thus creating the need for fewer teachers; and redistricting of school boundaries and the possible closing of school facilities. On the other hand, increasing enrollments can create overcrowded classrooms and a need for rapid staff and facilities expansion (Ubben et al., 2016).

Therefore, accurate enrollment projections are vital to budgetary allotments, staff planning, and facilities utilization. Over the years, numerous methods have been incorporated by school districts to project student enrollment. The most common model to date remains the *ratio retention* or *cohort survival method,* which provides sufficiently accurate results. Today, the cohort survival method is frequently utilized by schools and/or school districts in the form of computer software programs. Examples of cohort survival method worksheets and presentations can be examined online (on YouTube®, for example) by typing "cohort survival method" into a search engine.

School leaders must recognize many district office administrators prefer to underestimate enrollment projections because the potential negative impact on cost to a school district is lower. This is important to know since underprojections can equate to less than an appropriate and necessary allocation to the school. Moreover, underprojecting student enrollment equates to understaffing a school.

It is important to note that three types of procedures are required to project student enrollments: gathering demographic data, analyzing the data for possible trends, and then projecting student enrollment on the basis of the evaluated findings. In addition, a careful review and examination of all external environment information is critical to ensure accurate enrollment projections. External environment considerations include the following:

- emerging communities, including the building of new homes, rental properties such as apartment complexes, and the development of mobile home parks
- changing population patterns
- private nonpublic or charter school enrollments
- open school enrollment policies
- initiation of voucher plans
- governmental reduction of federal and/or state education funds
- a significant public event, such as the loss of a major community employer
- mobility rate

The cohort survival method accounts for the number of students enrolled in each grade level in a school or across a district over a specified number of years. Moreover, it requires a school to account for the number of students expected to enroll in kindergarten over the next five years. This accounting of potential kindergarten students is frequently based on housing surveys of children between birth and four years of age who reside in the school or district attendance zone. This information drives an average ratio calculation for each class from year to year, thus allowing for future enrollment projections.

Effective budget development is based on continuous evaluation. This recognition also brings about the need for the development of a detailed budget calendar. The budget calendar lists critical dates for the preparation, submission, review, and approval of the school budget.

The Budget Calendar

School administrators recognize effective budget development is based on continuous evaluation. This recognition also brings about the need for the development of a detailed budget calendar. The budget calendar lists critical dates for the preparation, submission, review, and approval of the school budget. A variety of straightforward techniques are generally used in developing a budget calendar. While the details involved in developing a school budget are not the same in all districts, it is recommended the following five steps be considered for incorporation when preparing a budget calendar:

1. Develop a master district calendar to ensure all budgetary actions and activities are consistent and compatible across the district and from school to school.
2. Identify specified budgetary actions and activities for inclusion in the calendar and arrange them in chronological order.
3. Assign completion dates for each action and activity and note said dates on the budget calendar. Completion dates should be assigned by working backward through the actions and activities from legally mandated dates as stipulated by state law and local district policy.
4. Assign dates and space accordingly to ensure sufficient time is allowed for the completion of each action and activity listed on the budget calendar.
5. Identify on the budget calendar the person(s) specifically responsible for each action or activity listed. This procedure is particularly useful to school administrators because it identifies their own detailed responsibilities and task completion dates.

A Proposed Budget Calendar Exemplified

Again, the budget development process and proposed calendar will vary from state to state and district to district, as fiscal year beginning dates typically start anywhere from July 1 to September 1. School officials who fail to establish a budget calendar or who procrastinate the budget development process are making a serious miscalculation, because the avoidance of approaching deadlines will definitely interfere with conscientious budget-building efforts (Brimley et al., 2020). Outlined in Table 9.6 is a proposed budget calendar with specified considerations as related to the budget development process.

TABLE 9.6 Proposed Budget Calendar

SCHEDULE	PROCEDURE
Prior to February 1	The superintendent of schools establishes the budget-planning format and schedule for preparation of the next fiscal year budget.
	Person responsible: superintendent or designee
February 1	A budget request by function and object form should be distributed to school administrators for completion by March 1. Columns for *Actual Previous Year* and *Estimated Current Year* should be completed prior to the form being disseminated to the administrators responsible.
	Person responsible: associate superintendent for finance
February 15	Projected student enrollments should be developed.
	Person responsible: associate superintendent for district administration in collaboration with school-site leaders
March 1	School administrators should return the completed budget request by function and object form to the district administrator responsible for the initial review and consideration of school needs. The school budget preparation process begins with the involvement of the budget development team.
	Person responsible: school-site leaders and SBDM team members.
April 1	Completed school budgets should be submitted to the district administrator responsible for the consolidation of the organizational budget.
	Person responsible: school-site leaders
April 15	The district administrator should submit the overall organizational budget to the superintendent of schools for review along with suggested revisions prior to consolidation into a total district budget.
	Person responsible: associate superintendent for finance
May 15	The accepted budget for the entire school district should be prepared and ready for adoption in its final form.
	Person responsible: associate superintendent for finance and superintendent
June 1	The superintendent of schools should have completed the review of the accepted budget in its final form.
	Person responsible: superintendent
Months of June/July	Budget workshops are scheduled for school board members.
	Person responsible: superintendent and school board
No later than August 15	The district budget should be submitted to the local school board for public hearings and final approval. This final date will vary from district to district. However, the final approval date is typically prescribed by state law, as any district and school budget must be approved prior to the expenditure of public funds.
	Person responsible: school board, superintendent, and associate superintendent for finance
No later than August 31	Budget adopted
	Person responsible: school board

The development and utilization of a budget calendar assists in the formulation of an integrated plan of fiscal operations and further provides a means of communication between the various levels of the organization. Finally, the budget calendar effectively provides each administrator within the organization with appropriate information and deadlines necessary to perform specified budget development duties and responsibilities.

The Budget Hearing and Defense

Many districts require school-site leaders, department directors, and other school personnel responsible for the development of budgets to formally meet and independently defend their budgets. This process can be quite stressful if the administrator has not properly prepared the budget. Preparation for the budget hearing and defense requires the school leader to devise an interesting and informative manner of presenting the fiscal and budgetary facts. This is often accomplished with visual aids presenting the necessary budgetary points and justifications.

The school leader, when preparing for and presenting at a budget hearing, must comprehend the budgetary components (accounting codes and descriptors), have been intimately involved in the budget development process, and understand the rationale for the monetary requests accompanying the proposed budget. Some districts require the school leader to meet with the superintendent or a designee and, in some instances, a committee of supervisors or peers. In any case, the process typically includes the necessary justification of questioned budgetary items, with final approval coming only after adjustments or revisions have been made to the proposed budget.

Finally, it is advised that the school leader heed a useful twist to an old football adage: "The best defense is a good offense." In other words, work hard at developing an effective budget, do the necessary homework (the behind-the-scenes work) associated with the budgetary tasks, and be prepared. Then all should go well at the budget defense hearing. That noted, also expect the unexpected when defending the budget. Remember, failing to prepare is preparing to fail!

Work hard at developing an effective budget, do the necessary homework (the behind-the-scenes work) associated with the budgetary tasks, and be prepared. Then all should go well at the budget defense hearing.

Final Thoughts

The effective school leader understands the importance of budgeting, especially as schools and school districts realize the function of a budget is more than mechanics and mathematics. The development of a school budget today, especially in this era of fiscal constraint, academic accountability, and frequent political intrusion, requires strong leadership skills, a vision with a purpose, and an action plan for the future. The development of an effective school budget calls for teamwork, dedicated efforts, and proper coding. Budget development demands considerations that increase opportunities for all stakeholders to play an active role in defining school issues and addressing problems. This process generates appropriate decisions and solutions.

Effective leadership enables a school administrator to develop a budget that projects the school's vision and academic action plan. Moreover, the effective school leader informs the general public regarding the direction of the school program and provides the framework for appropriate accounting and wise expenditure of educational dollars—all for the benefit of students. While no budget is ever perfect, proper visioning, regular planning, and continuous evaluation transform a common ledger of revenue and expenditures into a supportive document, leading students to academic success and fulfilling the campus and district visions or missions.

Building a school budget is never an easy task. Budgeting provides the necessary framework, as detailed in Tables 9.1 through 9.6, to help make a school's vision become a reality. With the institutionalization of site-based decision making in schools today, educational leaders have the opportunity and the obligation to engage the learning community in the budget development process by working collaboratively with all stakeholders to incorporate visioning and planning as necessary components in better budgets for better schools. By applying proven budgetary theory and techniques, administrators today—working with an attitude of "All of us are smarter than any one of us"—can utilize budgeting applications so the final budget compilation can positively impact the overall educational program and, most importantly, increase student achievement.

Discussion Questions

1. Who must be responsible for student enrollment projections, school district administration or school principals? Explain your answer.
2. What aspects of the school budget applications as detailed within this chapter might serve to aid a school leader relative to an increase or decrease in student enrollment?
3. Why are certain budget allotments more restrictive than others? Enlighten by providing examples.
4. How might the school budget applications detailed previously within the chapter serve the school leader at the budget defense hearing?
5. Why is the incorporation and utilization of a budget calendar important in building an effective school budget?

(Continued)

(Continued)

6. The thirteen identified school budget applications are designed to aid a school leader in developing an effective and efficient school budget. Examine each of the applications with special focus on Tables 9.1 to 9.5. Which one of these five tables do you perceive to be the most beneficial to a school leader attempting to create a campus budget? Justify your response.
7. How does this chapter relate to the Professional Standards for Educational Leaders (PSEL) as documented in Chapter 1? Which standard(s) are specifically relevant and why?

Case Study

Perplexing, Is It Not?

Alan Swann, school leader of Karl Rojek Memorial School, was sitting in his office in late January during the second semester of school. The budget season was hastily approaching. Alan, working with his assistant principal, Lainie Carroca, recognized his school enrollment had been rapidly increasing over the past few years. The associate superintendent for finance called to meet with Alan and Lainie. Arriving at the school, the chief financial officer informed the administrators that their school's budget allotment would be reduced for the upcoming fiscal year because district facilities were in serious need of upgrades and improvements.

Later, both principal and assistant principal were contemplating their discussion with the district's chief financial officer. Lainie spoke up first, saying, "The situation is perplexing, is it not?" Alan looked up and replied, "Yes, Lainie, I most certainly agree. We must do something and quick!" The assistant principal then asked, "What do you recommend, Alan?"

The principal responded, "Let's look at the data first before we do anything else. Data is always informative, and facts do not lie. If we have the basis for an argument for an increase in our school budgetary allocation—most importantly, an increase that will benefit of our students and teachers—the answer will be found in the numbers! Lainie, we have an obligation to respond!"

The current enrollment at Karl Rojek Memorial School is 815 students. In the last school year, the campus enrollment was 796. The year prior to that, the enrollment was 779. Three years ago, the enrollment was 761. For the previous years four, five, and six, student enrollment was 761, 757, and 752, respectively.

Case Study Application

1. What makes the situation in this case study so perplexing? Explain.
2. Utilizing Table 9.3 on allocation statements as a template, incorporate the following data as well as associated school allocation funds as identified below and respond to the questions that follow.

Last school year's per-pupil allocation for Karl Rojek Memorial School was $2,537.00. Student per-pupil allocations (based on average daily attendance) over the last few years have not changed to any noticeable degree. Use the forthcoming per-pupil funding amounts as the basis for further calculations.

The following figures represent the school's current demographic data as well as the associated allocation dollars[1]:

- Current student population is 815 students.
- Average daily attendance (ADA) has remained approximately the same over the previous six years at 94 percent.
- There are sixty-seven students served in special education, and they receive a funding amount of $7,125.00 per student.
- Gifted and talented students are thirty-eight in number and receive $285.00 per student.
- Bilingual/ESL students number 148 and receive $237.00 per pupil.
- Ninety-three percent of the student population is identified as Title I eligible and receive $262.00 per student in the ADA calculation.
- State compensatory funding equates to $396.00 per student (568 identified students).

Now answer the following questions:

a) Determine the total campus per-pupil allocation amount.

b) Compare this amount with the previous six years and determine if the reduction of per-pupil dollars is equal. Equitable?

[1]In reality, the annual per-pupil allocation and number of students qualifying for different services would have changed over the course of the previous six school years. However, as part of this experiential exercise, current per-pupil funding amounts will remain the same in all categories and for all previous school years.

c) Challenge the current per-pupil allocation, explaining why a greater total allocation is required. Do you have a logical argument for the budget defense hearing? Clarify why or why not.

d) As previously noted, incorporate Table 9.3 as a guide and determine if the students and faculty at Karl Rojek Memorial School are deserving of a greater allocation. Explain why or why not.

3. Can student instructional funds be utilized for district facilities improvements? Check with your principal and/or district chief financial officer for an explanation. Is there a budgetary defense relative to this consideration?
4. How should Principal Alan Swann address the possibility of a decrease in the school's budgetary allotment? Is an argument in defense of more campus dollars worthwhile/appropriate? What's a principal to do? Be specific in your answer.
5. What strategies or methods must Principal Swann and his assistant principal, Lainie Carroca, apply and specifically utilize to resolve this budgetary issue at the upcoming budget defense hearing?
6. Which of the budget applications identified within this chapter are relevant in building an effective argument to better increase the school's budgetary allotment? Which of the Tables 9.1 through 9.5 could be most beneficial in this situation and the upcoming budget defense? Explain.
7. Stakeholders must be informed about the fiscal situation and their ideas, suggestions, and/or recommendations invited. Collaboration is always important. What can Principal Swann tell his team? How can the "perplexing" issue be explained? Place yourself in this situation. Become his assistant principal, Lainie Carroca, and offer advice, if not serious recommendations.

Important note: You are now prepared and ready to begin the experiential learning activity found in Resource A titled "The Budget Development Project." Good luck and good budgeting!

Resource A

The Budget Development Project: A Hands-On Experiential Exercise

Information and Instructions

The budget development project detailed here provides the reader with a comprehensive examination of a fictious school and school district. The school will be known as Mountain Vista Elementary School, and the district will be named Mesa Valley Independent School District (ISD).

Mesa Valley ISD serves a major suburban area just north of a large urban center. The school district has earned an outstanding reputation over the years for its strong academic and extracurricular programs, its effective school leadership, and its financial stability.

The district's tax base, while more than adequate, remains most interestingly diverse, with local revenues generated from the agribusiness industry, which includes pecan growing, milk and dairy products, cotton farming, and cattle ranching, as well as from an infusion of high-tech industries that ultimately attracted the now-famous computer software company, Styl-USA, Inc.

With a diverse tax base comes a diverse population, with socioeconomic levels representative of the poor agribusiness workers, the medium-income urban-flight families, and the independently wealthy CEOs, the latter of whom all reside in what has become known as Technology Valley.

Mesa Valley ISD serves 25,502 students. The district has three high schools, five middle schools, and fifteen elementary schools. Mountain Vista Elementary School is the fifth-oldest elementary school in the district, with a population of 818 students enrolled for the current school year. Listed in Table A.1 are total student enrollments for the previous five school years.

TABLE A.1 Student Enrollment

SCHOOL YEAR	STUDENT ENROLLMENT
Previous year #1	831
Previous year #2	845
Previous year #3	850
Previous year #4	826
Previous year #5	808

The campus has a free and reduced-price lunch population of 87 percent and is thus considered a Title I schoolwide project. The average daily attendance (ADA) is 90 percent. Mountain Vista has a unique student population that ranges from those of a high socioeconomic background to students of high-poverty status. The school is also home to a large English language learner (ELL) population since many of the families living within the attendance zone are resident or migrant farm workers employed by the numerous agribusinesses.

Mountain Vista Elementary School houses prekindergarten through Grade 5, with a student population of 80 percent Hispanic, 10 percent Anglo, 5 percent African American, and 5 percent Asian American. Gifted and talented students make up 4 percent of the population, 5 percent of the student body is identified as special education, and 25 percent of students are served in the bilingual education program. The school has forty-two teachers, one counselor, one nurse, one nurse assistant, one instructional facilitator, one librarian, thirteen instructional aides, two clerical aides, one secretary, one attendance clerk, one assistant principal, and one principal.

Each of the grade levels at Mountain Vista Elementary School has six sections of students with the exception of prekindergarten (which has two sections—one bilingual and one monolingual), Grade 2 (five sections), and Grade 4 (five sections). Every grade level has one section of bilingual students and one section of special education inclusion–monolingual students (except prekindergarten), with the remaining sections serving monolingual students. Each section of bilingual students at every grade level is served by one teacher and one instructional aide. The prekindergarten sections are served by one teacher and one instructional aide each. Finally, the special education students are served by two teachers and five instructional aides.

Mountain Vista Elementary School also employs one gifted and talented teacher (half time) and one speech therapist (half time) as well as a full-time physical education teacher, music teacher, and Title VI aide. There are four custodians and five food services employees. Finally, both faculty and administration agree Mountain Vista Elementary School is in need of a full-time campus diagnostician and a second school counselor. Administration hopes to convince the superintendent of these educational needs during the budget defense hearing.

The Mesa Valley ISD associate superintendent for finance has indicated each elementary school will be provided a per-pupil campus budget allocation of $2,537 for the next school year. This allocation is to support the school's academic programs, salaries, and any supplemental stipends ($2,000) for special education teachers, bilingual teachers, math and science teachers, testing coordinators, and head librarian, counselor, nurse, head custodian, and grade-level chairs. Table A.2 lists the annual salaries of all school personnel.

TABLE A.2 Salaries

PERSONNEL POSITION	SALARY PER YEAR ($)
Teachers, nurse, librarian	51,500
Principal	110,000
Assistant principal	97,000
Counselor	65,000
Diagnostician	75,000
Instructional coach	60,000
Speech therapist	58,000
Testing coordinator	53,000
Security officer	51,000
Secretary	40,000
Instructional and clerical aides	31,000
Nurse assistant	41,000
Custodian (head)	37,000
Custodians	30,000
Food services	21,000
Consultant(s) per day	2,500

Mountain Vista Elementary School has been experiencing problems with reading achievement and, consequently, low problem-solving skills in the area of mathematics as measured by the state assessment of essential skills (SAES). This problem affects most of the content areas since reading is the primary factor for academic success. The SBDM committee believes the promotion of literacy at school and within the community should be a campus priority. Other academic considerations have been included within the proposed campus action plan (CAP) or campus improvement plan (CIP) for the next school year. However, a needs assessment and priority analysis have not been conducted in relation to the action/improvement plan. Identified on the subsequent pages is the Mountain View Elementary School's CAP or CIP.

Finally, the school has recently experienced a turnover in campus leaders. The prior principal replaced a strong and effective instructional leader who had gained the trust, confidence, and respect of the learning community. However, this principal—Dr. Savannah Grace—retired after leading the school to the highest accountability rating according to the state's education agency. Dr. Grace's replacement for the previous two years was a less-than-effective instructional leader, and both he and his assistant principal resigned to pursue other educational interests.

During the two years following Dr. Grace's retirement, the instructional program at Mountain Vista Elementary School suffered, and just this school year, Dr. Jenda Taft and her assistant, John Steven Leakey, assumed the roles of principal and assistant principal. They realize they have their work cut out for them, but both are ethical and moral professionals with excellent credentials and reputations. Both leaders, after reviewing the state academic performance report (SAPR), understood the charge that had been issued to them by Dr. Leroy J. Thedson, the Mesa Valley ISD superintendent: "Turn Mountain Vista around and get those scores back on track. I expect all of your test groups and subpopulation scores to be at 90 percent or higher in the next two years!"

Directions: To best complete the budget development project, the following process is suggested: Carefully read, in sequence, each information guideline along with its supporting materials and then complete the noted tasks before moving on to the next set of instructions. Refer to Information Guideline #4 only after completing the first three directives and activities.

This particular project has been an extremely successful activity for many years and is often considered the most popular aspect of our instruction as it permits the prospective school leader to gain significant and practical insights into and experience with building a school budget.

While no clinical practicum can ever be as true to life as the on-site experience, the processes detailed within this budget development project are intended to present the reader and student of the budgeting process with a meaningful and relevant experience that is as close as possible to the actual budgetary practices of a real school and school district.

1. Follow the Sorenson-Goldsmith Integrated Budget Model, as identified in Chapter 3, which showcases the eight components necessary to define and select the appropriate stakeholders, conduct a needs assessment, analyze the data presented,

prioritize needs, set goals and objectives, and develop an action or improvement plan.

2. Review all information and data provided (including the Mountain Vista Elementary School's action plan and the SAPR) to determine if the information and data are being appropriately, effectively, and efficiently utilized. If not, make any and all necessary changes.
3. Develop a campus budget for Mountain Vista Elementary School by reflecting upon the budgetary applications detailed in Chapter 9. A careful review of the preceding chapters is also recommended.
4. Your completed budget project should include (1) a descriptive narrative, (2) programmatic identifiers, (3) a mission statement, (4) student enrollment projections, (5) an analysis of the academic action plan, (6) a needs assessment and priority analysis, (7) a teacher/student distribution table, (8) a faculty apportionment table, (9) a forecast of population trends utilizing the cohort survival method, (10) any above-basic personnel requests and justifications, (11) an allocation statement, (12) a salaries for personnel table, and (13) the final budget compilation utilizing accounting codes, descriptors, and dollar totals.

   Now it is time to begin the budget development project! Good luck and good visioning, planning, and budgeting!

   After, and only after, completing the first four information directives and activities, move to Informational Guideline #5.

5. Finally, after completing Information Guidelines #1-#4, you may turn to the Mesa Valley ISD memorandum found at the conclusion of this case study. Remember this memorandum is to be read and complied with only after you have completed the first four information guidelines.

Campus Action Plan

Mountain Vista Elementary School

Mesa Valley Independent School District Campus Action Plan

SBDM Committee

BELINDA DEL MONTE, PRESCHOOL TEACHER	JAYE MINTER, MUSIC TEACHER
Karla Billingsly, Grade 1 teacher; Leslie Lovington, Grade 2 teacher; Dianna Sanchez, Grade 3 bilingual teacher	Melissa Alfond, instructional aide, and Suzan Rollins, PTA president
Donya Harbrook, Grade 4 Title I teacher	Molly Corlioni, parent

(Continued)

(Continued)

BELINDA DEL MONTE, PRESCHOOL TEACHER	JAYE MINTER, MUSIC TEACHER
Susie Wigington, Grade 5 teacher	Flo Cortez, parent
Lisa Nachin, counselor	Denise Acrer, parent
Norma Garcia, special education teacher	Xavier Bacerra, district administrator
Randy Woodson, chief of police and community member	John Steven Leakey, assistant principal
Dr. Jenda Taft, principal	

Mission Statement

Mountain View Elementary School will provide a safe environment for all students by fostering productive citizens for a better tomorrow.

Goal 1: Increase student achievement after a review and analysis of SAES data.

Objective 1: Develop strategies that will increase student achievement for specific student populations—gender, ethnicity, and educationally disadvantaged (at risk).

Strategy 1: Target specific instructional objectives.

ACTION(S) IMPLEMENTATION(S)	RESPONSIBLE STAFF ASSIGNED	TIMELINE START/ END	RESOURCES (HUMAN, MATERIAL FISCAL)	AUDIT (FORMATIVE)	REPORTED/ DOCUMENTED
Identify instructional areas of strength, areas needing improvement, and areas of weakness with regard to specific SAES objectives.	Principal and teachers	August–May (current year)	SAES English language arts reading objectives and measurement specifications booklet, SAES mathematics objectives and measurement specifications booklet, MVISD curriculum guides, instructional resource center materials, teacher-made materials, SAES disaggregated data, Mountain Vista SAES booklet *Time on Target* criterion-referenced pretests	Disaggregated data information sheets, SAES ATTACK skills worksheets, diagnostic and screening results, and lesson plans	Principal's office

Evaluation (Summative): All disaggregated student groups will obtain 90 percent or greater mastery on SAES.

Goal 2: Provide a curriculum that addresses higher-order thinking skills to increase student academic performance.

Objective 1: Explore and implement programs that will increase overall student achievement.

Strategy 1: Continue current instructional programs.

ACTION(S) IMPLEMENTATION(S)	RESPONSIBLE STAFF ASSIGNED	TIMELINE START/ END	RESOURCES (HUMAN, MATERIAL, FISCAL)	AUDIT (FORMATIVE)	REPORTED/ DOCUMENTED
Develop staff development programs for Grade 4 process writing. Enhance the reading program by implementing: ___phonemic/phonetic instruction ___increased reading time per day ___learning centers ___subgrouping ___integrated units ___reading styles inventories. Continue cross-grade-level planning during the first six weeks of school.	Principal, teachers, and director of elementary education	August–May (current year)	Integrated reader library books and software, phonetic readers teaching resources, SOAR With Knowledge instructional materials, Maria Carlo reading styles inventory, and teacher-made resources	Integrated reader participation charts and printout reports, lesson plans, teacher observation of student performance, principal visitation and participation in classroom	Principal's office, lesson plans, and library circulation records

Evaluation (Summative): All disaggregated student groups will obtain 90 percent or greater mastery on SAES.

Goal 3: Provide a curriculum that addresses higher-order thinking skills to increase student academic performance.

Objective 1: Explore and implement programs that will increase overall student achievement.

Strategy 1: Continue current instructional programs.

ACTION(S) IMPLEMENTATION(S)	RESPONSIBLE STAFF ASSIGNED	TIMELINE START/END	RESOURCES (HUMAN MATERIAL, FISCAL)	AUDIT (FORMATIVE)	REPORTED/ DOCUMENTED
Continue the On-To-It Math program. Develop a math curriculum cross-referenced guide incorporating On-To Math, Maxim Math, and Math This Way instructional programs. Design math diagnostic tests to be administered in Grades 1–5. Integrate science and social studies into the math instructional program with the extensive implementation of SOAR With Knowledge. Plan lessons to incorporate the Living Science Center into the instructional program at least twice each six weeks throughout the school year.	Principal, teachers, resource center coordinator, and the director of elementary education	August–May (current year)	On-To-It Math and Maxim Math teaching resources, MVISD curriculum guides, library books, classroom libraries and readers, periodicals, newspapers, other reading materials, teacher-made resources	Software reports and lesson plans, teacher observations of student performance, principal visitation and participation in classrooms	Principal's office, lesson plans, library circulation records

Evaluation (Summative): All disaggregated student groups will obtain 90 percent or greater mastery on SAES.

Goal 4: Develop methods and strategies to assist at-risk students to achieve academic success.

Objective 1: Identify and serve students in at-risk situations in order that they obtain 80 percent or greater mastery on SAES.

Strategy 1: Extend learning opportunities and intervention programs for at-risk students.

ACTION(S) IMPLEMENTATION(S)	RESPONSIBLE STAFF ASSIGNED	TIMELINE START/END	RESOURCES (HUMAN, MATERIAL, FISCAL)	AUDIT (FORMATIVE)	REPORTED/ DOCUMENTED
Follow guidelines for identification of at-risk students as mandated by the state education agency and the MVISD at-risk plan. Continue tutoring, counseling, special education, and 504 referral programs and interagency involvement referrals. Enhance the student mentoring program between Grades 3 and 4 for at-risk students and Grades PreK–2 for at-risk students. Implement Title I compacts to encourage parental involvement and awareness as well to as increase student achievement and teacher responsibility.	Principal, teachers, counselor, instructional aides, and security officer	August–May (current year)	Principal, counselor, at-risk coordinator, campus at-risk committee	At-risk student activity and identification sheets	Principal's office

Evaluation (Summative): All disaggregated student groups will obtain 90 percent or greater mastery on SAES.

Goal 5: Develop methods and strategies to assist at-risk students to achieve academic success.

Objective 1: Identify and serve students in at-risk situations in order they obtain 90 percent or greater mastery on SAES.

Strategy 1: Offer parent training and information sharing opportunities.

ACTION(S)	RESPONSIBLE STAFF		RESOURCES (HUMAN,		REPORTED/
IMPLEMENTATION(S)	ASSIGNED	TIMELINE START/END	MATERIAL, FISCAL)	AUDIT (FORMATIVE)	DOCUMENTED
Conduct a parent classroom orientation program during the first six weeks of the school year. Provide for a "Parent University" each school year. Survey parents to determine needs to be addressed during the Parent University program.	Principal, counselor, at-risk coordinator and committee, and teachers	August–May (current year)	Newsletters, meeting notices, parent survey and evaluation forms, childcare, phone bank, door prizes	Parent newsletters, parent training workshop notifications, parent classroom orientation sign-in sheets, parent evaluation forms	Principal's office

Evaluation (Summative): Parent training opportunities and orientations will be held in order that all disaggregated student groups will obtain 90 percent or greater mastery on SAES.

State Academic Performance Report (SAPR)—Abbreviated Form

Campus Report

District Name: **MESA VALLEY ISD**

Campus Name: **MOUNTAIN VISTA ES**

Campus Number: **105**

Accountability Rating: **Met Standard**

Met Standard

Improvement Required

Not Rated

Distinction Designations:

Academic Achievement in Science

State Education Agency

DISTRICT NAME: MESA VALLEY ISD CAMPUS NAME: MOUNTAIN VISTA ES CAMPUS #: 105			STATE ACADEMIC PERFORMANCE REPORT CAMPUS ACCOUNTABILITY RATING: MET STANDARD			TOTAL ENROLLMENT: 831 GRADE SPAN: PREK–5 SCHOOL TYPE: ELEMENTARY		
INDICATOR:	**STATE, %**	**DISTRICT, %**	**CAMPUS, %**	**AFRICAN AMERICAN, %**	**HISPANIC, %**	**WHITE, %**	**ASIAN AMERICAN, %**	**ECON. DISADV., %**
SAES %								
Passing								
Grade 3								
Reading	71.3	78.9	74.2	75.6	69.7	80.5	83.2	67.4
Math	74.6	79.2	73.8	65.7	61.7	84.2	86.3	63.7
SAES %								
Passing								
Grade 4								
Reading	78.7	81.0	70.7	70.2	61.5	78.6	81.2	60.9
Math	68.3	71.6	62.3	58.4	57.7	66.0	71.3	40.0
Writing	78.6	84.7	75.2	70.7	69.6	80.6	83.2	60.7
SAES %								
Passing								
Grade 5								
Reading	75.5	77.2	60.1	57.6	52.9	69.3	72.4	40.0
Math	77.3	78.0	67.3	58.6	47.6	70.2	73.5	47.2
Science	74.7	83.4	84.7	81.2	79.0	95.1	93.2	77.0
Attendance	94.5	95.6	90.1	88.5	85.3	95.4	98.7	82.3

Student Information

Total Students: 831

Students by Grade:	Prekindergarten	32
	Kindergarten	124
	Grade 1	121
	Grade 2	102
	Grade 3	123
	Grade 4	105
	Grade 5	181
	Special education	43

Retention Rates by Grade, %

	STATE	DISTRICT	CAMPUS
Kindergarten	1.7	0.7	2.2
Grade 1	4.7	3.9	5.1
Grade 2	1.7	0.7	1.9
Grade 3	1.1	0.6	1.3
Grade 4	0.9	0.7	1.2
Grade 5	0.8	0.3	0.9

Budgeted Operating Expenditure Information

BUDGETED OPERATING EXPENDITURE INFORMATION				
CAMPUS PCT.	DISTRICT	PCT.	STATE	PCT.
Total campus budget $2,108,247; 100	$116,168,713	100	$12,711,996,407	100
By Function				
Instruction $1,486,314; 70.5	$88,520,559	76.2	$9,559,421,298	75.2
Administration $215,041; 10.2	$8,596,486	7.4	$953,399,731	7.5
Other campus costs $406,892; 19.3	$19,051,668	16.4	$2,199,175,378	17.3
Budgeted Instructional Operating Expenditures by Program				

BUDGETED OPERATING EXPENDITURE INFORMATION				
CAMPUS PCT.	DISTRICT	PCT.	STATE	PCT.
Regular education $1,142,975; 76.9		86.9		86.8
Special education $84,720; 5.7		11.4		11.2
Title I education $219,974; 14.8		15.0		14.9
Bilingual education $11,891; 0.8		4.7		3.6
Gifted/talented ed. $26,754; 1.8		1.3		0.6

Data linked to state Fiscal Education and Information System (FEIMS) financial standard reports (see Chapter 4 for more information).

Important note: The memorandum which follows is not to be read or reviewed until completion of the previously identified and listed information directives, guidelines, and activities.

Memorandum

MESA VALLEY INDEPENDENT SCHOOL		COMMITTED TO
DISTRICT		EXCELLENCE IN EDUCATION
TO:	Dr. Jenda Taft, principal of Mountain Vista Elementary School, and the budget team members	
FROM:	Dr. Leroy J. Thedson, superintendent of schools	
DATE:	Spring (current year)	
SUBJECT:	Budgetary constraints and reductions	

Due to the recent closure of the Mountain Stream Manufacturing Plant, a significant loss of district revenue has occurred. To ensure the district budget and reserves remain solvent, all schools and departments are being asked to include a 9 percent reduction (see specified accounts) within their organizational budgets for the upcoming fiscal year.

Specified line item accounts by code/description:

199-11/13-6112.00	Substitutes
199-11/13-6118.00	Extra duty pay

199-11/23-6269.00	Rentals—operating leases (copiers)
199-11/13/23/31/33-6411.00	Travel

Please note the school district and board of trustees remain genuinely concerned about this temporary financial setback. However, be aware all areas of the district budget are being reduced, and expected revenue to be generated from the Mesa Vista Valley Packing Company—which is scheduled to open within the next two to three years—will hopefully compensate for this unexpected budgetary reduction. Your continued commitment to the students of this school district is most appreciated.

Resource B

Selected Forms

FORM B.1 Budget Development Spreadsheet

FUND	FUNCTION	OBJECT/ SUB-OBJECT	ORGANIZATION	FISCAL YEAR	PROGRAM INTENT	DESCRIPTION	TOTAL
						Grand Total	$

This form is also available for viewing and printing purposes at the following Corwin web link: http://resources.corwin.com/schoolbudget.

FORM B.2 Strategy Page

Goal 1:

Objective 1:

Strategy 1:

ACTIONS	RESPONSIBILITY	TIMELINE START/END	RESOURCES (HUMAN, MATERIAL, FISCAL)	REPORTED/AUDIT (FORMATIVE)	DOCUMENTED

Evaluation (Summative):

This form is also available for viewing and printing purposes at the following Corwin web link: http://resources.corwin.com/schoolbudget.

Resource C

Experiential Exercises

The Budgeting Codes Activity

Carefully read and assess each scenario presented and then refer to the Accounting Codes Reference Sheet (within the pages of this resource) to complete the activity. Fill in the blanks with the proper accounting codes. For the purpose of this exercise, utilize the current school year for fiscal year coding and .00 for the sub-object code.

Note that accounting codes vary from state to state and from district to district. The codes utilized within this resource represent one particular example.

1. Smyler Grogan, assistant principal at Desert Valley Elementary School, had been given the responsibility of budget manager and was working with the budget development team to prepare the school budget for the next fiscal year. In the course of the budget preparation process, Mr. Grogan was contemplating which accounting codes would best correlate with the budgetary decisions made by him and the team. He knew the school's guidance counselor, Mrs. Vestal Umberger, needed a new filing credenza for her office. Desert Valley was built in 1962 and was the third elementary school in the district at the time, and Mr. Grogan realized much of the furniture in Mrs. Umberger's office had never been replaced in all those years.

   Fill in the blanks with the proper coding:

   ________-______-____________.______-______-______-________

2. Dr. Yvette Méndez, principal at the Mission Hills Alternative Center for Education, was reviewing the monthly budget report when she realized she had not budgeted for the additional $2,000 that would be needed to pay for the honorarium to be provided to the staff development presenter who was coming next week. The presenter was a known expert in the area of teaching methodologies as associated with effective alternative school

settings. Quickly Dr. Méndez began completing a district budget amendment and transfer form to ensure the budgeted dollars would be available in the correct account. She finished the budget amendment, making certain the appropriate funds were budgeted for the coming summer school program. She then called the presenter to verify his acceptance of the district contract.

Fill in the blanks with the proper coding:

_______-_____-___________._____-_____-_____-_______

3. Steve Mohyla, teacher and site-based committee chair at Western Ridge Middle School, was just finishing his lunch when Letty Muñoz, the school secretary, came by and told Steve he needed to provide her with an accounting code for a recent purchase he had made. Letty had to track down Steve this particular time because he had spent money out of the school's activity account for items associated with the journalism department. She knew Steve was an exceptional teacher, but it was essential he provide an accounting code associated with activity fund expenditure.

Letty thought to herself, *It's a challenge keeping up with all that's happening around campus at this old school!* (Western Ridge was the second middle school built in the district.) She told Steve he also needed to allocate funding for the copy machine the department was leasing from the Whatacopy Shop. Letty asked Steve to come by the office after he had finished his deviled egg sandwich as they both needed to ensure the accounting code was properly identified!

Fill in the blanks with the proper coding:

_______-_____-___________._____-_____-_____-_______

_______-_____-___________._____-_____-_____-_______

4. Bayou Elementary School was the newest elementary campus in Pecan Grove Independent School District. It had just opened four months ago to accommodate the growing population of students in the greater Hudston metropolitan area. The seven other elementary schools were highly rated according to statewide accountability standards. Susan Dianes knew she had quite a task on her hands as she assumed her new role of the school's first principal.

Previously Dr. Dianes had been a strong assistant principal for four years at Enchanted Path Elementary School and had been an outstanding special education teacher for seven years in a nearby school district. However, today she had to work with the site-based team and some difficult decisions had to be made.

Dr. Dianes had received word earlier in the week the school budget was about to be cut in the area of student field trips. Student travel had become a school board issue, and starting next semester, any new student travel requests would be denied. Dr. Dianes knew the fourth-grade class always made a major end-of-the-year trip to Seaside Kingdom located down on the coast. Monies must be encumbered now or any attempt next semester to fund the trip would be met with stiff resistance from central office administration, not to mention the school board.

Later that afternoon, Dr. Dianes and the site-based team met, and all agreed funds must be amended from other budgetary accounts. Thus, Dr. Dianes and the team reviewed the budget and determined where the cuts would come from, and then Dr. Dianes completed the necessary budget amendment/transfer forms.

Fill in the blanks with the proper coding:

_______-_____-____________._____-_____-_____-_______

Accounting Codes Reference Sheet

State education codes across the nation require a standard fiscal accounting system be adopted by each school district. A major purpose of any accounting code structure is to ensure the sequence of codes uniformly applies to all school districts. Utilize this coding structure when responding to the scenarios presented in Chapter 8 of this text as well as to the above experiential exercises.

199—11—6399.00—001—Current Year—11

1 2 3 4 5 6 7

1. Fund Code (500+)*

185 = State compensatory education

199 = General fund

204 = Title IV (safe and drug-free schools)

205 = Head start

211 = Title I (funding for low-achieving students in high-poverty schools)

212 = Title I (funding for migrant students)

219 = Bilingual education

224 = Special education

243 = Vocational education (career and technical/tech-prep)

255 = Title II (funding to hire, train, and retain quality educators)

461 = Campus activity fund

2. Function Code (27)

11 = Instruction

12 = Instructional resources and media services

13 = Curriculum and staff development

21 = Instructional leadership (instructional specialist/district office directors)

23 = School leadership (administration)

31 = Guidance counseling and evaluation services

32 = Social work services

33 = Health services (nurse)

35 = Food services

36 = Extracurricular (stipends and travel—athletics, drama, choir, band, etc.)

51 = Maintenance and operations (custodial supplies)

52 = Security

53 = Computers/maintenance and repair (students/teachers)

61 = Community services

3. Object Code (35)

6100 = Payroll costs

6110 = Teachers and other professional personnel

6112 = Salaries or wages for substitute teachers

6117 = Extra duty pay—professional (expenditures for professional development/curriculum writing as related to Function 12)

6118 = Professional personnel stipends and extra duty pay

6119 = Salaries or wages—teachers and other professional personnel (summer/evening classes, for example)

6121 = Paraprofessional personnel/extra duty pay (overtime)

6129 = Salaries for support personnel (paraprofessionals, etc.)

6200 = Professional and contracted services

6219 = Other professional contracted services (architecture, landscaping, engineering, etc.)

6239 = Contracted services (education service centers, for example)

6249 = Maintenance and repair

6269 = Rentals/operating leases (copiers, etc.)

6291 = Consulting services

6300 = Supplies and materials

6321 = Textbooks

6325 = Magazines and periodicals

6329 = Reading materials

6339 = Testing materials

6395 = Technology supplies/equipment under $5,000 (per-unit cost)

6396 = Technology furniture and equipment under $5,000 (per-unit cost)

6398 = Technology site licenses

6399 = General supplies (everything from paper clips to staples to postage)

6400 = Other operating costs

6411 = Travel/subsistence (employees)

6412 = Travel/subsistence (students)

6494 = Transportation (buses)

6498 = Hospitality expenses

6600 = Capital outlay—equipment

6636 = Technology equipment over $5,000 (per-unit cost)

6637 = Computer labs

6639 = Furniture and equipment over $5,000 (per-unit cost)

6649 = Furniture and equipment under $5,000 (per-unit cost)

6669 = Library books

4. Sub-Object Code

This code is often used to delineate, for example, local departments. (For the purpose of the exercises and activities within this book, utilize .00 for the sub-object code).

5. Organization Code (School) (900)

001–040 = High school campuses

041–100 = Middle school campuses

101–698 = Elementary school campuses

699 = Summer school organizations

6. Fiscal Year Code

24 = 2023–2024

25 = 2024–2025

26 = 2025–2026

27 = 2026–2027

28 = 2027–2028

29 = 2028–2029

30 = 2029–2030

31 = 2030–2031

32 = 2031–2032, etc.

7. Program Intent Code (13)

11 = Basic educational services

21 = Gifted and talented

22 = Career and technology

23 = Special education

24 = Accelerated instruction

25 = Bilingual education

28 = Disciplinary alternative education placement (AEP) services

30 = Title I (schoolwide programs/projects)

91 = Athletics

99 = Undistributed (charges not distributed to specific programs, e.g., employee allowance for cell phones or band, choir, drama, or other extracurricular programs)

Additional Fund Code Information

It is not unusual for different programs and/or specified service agreements to be categorized by code funding numbers that are sequentially based. Listed below are several examples. Your state coding may be identical to the examples identified. However, to best ensure accuracy in coding, it is always recommended school leaders check with their school systems and/or state education department for absolute coding accuracy.

200–289 = Federal programs (examples include Title I—211, bilingual education—219, special education—224, school breakfast and lunch programs—240)

290–379 = Federally funded shared services agreement[1] (examples include a rural special education co-op or Part B discretionary deaf shared services, both 315)

380–429 = State programs (examples include adult basic education—381, successful schools program—393, life skills programs—394, advanced placement incentives—397, state reading initiative—414)

430–459 = State-funded shared services agreement[2] (an example would be Regional Day School for the Deaf—435)

460–499 = Local programs (an example would be a high school culinary arts program—481)

Notes

* The number in parenthesis represents the total number of different accounting codes that might be utilized when developing a school budget. The codes listed within the Accounting Codes Reference Sheet represent the most commonly utilized at the school site level.

1. A federally funded shared services agreement/arrangement exists when two or more school systems enter into an agreement for the performance and administration of a program. An example would be school systems who enter into a written contract to jointly operate their special education programs as a shared services agreement and must follow procedures developed by the U. S. Department of Education.
2. A state-funded shared services agreement/arrangement exists when a school system enters into an agreement with another school system or other state-funded institution for the performance and administration of a program. For example, schools systems may enter into a written contract to jointly participate in a Regional Day School for the Deaf as part of a state shared services agreement and therefore must follow procedures developed by the state department of education.

Resource D

Budgeting Checklist for School Administrators

School administrators have numerous tasks and responsibilities related to the school budget and other bookkeeping procedures. This checklist is intended to assist the school leader in mastering those tasks and responsibilities. Furthermore, it is anticipated each of these checklist items will further serve to ensure a successful budgetary year as well as the overall success of those individuals involved in a most demanding yet essential process.

Bookkeeping Tasks and Responsibilities

- ☐ Review all receipt books.
- ☐ Reconcile all bank statements on a monthly basis (if applicable at the school-site level).
- ☐ Account for petty cash funds and reconcile these accounts on a monthly basis.
- ☐ Ensure each month all checks have been signed with proper signatures (if school is not a cashless entity). Account for all credit card expenditures.
- ☐ Visit on a regular (weekly) basis with the bookkeeping clerk regarding all budgetary considerations.
- ☐ Ensure all bookkeeping personnel are bonded.
- ☐ Monitor all payments of bills and potential discounts for early or timely payments.
- ☐ Review any bookkeeping or budgetary issues requiring your approval or signature. Examples include the following:
  - ☐ checks and credit cards
  - ☐ purchase orders

- ☐ financial reports
- ☐ fundraising requests
- ☐ amendments and transfers
- ☐ field trip requests

Budget Manager Tasks and Responsibilities

- ☐ Examine and review the budget on a monthly basis.
- ☐ Ensure all requisitions are prepared. Specifically list and identify the quantity ordered, the proper accounting code(s), the description of the item(s) ordered, and the unit cost per item(s) ordered. Ensure subtotals and grand totals are reflected on the requisition, the originator is identified, and the approval signature is noted.
- ☐ During the requisition or budget season, ensure all requisition forms are prepared by faculty and staff and submitted on a timely basis.
- ☐ Ensure all accounts have been properly audited by authorized outside accounting firms.
- ☐ Update the faculty handbook annually regarding any fiscal and/or budgetary topics or issues.
- ☐ Hold a faculty meeting prior to the budget development and requisition season to ensure all parties understand the allocations provided as well as the proper procedures associated with requisition supplies, materials, and all other budgetary considerations.
- ☐ Develop a school academic action or improvement plan and integrate the plan with the school budget.
- ☐ Review the different budget accounts each month. Do not allow overexpenditures to roll forward from one month to the next.
- ☐ Amend the school budget and make associated transfer(s) of funds as necessary and in accordance with the school academic action or improvement plan.
- ☐ Be aware of all district guidelines and deadlines associated with the school budget.
- ☐ Spend all school funds wisely, appropriately, legally, timely, and with a student-centered approach/application.

Fundraising and Crowdfunding Considerations

- ☐ All fundraising and crowdfunding must comply with local board policy and/or administrative regulations.

☐ All fundraising and crowdfunding requests/projects must be monitored and approved prior to initiating any student-focused efforts. Crowdfunding, if school board/district approved, is an alternative method of raising funds and serves as a means of enhancing schools and classrooms in terms of supplies and materials. Crowdfunding can also be utilized for more creative projects such as start-up funding for student films, music, small business ventures, and field trips, for example. (See Chapter 6 for further information regarding fundraising and crowdfunding.)

☐ Identify and monitor additional outside sources of revenue (Adopt-A-School businesses, grants, foundation dollars, etc.) that can further facilitate and enhance the budgetary allotment.

Site-Based Team and Budget Development

☐ The budget development season typically begins each January with a meeting with the site-based team to initiate discussions about issues and considerations that will impact the budget proposed for the next school year.

☐ Establish a budget calendar and begin regular meetings for the purpose of developing the school budget.

☐ Plan to spend the time necessary for proper budget development. In most cases, this will require several after-school meetings, at least two half-day sessions, and at least one full-day meeting.

☐ Provide the site-based team with the proper accounting codes and categories to begin the school budget development process.

☐ Establish all revenue and expenditure targets for the next fiscal year budget with the team.

☐ Enter all revenue and expenditure funds on the appropriate school form to be submitted to the district business department.

☐ Examine any budgetary concerns that might have been problematic during the previous year budget cycle. Review the budget on an account-by-account basis.

Important Budgetary Questions

☐ What is the budgetary allotment for the next fiscal year?

☐ What is the basis for the upcoming budgetary allotment?

☐ What is the projected student enrollment for next year and what is the per-pupil allotment?

☐ Are there any money or budgetary concerns or considerations to be aware of this week?

- ☐ Are any employees not following proper fiscal procedures as related to the budget or bookkeeping management, receipts, purchase orders, reimbursements, or financial reports, including credit card and bank reconciliation processes?
- ☐ Do any potential credit card or check purchases or purchase orders need approval and/or authorized signature?
- ☐ Are daily bank deposits being made (if applicable at the school-site level)?
- ☐ Are there any other items related to the school budget or bookkeeping procedures that need to be discussed or examined?
- ☐ What bookkeeping or budgetary improvements need to be made?
- ☐ When do I get a well-deserved vacation?

References

ACERCA. (2022). *Vouchers hurt: The truth about academic outcomes.* https://www.sosaznetwork.org/tag/education/

Allegretto, S., Garcia, E., & Weiss, E. (2022). *Public education funding in the U.S. needs an overhaul.* Economy Policy Institute. https://www.epi.org/publication/public-education-funding-in-the-us-needs-an-overhaul/

American Association of School Administrators (AASA). (2002). *Using data to improve schools: What's working.*

American Society of Civil Engineers. (2022). *2021 infrastructure report card.* https://infrastructurereportcard.org/cat-item/schools-infrastructure/

Asif, A. (2013). *As schools become more technologically advanced, who is in charge?* hechingered.org/content/as-schools-become-more-technologically-advanced-who-is-in-charge_6469/

Ball, D. (2022). *Adjusting the sails: Weathering the storms of administrative leadership.* Rowman & Littlefield.

Bambrick-Santoyo, P. (2018). *Leverage leadership 2.0: A practical guide to building exceptional schools.* Jossey-Bass.

Banks, T., & Obiakor, F. E. (2015). Culturally responsive positive behavior supports: Considerations for practice. *Journal of Education and Training Studies, 2*(2), 83–90.

Barnum, M. (2022). *As pandemic aid runs out, America is set to return to a broken school funding system.* Chalkbeat. https://www.chalkbeat.org/2022/8/25/23318969/school-funding-inequality-child-poverty-covid-relief

Barrington, K. (2022). *New study confirms that private schools are no better than public schools.* Public School Review. https://www.publicschoolreview.com/blog/new-study-confirms-that-private-schools-are-no-better-than-public-schools

Black, D. W. (2021). *Educational law: Equity, fairness, and reform* (3rd ed.). Aspen Publishing.

Blanchard, K., Broadwell, R., Hoyt, N., & Hoyt, J. (2018). *Servant leadership in action: How you can achieve great relationships and results.* Berrett-Koehler Publishers.

Blinder, A. (2015). Atlanta educators convicted in school cheating scandal. *New York Times.* https://www.nytimes.com/2015/04/02/us/verdict-reached-in-atlanta-school-testing-trial.html

Boser, U., Benner, M., & Roth, E. (2018). *The highly negative impacts of vouchers.* Center for American Progress.

Bracey, G. W. (2002). *The war against America's public schools: Privatizing schools, commercializing education.* Allyn & Bacon.

Brady, K. P., & Pijanowski, J. C. (2007). Maximizing state lottery dollars for public education: An analysis of current state lottery models. *Normes, 7*(2), 20–37.

Brainy Quote. (2001–2023). *Samuel Johnson quotes.* https://www.brainyquote.com/quotes/authors/s/samuel_johnson.html

Brimley, V., Jr., Verstegen, D. A., & Knoeppel, R. C. (2020). *Financing education in a climate of change* (13th ed.). Pearson Education.

Brown, M. (2022). *States that spend the most on education*. Learner. https://www.learner.com/blog/states-that-spend-the-most-on-education

Carnoy, M. (2017). *School vouchers are not a proven strategy for improving student achievement*. Economic Policy Institute.

Carroll, L. (1993). *Alice's adventures in wonderland* (Dover Thrift ed.). Dover Publications. (Original work published in 1865.)

Casner, T. (2021). *From fishing trips to phishing scams: Today's top school district fraud traps and how to avoid them*. Weaver. https://weaver.com/blog/fishing-trips-phishing-scams-todays-top-school-district-fraud-traps-and-how-avoid-them

Center on Education Policy. (2016). *Keeping informed about school vouchers: A review of major developments and research*.

Chen, G. (2022). *Do lotteries really benefit schools? The answer is hazy*. Public School Review. https://www.publicschoolreview.com/blog/do-lotteries-really-benefit-public-schools-the-answer-is-hazy

Childress, M. (2014, May–June). Building teacher capacity. *Principal*, 8–12.

Cizek, G. J. (1999). *Cheating on tests: How to do it, detect it, and prevent it*. Lawrence Erlbaum.

Common Ground. (2022). *Paying for special education*. https://njcommonground.org/paying-for-special-education/

Cooper, T. L. (2012). *The responsible administrator: An approach to ethics for the administrative role*. Jossey-Bass.

Cover, D. (2023). *There is always hope*. Unpublished Interview, Department of Educational Leadership and Foundations, The University of Texas at El Paso, El Paso, TX.

Covey, S. R. (2020). *The seven habits of highly effective people*. Simon & Schuster.

Curacubby Team. (2020). *The comprehensive guide to accounting for school administrators*. https://www.curacubby.com/resources/accounting-for-school-administrators

Darling-Hammond, L., & McLaughlin, M. W. (1995). Policies that support professional development in an era of reform. *Phi Delta Kappan, 76*(8), 597–604.

Deal, T. E., & Peterson, K. D. (2016). *Shaping school culture: Pitfalls, paradoxes, and promises* (3rd ed.). Jossey-Bass.

Deming, W. E. (2000). *Out of crisis*. MIT Press.

DePree, M. (2003). *Leading without power: Finding hope in serving community*. Jossey-Bass.

DeSchryver, D. (2021). *The DonorsChoose blog: What school business officials need to know about crowdfunding*. DonorsChoose. https://blog.donorschoose.org/articles/what-school-business-officials-need-to-know-about-crowdfunding

DiMarco, B., & Cohen, L. (2023). *The new wave of public funding of private schooling explained*. FutureEd. https://www.future-ed.org/the-new-wave-of-public-funding-of-private-schools-explained/

Donahue, W. E. (2022). *Professional ethics: A competency-based approach to understanding and applying professional ethics*. Centrestar Learning.

Donaldson, E. (2022). What to know about vouchers and the school choice movement in Texas. *Dallas Morning News*. https://www.dallasnews.com/news/education/2022/07/26/what-to-know-about-vouchers-and-the-school-choice-movement-in-Texas

Donaldson, E., Ayala, E., & Richman, T. (2023). What are school vouchers and how are they different from ESA effort pushed in Texas? *Dallas Morning News*. https://www.dallasnews.com/news/education/2023/02/01/what-are-education-savings-accounts-abbott-calls-for-esas-in-texas-school-vouchers-fights/

Douglas, K. (2022). *These are the top issues facing Texas public schools right now*. Texas Association of School Boards. https://www.tasb.org/members/advocate-district/lege-update-april-2022/

Durrani, A. (2023). *What school choice is and how it works*. U.S. News and World Report. https://www.usnews.com/education/k12/articles/what-school-choice-is-and-how-it-works

Earl, L. (1995). Moving from the political to the practical: A hard look at assessment and accountability. *Orbit, 26*(2), 61–63.

edCHOICE & Morning Consult. (2022). *The public, parents, and K-12 education: A national polling report.* https://edchoice.morningconsultintelligence.com/assets/203341.pdf?utm_source=substack&utm_medium=email

Edmonds, R. R. (1979). Effective schools for the urban poor. *Educational Leadership, 37*(2), 15–24.

Education Law Center. (2022). *Making the grade.* https://edlawcenter.org/research/making-the-grade-2020.html

Education Week. (2023). *Tips for nurturing a thriving school culture.* https://www.edweek.org/leadership/downloadable-a-recipe-for-creating-a-school-culture-teachers-dont-want-to-leave/2023/09?utm_source=nl&utm_medium=eml&utm_campaign=popweek&utm_content=list&M=7895655&UUID=14f3b062c0baef467fd6eefe3a4d6cd4&T=10496041

Eliot, T. S. (1935). *Murder in the cathedral.* Harcourt Brace.

Erekson, O. H., DeShano, K. M., Platt, G., & Zeigert, A. L. (2002). Fungibility of lottery revenues and support for public education. *Journal of Education Finance, 28*(2), 301–311.

ESEA Network. (2022). *National ESEA distinguished schools.* https://www.eseanetwork.org/ds

Essex, N. L. (2015). *School law and the public schools: A practical guide for educational leaders.* Pearson Education.

Farrie, D., Kim, R., & Sciarra, D. G. (2019). *Making the grade 2019: How fair is school funding in your state?* Education Law Center.

FasterCapital. (2023). *The advantages and disadvantages of crowdfunding for your small business needs.* https://fastercapital.com/content/The-Advantages-And-Disadvantages-Of-Crowdfunding-For-Your-Small-Business-Needs.html

Fiddiman, B., & Yin, J. (2019). *The danger private school voucher programs pose to civil rights.* Center for American Progress.

Garrett, T. A. (2001). Earmarked lottery revenues for education: A new test of fungibility. *Journal of Education Finance, 26*(3), 219–238.

Goldsmith, L. M., & Sorenson, R. D. (2005). Ethics, integrity and fairness: Three musts for school vision and budgeting. *Texas Study of Secondary Education, 15*(1), 7–9.

Gordon, M. F., & Louis, K. S. (2009). Linking parent and community involvement with student achievement: Comparing principal and teacher perceptions of stakeholder influence. *American Journal of Education, 116*(1), 1–32.

Graham, E. (2022). *Educators push back against school voucher legislation.* National Education Association. https://www.nea.org/advocating-for-change/new-from-nea/educators-push-back-against-school-voucher-legislation

Gray, L., & Lewis, L. (2021). *Use of educational technology for instruction in public schools: 2019–20* (NCES 2021-017). U.S. Department of Education. National Center for Education Statistics. https://nces.ed.gov/pubsearch/pubsinfo.asp?pubid=2021017

Green, L. (2016). *Booster club embezzlement: Legal issues, preventive strategies.* National Federation of State High School Associations. https://www.nfhs.org/articles/booster-club-embezzlement-legal-issues-preventive-strategies/

Green, R. L. (2016). *Practicing the art of leadership: A problem-based approach to implementing the professional standards for educational leaders.* Pearson Education, Inc.

Hadderman, M. (2002). School-based budgeting. *Teacher Librarian, 30*(1), 27–30.

Halsne, C., & Koeberl, C. (2016). *Denver public schools crack down on employee credit card use.* Fox 31. http://kdvr.com/2016/03/02/dps-cracks-down-on-employee-credit-card-use/

Hanson, M. (2022). *U.S. public education spending statistics.* Education Data Initiative. https://educationdata.org/public-education-spending-statistics

Harsha, K. (2015). *Former EPISD superintendent begins new career after prison sentence.* KTSM.com. https://www.ktsm.com/news/former-episd-superintendent-begins-new-career-after-prison-sentence/

Hattie, J. (2012). *Visible learning for teachers: Maximizing impact on learning.* Routledge.

Henderson, A. T., Marburger, C. L., & Ooms, T. (1986). *Beyond the bake sale: An educator's guide to working with parents.* National Committee for Citizens in Education.

Hoban, G., Tyler, C., Salice, B., & Cunniff, D. T. (2018). *Ethics for visionary school leaders: Setting your ethical compass* (3rd ed.). Kendall-Hunt Publishing.

Holcomb, E. L. (2017). *Getting more excited about using data.* Corwin.

Hoy, W. K., & Miskel, C. G. (2012). *Educational administration: Theory, research, and practice.* McGraw-Hill Humanities/Social Sciences/Languages.

Hughes, R. L., Ginnett, R. C., & Curphy, G. J. (2021). *Leadership: Enhancing the lessons of experience.* McGraw-Hill Education.

Husarevich, K. (2023). *How modern technology impacts education.* DealRoom. https://dealroom.net/blog/how-technology-affects-education

Hutchinson, S. (2022). *Supreme Court ruling brings an altered legal landscape for school choice.* The Hechinger Report. https://hechingerreport.org/supreme-court-ruling-brings-an-altered-legal-landscape-for-school-choice/

Independent School Management (ISM). (2017). *Strategies for strengthening ties with feeder schools.* https://isminc.com/advisory/publications/the-source/strategies-strengthening-ties-feeder-schools

Ishimaru, A. M. (2020). *Just schools: Building equitable collaborations with families and communities.* Teachers College Press.

Jewison, N. (Director). (1971). *Fiddler on the Roof* [Film]. The Mirisch Company and Cartier Productions.

Jochim, A., Diliberti, M. K., Schwartz, H., Destler, K., & Hill, P. (2023). *Navigating political tensions over schooling: Findings from the American school district panel survey.* CRPE. https://crpe.org/asdp-2023-politics-brief/

Johnson, C. E. (2020). *Meeting the ethical challenges of leadership.* Sage.

Johnson, R. S. (2002). *Using data to close the achievement gap: How to measure equity in our schools* (2nd ed.). Corwin.

Jones, T. H., & Amalfitano, J. L. (1994). *America's gamble: Public school finance and state lotteries.* Technomic.

Jordan, P. (2023). *Attendance playbook: Smart strategies for reducing student absenteeism post-pandemic.* Future-ed.org. https://www.future-ed.org/wp-content/uploads/2023/05/Attendance-Playbook.5.23.pdf

KEVGroup.com. (2020). *School fraud: Avoiding financial fraud in schools.* https://kevgroup.com/wp-content/uploads/2020/01/School-Fraud.pdf

Khalifa, M. A., Gooden, M. A., & Davis, J. E. (2016). Culturally responsive school leadership: A synthesis of the literature. *Review of Educational Research, 86*(4), 1272–1311.

Knight, D. (2023). *The David Knight Show.* PodcastAddict.https://podcastaddict.com/podcast/the-david-knight-show/2448666

Kouzes, J. M., & Posner, B. Z. (2023). *The leadership challenge* (7th ed.). Jossey-Bass.

KVIA.com. (2011). *EPISD superintendent on list of highest paid superintendents in Texas.* https://kvia.com/news/2011/04/22/episd-superintendent-on-list-of-highest-paid-superintendents-in-texas/

Laffee, S. (2002, December). Data-driven districts. *The School Administrator, 59,* 6–15.

Lai, E. (2014). Principal leadership practices in exploited situated possibilities to build teacher capacity for change. *Asia Pacific Education, 15,* 165–175.

Lazear, J. (1992). *Meditations for men who do too much.* Fireside/Parkside, Simon & Schuster.

Learning Policy Institute. (2022, September 28). *Attendance is an essential ingredient for educational equity* (Blog by Hedy N. Chang). https://learningpolicyinstitute.org/blog/attendance-essential-ingredient-educational-equity

Lemov, D. (2021). *Teach like a champion 3.0.* Jossey-Bass.

Levin, H. M. (2011). Waiting for Godot: Cost-effectiveness analysis in education. *New Directions for Evaluation, 90*, 55–68.

Linder, D. (n.d.). *Regulation of obscenity and nudity*. Exploring Constitutional Conflicts. http://law2.umkc.edu/faculty/projects/ftrials/conlaw/obscenity.htm

Lopez, B. (2022). Some Republicans are optimistic about enacting school choice in next year's session—But it might not be so easy. *Texas Tribune*. https://www.texastribune.org/2022/11/28/texas-school-choice-vouchers/

Lunenburg, F. C., & Irby, B. J. (2022). *The principalship*. Rowman & Littlefield.

Martinez, A. (2017, June 14). Murphy details role in cheating plan. *El Paso Times*. http://www.elpasotimes.com/story/news/crime/2017/06/13/defense-episd-case-says-inquiry-politically-motivated/393867001/

Mead, J. F., & Eckes, S. E. (2018). *How school privatization opens the door to discrimination*. National Education Policy Center.

MIP Fund Accounting. (2023). *Guide to funding accounting for educational institutions*. https://www.mip.com/resource/guide-to-fund-accounting-for-educational-institutions/

Miranda, A. (2012). *Excellent leadership in budgeting strategies*. Unpublished Interview, Department of Educational Leadership and Foundations, The University of Texas at El Paso, El Paso, TX.

Modan, N. (2022). *Finance experts: School district budgets 'headed for a wild ride'*. K-12 Dive. https://www.k12dive.com/news/finance-experts-school-district-budgets-headed-for-a-wild-ride/630094

Mungal, A. S., & Sorenson, R. D. (2020). *Steps to success: What successful principals do every day*. Rowman & Littlefield.

Munna, A. S. (2023). *Instructional leadership and role of module leaders*. Sage Journals. https://journals.sagepub.com/doi/full/10.1177/10567879211042321

Mutter, D. W., & Parker, P. J. (2012). *School money matters: A handbook for principals*. Association for Supervision and Curriculum Development (ASCD).

Nasdaq. (2020). *Nasdaq CEO Adena Friedman shares 3 principles in leadership amid times of turmoil*. https://www.nasdaq.com/articles/nasdaq-ceo-adena-friedman-shares-3-principles-in-leadership-amid-times-of-turmoil-2020-05

National Center for Education Statistics (NCES). (2016). *Financial accounting for local and state school systems*. https://nces.ed.gov/pubsearch/pubsinfo.asp?pubid=2015347

National Center for Education Statistics (NCES). (2019). *Study of the Title I, Part A grant program mathematical formulas*. https://nces.ed.gov/pubs2019/titlei/summary.asp

National Center for Education Statistics (NCES). (2020). *Digest of education statistics*. http://nces.ed.gov/pubs2016/2016006.pdf

National Center for Education Statistics (NCES). (2022). *Report on the condition of education 2022*. https://nces.ed.gov/pubs2022/2022144.pdf

National Center for Education Statistics (NCES). (2023). Violent deaths at school and away from school, school shootings, and active shooter incidents. *Condition of Education*. U.S. Department of Education, Institute of Education Sciences. https://nces.ed.gov/programs/coe/indicator/a01

National Conference of State Legislatures. (2016). *School finance*. http://www.ncsl.org/research/education/school-finance.aspx

National Education Association. (2022). *Rankings of the states 2021 and estimates of school statistics*. https://www.nea.org/sites/default/files/2022-04/2022%20Rankings%20and%20Estimates%20Report.pdf

National Policy Board for Educational Administration (NPBEA). (2015). *Professional standards for educational leaders*. Professional-Standards-for-Educational-Leaders_2015.pdf

Northouse, P. G. (2021). *Leadership: Theory and practice*. Sage.

Osborne, J., Barbee, D., & Suydam, J. A. (1999). FBI is asked to examine CCISD. *Corpus Christi Caller-Times*. http://www.caller2.com/1999/october/06/today/local_ne/1147.html

Ositelu, M. O. (2019). *Equipping individuals for life beyond bars*. https://d1y8sb8igg2f8e.cloudfront.net/documents/Research_Brief_Equipping_Individuals_Life_Beyond_bars.pdf

Ovsiew, L., & Castetter, W. B. (1960). *Budgeting for better schools*. Prentice Hall.

Owings, W. A., & Kaplan, L. S. (2020). *American public school finance*. Routledge.

Park, S., Hironaka, S., Carver, P., & Norgstrum, L. (2013). Continuous improvement in education. *Carnegie Foundations for the Advancement of Teaching*. White Paper.

PaySchools. (2016). *Creating a cashless school*. https://www.payschools.com/wp-content/uploads/2016/05/PaySchools%20Buyers%20Guide%20V8.pdf

Potter, H. (2017). *Do private school vouchers pose a threat to integration?* The Century Foundation.

Prison Bureau in Federal Register. (2021). *Annual determination of average cost of incarceration fee (COIF)*. Federal Register. https://www.federalregister.gov/documents/2021/09/01/2021-18800/annual-determination-of-average-cost-of-incarceration-fee-coif

Promethean. (2022). *The state of technology in education—2022*. https://www.prometheanworld.com/microsites/state-of-technolgy-in-education-report-2022-2023/

Ravitch, D. (2021a). *The dark history of school choice*. New York Review. https://www.nybooks.com/articles/2021/01/14/the-dark-history-of-school-choice/

Ravitch, D. (2021b). *Slaying Goliath: The passionate resistance to privatization and the fight to save America's public schools*. Knopf.

Reagan, R. (1987). *Remarks on signing the intermediate-range nuclear forces treaty, December 8, 1987*. http://www.reagan.utexas.edu/archives/speeches/1987/120887c.htm

Roe, W. H. (1961). *School business management*. McGraw-Hill.

Ronka, D., Lachat, M. A., Slaughter, R., & Meltzer, J. (2009). Answering questions that count. *Educational Leadership, 66*(4), 18–24.

Rowley, M. (2019). *Cashless societies: The pros and cons*. Cisco. https://newsroom.cisco.com/feature-content?type=webcontent&articleId=1750635

Roza, M. (2021). *There's a fiscal cliff coming, and some districts appear hell-bent on making it worse*. Thomas B. Fordham Institute. https://fordhaminstitute.org/national/commentary/theres-fiscal-cliff-coming-and-some-districts-appear-hell-bent-making-it-worse

Self-Walbrick, S., & Walsh, D. A. (2023). *Here's everything you need to know about school vouchers in Texas*. Texas Standard. https://www.texasstandard.org/stories/school-vouchers-choice-texas-legislature/#:~:text=Voucher%20opponents%20argue%20%E2%80%9Cschool%20choice,avoid%20the%20public%20school%20system

Severson, K. (2011, July 6). Systematic cheating is found in Atlanta's school system. *New York Times*. http://www.nytimes.com/2011/07/06/education/06atlanta.html

Shaker, G. G., Tempel, E. R., Nathan, S. K., & Stancyzykiewicz, B. (2022). *Achieving excellence in fundraising*. John Wiley & Sons.

Snopes. (2017). *If 99.9 percent is good enough, then . . .* http://msgboard.com/cgi-bin/ultimatebb.cgi?ubb=get_topic;f=47;t=000474;p=0

Sorenson, R. D. (2007, Winter). How sex and money ruined Dr. Ed U. Kator's career. *Leadership in Focus, 6*, 6–10.

Sorenson, R. D. (2021). *Responding to resisters: Tactics that work for principals*. Rowman & Littlefield.

Sorenson, R. D. (2022). *Equity, equality, and empathy: What principals can do for the well-being of the learning community*. Rowman & Littlefield.

Sorenson, R. D. (2024). *Essentials for new principals: Seven steps to becoming successful—Key expectations and skills*. Rowman & Littlefield.

Sorenson, R. D., & Goldsmith, L. M. (2006). Auditing procedures and ethical behaviors: Cures for the common scheme. *TEPSA Journal,Winter*, 10–14.

Sorenson, R. D., & Goldsmith, L. M. (2009). *The principal's guide to managing school personnel*. Corwin.

Sorenson, R. D., Goldsmith, L. M., & DeMatthews, D. E. (2016). *The principal's guide to time management: Instructional leadership in the digital age*. Corwin.

Sorenson, R. D., Goldsmith, L. M., Méndez, Z. Y., & Maxwell, K. T. (2011). *The principal's guide to curriculum leadership*. Corwin.

Southern Poverty Law Center (SPLC). (2021). *Inequity in school funding: Southern states must prioritize fair public school spending*. https://www.splcenter.org/southern-schools-funding-inequities

Statista Inc. (2023). *Number of victims of mass shootings in the United States between 1982 and August 2023*. Retrieved September 24, 2023, from https://www.statista.com/statistics/811504/mass-shooting-victims-in-the-united-states-by-fatalities-and-injuries/

Stein, J. (Ed.). (1967). *The random house dictionary of the English language* (Unabridged ed.). Random House.

Stokes, B. (2011). *America's first deflationary depression: Is a bigger one ahead?* Elliot Wave International. http://www.elliottwave.com/freeupdates/archives/2011/11/01/America-s-First-Deflationary-Depression-Is-a-Bigger-One-Ahead.aspx

Strauss, V. (2012, March 30). Mega millions: Do lotteries really benefit public schools? *The Washington Post*. https://www.washingtonpost.com/blogs/answer-sheet/post/mega-millions-do-lotteries-really-benefit-public-schools/2012/03/30/gIQAbTUNlS_blog.html?utm_term=.f70e58041303

Strauss, V. (2017, May 24). Analysis: Five startling things Betsy DeVos just told Congress. *The Washington Post*. https://www.washingtonpost.com/news/answer-sheet/wp/2017/05/24/five-startling-things-betsy-devos-just-told-congress/?utm_term=.f22282af510f

Toch, T., & Rothman, R. (2023). *Avoiding a rush to judgement: Teacher evaluation and teacher quality*. Scribd. https://www.scribd.com/document/534516367/kerwin-1

Tschannen-Moran, M. (2014). *Trust matters: Leadership for successful schools* (2nd ed.). Jossey-Bass.

U.S. Census Bureau. (2022). *2021 public elementary-secondary education finance data*. https://www.census.gov/data/tables/2021/econ/school-finances/secondary-education-finance.html

U.S. Department of Education. (2023). *Fiscal years 2022–2024 state tables of the U.S. Department of Education*. https://www2.ed.gov/about/overview/budget/statetables/index.html

U.S. Department of Justice Archives. (2020). *Embezzlement*. https://www.justice.gov/archives/jm/criminal-resource-manual-1005-embezzlement

Ubben, G. C., Hughes, L. W., & Norris, C. J. (2016). *The principal: Creative leadership for excellence in schools*. Pearson Education.

Urban, W. J., & Wagoner, J. L. (2019). *American education: A history*. Routledge.

Vamos, M., & Jackson, S. (Eds.). (1989, May 29). The public is willing to take business on. *Business Week/Harris Poll, 3107*, 29.

Walsh, D. A., & Self-Walbrick, S. (2023). *Here's everything you need to know about school vouchers in Texas*. Houston Public Media. https://www.houstonpublicmedia.org/articles/education/2023/02/09/443267/here's-everything-you-need-to-know-about-school-vouchers-in-texas/

Walsh, J., & Orman, S. (2022). *The educators guide to Texas school law* (10th ed.). University of Texas Press.

Walton, M. (1986). *The Deming management method*. Perigee.

Warren, M. R., Hong, S., Rubin, C. L., & Sychitkokhong, P. U. (2009). Beyond the bake sale: A community-based relational approach to parent engagement in schools. *Teachers College Record, 111*(9), 2209–2254.

Weiner, K. G., & Green, P. (2018). *Private choice and vouchers: Implications for students with disabilities*. National Council on Disability.

Wilder, F. (2022). *Inside the secret plan to bring private school vouchers to Texas*. Texas Monthly. https://www.texasmonthly.com/news-politics/inside-the-secret-plan-to-bring-private-school-vouchers-to-texas/

Wilhour, J. (1998). *I teach*. Unpublished Interview, Department of Educational Leadership and Foundations, The University of Texas at El Paso, El Paso, TX.

Wilkins, A. L., & Patterson, K. J. (1985). Five steps for closing culture-gaps. In R. H. Kilmann, M. J. Saxton, & R. Serpa (Eds.), *Gaining control of the corporate culture* (pp. 351–369). Jossey-Bass.

Will, G. (2005, February 17). These bones protected by muscle. *Abilene Reporter-News*, 4AA.

Williams, L. (2022). *What kind of education do lotteries fund?* American Institute for Economic Research. https://www.aier.org/article/what-kind-of-education-do-lotteries-fund/

Worth, J. (2015). *4 ways to protect your business against employee fraud and theft*. Entrepreneur. http://www.entrepreneur.com/article/244607

Yale School of Medicine. (2023). *Yale Center for Emotional Intelligence* (YCEI). https://medicine.yale.edu/childstudy/services/community-and-schools-programs/center-for-emotional-intelligence/

YARN. (2005–2023). *Citizen Kane film clip/quote*. https://getyarn.io/yarn-clip/ad8ddd36-e9a9-41da-894e-64420505a6bd

Yukl, G. A., & Gardner, W. L., III. (2019). *Leadership in organizations* (9th ed.). Pearson Education.

Zeitlin, S. G. (2021). Francis Bacon on imperial and colonial warfare. *The Review of Politics, 83*(2), 196–218.

Zhou, J. (2022). *State regulation of private schools*. Private School Review. https://www.privateschoolreview.com/blog/state-regulation-of-private-schools

Index

For leaders who need results now...
because our students can't wait

SPIRIT WORK AND THE SCIENCE OF COLLABORATION
Michael Fullan and Mark Edwards

LEADER CREDIBILITY
Douglas Fisher, Nancy Frey, Cathy Lassiter, and Dominique Smith

ENGAGE EVERY FAMILY
Steven M. Constantino

DE-IMPLEMENTATION
Peter M. DeWitt

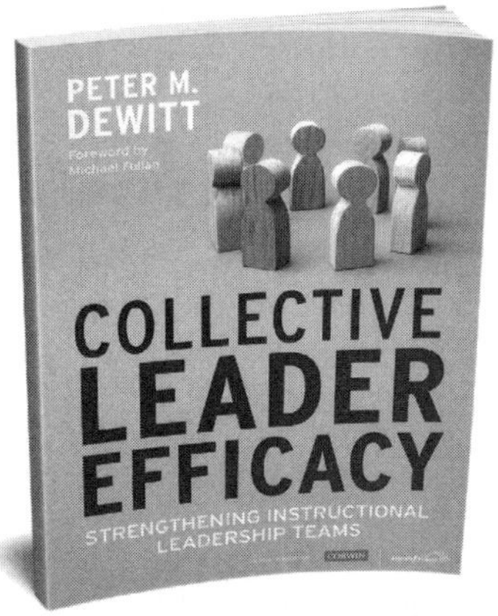

COLLECTIVE LEADER EFFICACY
Peter M. DeWitt

PUTTING FACES ON THE DATA
Lyn Sharratt and Michael Fullan

To find these and other best-selling books, visit **corwin.com/leadership**